AMERICAN HISTORY BY THE STATE

Interesting Stories And Random Facts About Texas, California And New York

History of The United States

BILL O'NEILL

The Great Book of Texas
The Great Book of California
The Great Book of New York

ISBN: 9781096803133

CONTENTS

THE GREAT
BOOK OF TEXAS

The Crazy History of Texas with
Amazing Random Facts & Trivia

**A Trivia Nerds Guide
to the History of the
United States Vol.1**

BILL O'NEILL

DON'T FORGET YOUR
FREE BOOKS

CONTENTS

INTRODUCTION

How much do you really know about Texas?

Sure, you know that Texas is a state that's chock full of state pride. You know that it's an oil state and is home to the Dallas Cowboys. But what else do you *really* know about it?

By now, you've most likely heard about the Texas Revolution and the Battle of the Alamo. You probably know of Davy Crockett and you may have even heard that he died during the Battle of the Alamo, but do you know what really happened to him?

Have you ever wondered how Texas came to be known as the Lone Star State? Do you know who first discovered Texas? Do you know how many different flags have flown over Texas?

You've heard of Bush family legacy, but do you know which United States presidents were actually born in Texas?

Do you know about some of the paranormal folklore and unsolved mysteries of the state? Are you aware of odd sci-fi phenomenon that is believed to have occurred here?

If you have ever wondered about any of these things or more, then this book is for you! It's full of stories about Texas's history.

This isn't your typical book about Texas. It will guide you through some of the historical events and facts that have formed Texas into the incredible state it is today. You'll learn facts about the state that you may have never even wondered about. Once you've finished this book, you are going to know all there is to know about Texas.

Texas is a state that's rich in its history and culture. We will go all the way back to when the state was first founded and when it gained its independence from Mexico. We'll also jump forward to 2018 and take a closer look at some of the more recent historical icons whose roots were planted in Texas.

While this book will mostly follow a timeline of historical events, we will jump around some as we talk about Texas's history and other interesting facts about the state and the people who live in it.

This book is broken up into three easy-to-follow chapters to help you gain a better understanding of the Lone Star State. You'll learn some interesting facts about Texas that you'll be able to discuss with your friends or that may even make you want to visit this state!

Some of the facts you're about to learn are sad and some of them are shocking, but all of them are fascinating.

So, get ready to learn the following...

How did Texas get its name?

Why is it nicknamed the Lone Star State?

Who were the key players in the Battle of the Alamo?

Which *Disney* childhood stars came from Texas?

What sporting events got their start in Texas?

What animal did farmers and ranchers intentionally try to kill off?

And so much more!

CHAPTER ONE

TEXAS'S HISTORY AND RANDOM FACTS

Texas was the 28th state to enter the Union. The state is often represented by the Longhorn since it is the leading state in cattle production. But there's so much more to this state than its Longhorns. It's rich in both history and culture. Do you want to learn some interesting facts about Texas and its history? If so, then read on!

The Indians of Texas Gave the State Its Name

Before the Europeans settled in what is now known as Texas, the region was home to a number of different Native American tribes, now commonly known as the Indians of Texas. The area they occupied spanned from the Red River in Northern Texas to the Rio Grande in Southern Texas. Some of the major Native American tribes inhabiting Texas during this time included the Caddo, the Karankawa, the Coahuiltecan, the Lipan (Lipan-Apache), the Tonkawa, and the late-arriving Comanche.

Spanning across different regions of Texas, there was a world of cultural differences between these Native American tribes. Of all the Indians of Texas, the Caddo were the most well-developed tribe. They were known to be successful agriculturists.

It is from the Caddo that the state of Texas earned its name. Early Spanish authorities referred to a group within this tribe as the

"Tejas," which was the Caddo's word for "friend." Texas was the Spanish pronunciation of the word Tejas.

The word "Tejano" also stemmed from the word "Teja." Tejano means a Mexican-American residing in Southern Texas.

The Last Battle of the Civil War Took Place in Texas

The last battle of the Civil War is highly controversial. Technically, the last major Civil War battle was the Battle of Appomattox Court, which took place in April 1865. During this battle, Confederate General Robert E. Lee surrendered.

However, most Americans recognize the Battle of Palmito Ranch as the last battle of the Civil War. It took place on May 12-13, 1865, in Brownsville, Texas. Although the Union and Confederates were already commencing upon a truce, Union Colonel Theodore H. Barrett ordered an attack, which took place near Fort Brown. It's been said that Barrett wanted to witness a battle before the war came to an end. The following day, the Confederacy retaliated and attacked near Palmito Ranch.

It may be surprising to some that the Confederates actually won this final battle, killing or wounding 30 Union soldiers. They also captured 100 other opponents. The Confederates were said to have been supplied by the French Army, which was occupying a nearby town in Mexico. Although it cannot be verified, it is also believed that the French Army provided the Confederates with a steam-powered gunboat that they used to patrol the Rio Grande.

The Confederates may have won the Battle of Palmito Ranch, but their victory didn't last too long. They officially surrendered and President Andrew Jackson ended the Union blockade of the Southern states in June of 1865.

Davy Crockett's Death Remains a Mystery

Legendary frontiersman and U.S. Congressman, David "Davy" Crockett, was one of the most famous people to fight in the Battle of the Alamo. He was a Congressman in Tennessee and had recently

14

lost his seat. It's believed that he headed to Texas to help boost his political career, as his participation in the Battle of the Alamo could have worked to his advantage.

When Davy Crockett arrived at the Alamo in early 1836, he was quickly identified as its leader. This was mostly due to his popularity, but the fact that he and his volunteers brought rifles with them helped to secure his position because the fort was poorly defended at the time of their arrival. His fame helped boost morale at the Alamo and he used his level-headed skillfulness in politics to help diffuse tensions that were occurring within the fort.

So, what exactly happened to Davy Crockett? Well, no one knows for sure. Davy Crockett was at the Alamo when the Mexican Army attacked on March 6, 1836. Most of the 200 men who were inside the fort perished during this attack, and although some of the soldiers surrendered, they were later killed. After the battle was over, it was rumored that Davy Crockett was one of them. However, other accounts at the time claimed that he was found dead inside the Alamo. To this day, Crockett's death remains a mystery.

Regardless of how Crockett died, word of his death spread all across Texas and the United States. Davy Crockett's participation in the battle was highly influential. Since he was such a famous person, it inspired others to come to continue to fight in the Battle of the Alamo.

Tejanos Fought in the Battle of the Alamo

Since the Battle of the Alamo was an attack instigated by the Mexican Army, it may be surprising for some to know that Tejanos fought as defenders in the battle.

Some historians regard the Tejanos who fought in the battle as the unsung heroes, as they often weren't idolized the same way Anglo-American defenders like Jim Bowie, Davy Crockett, and William Travis were. In fact, in many retellings of the Battle of the Alamo, the Tejanos' role was left out completely.

Before we discuss the battle, let's talk more about the Tejanos. The Tejanos who lived in San Antonio, which was then northeastern Mexico, lived apart from the rest of Mexico. They had formed a ranching community and a culture that was distinct from that of Mexico.

In 1821, Mexico gained its independence from Spain. During this time, Mexico welcomed U.S. settlers to inhabit Texas, which was under the control of the Mexican government. Most of the Tejanos recognized the financial benefits of immigrants and welcomed the U.S. settlers with open arms.

There's a bit of controversy among historians regarding what the objectives of the Tejanos really were. Some historians feel the Tejanos wanted their independence from Mexico and invited U.S. settlers to fight for their cause. Other historians think that the Tejanos wanted Texas to have rights but they didn't want to actually break away from Mexico.

Regardless of their motivations, Tejanos played a critical role in Texas's independence. Some of the Tejanos who played a key role in the Battle of the Alamo included Juan Seguin, Gregorio Esparza, and José Toribio Losoya.

Six Flags Have Been Flown Over Texas

Have you ever heard the saying "six flags over Texas?" You may have seen the slogan at theme parks, shopping malls, and other places.

Maybe you have even heard that six flags have flown over Texas, but do you know the reason why?

Well, it all stems from 1519 when Spanish explorers first arrived in Texas. For a long time, the Spanish explorers had actually ignored Texas before their arrival in 1519. They didn't think there was anything in the area worth exploring.

It wasn't until the 1680s, when the Spanish found out that the French had established an outpost in Matagorda Bay, that the

Spanish claimed ownership of Texas. The Spanish founded San Antonio in 1718.

In 1821, Mexico gained its independence from Spain and pushed them out of Texas. However, Texas did not remain under Mexico's control for very long after that.

In 1836, Texas became its own country, during which time it was called the Republic of Texas. Again, this didn't last too long. Texas agreed to become a part of the United States in 1845. But in 1861, it was one of 10 states that seceded to form the Confederacy. After the Civil War, Texas rejoined the Union in 1865, which it continues to remain a part of to this day!

As you've probably guessed by now, the six flags that have flown over Texas were from each of the countries that have ruled over the state.

The six flags that have flown over Texas are:

1. The flag of Spain (1519-1821)

2. The royal banner of France (1685-1690)

3. The flag of Mexico (1821-1836)

4. The flag of the Republic of Texas (1836-1845)

5. The flag of the United States of America (1845-1861 and 1865-present)

6. The flag of the Confederate States of America (1861-1865)

Many places throughout Texas continue to display the six flags today. However, some have removed the Confederate flag in recent years.

Why Texas is Nicknamed "The Lone Star State"

Have you ever wondered why Texas was nicknamed the Lone Star State? It got the nickname from its flag. The Texas state flag, which was adopted when the state became the Republic of Texas, is called the Lone Star Flag. The reasoning for this is pretty simple: the flag has a single or "lone" white star.

The Lone Star Flag is made up of three colors: red, white, and blue. Each color on the flag embodies a different meaning. The red represents bravery, the white represents purity, and the blue represents loyalty.

There's also a meaning behind the lone star on the flag. The star is meant to represent "ALL of Texas and stands for our unity under God, State, and Country."

Many Texans still hang the Lone Star Flag as a reminder of Texas's independence.

Camels Were Once Brought to Texas

You might think that camels are only found in the Eastern hemisphere, zoos, or circuses, but this hasn't always been the case. In fact, at one point, camels were commonly seen in Texas!

In 1856, the United States Army began a program called the United States Camel Corps. Camels were brought in from countries such as Greece, Egypt, Turkey, and Malta. They were transported by boat to Indianola, Texas and were taken to Camp Verde.

Why would the U.S. Army bring camels to Texas? They wanted to experiment with using the camels as pack animals in the desert of Southwestern Texas.

In certain aspects, the camels did a great job in Texas. Not only did they fare well on a diet of prickly plants and scrubs, but the camels were also useful in areas where horses and mules weren't. They were able to go days at a time without water and even led soldiers to water holes, which saved lives.

As a whole, however, the United States Camel Corps experiment was largely unsuccessful. The camels didn't get along with the horses and mules. The horses and mules were so afraid of the camels that they would bolt. The camels were also difficult to handle and their odor was bothersome to the soldiers.

The U.S. Army stopped using camels in Texas during the Civil War after a failed attempt to carry mail between New Mexico and California.

So, what happened to those camels? While the government was able to round up 66 camels from the population, of which more than 100 had resided at Camp Verde and still more roamed the countryside, no one knows for sure what happened to those that remained uncaptured. The ones that were rounded up were sold off to circuses in the United States and Mexico in 1866.

But what about the camels that weren't rounded up? Well, they're a bit of a legend. It has been said that those camels may have continued to breed out in the wild. Some people even claim to see them today, but there are plenty of people who are skeptical about their existence. A camel sighting in Texas is often compared to a Chupacabra or Bigfoot sighting. If you happen to see a camel in Texas, just know that people might not believe your tale.

Sam Houston May Be Texas's Hero, But He Wasn't Even from Texas!

Sam Houston is by far the most well-known Texan in history. He has long been viewed as Texas's hero—and for good reason. Without him, Texas wouldn't be the state it is today. In fact, if it weren't for him, it wouldn't be a state *at all*.

After the deadly attack at the Alamo, Sam Houston and his troops caught the Mexican Army off-guard while they were sleeping on the banks of the San Jacinto River. Eight-hundred soldiers defeated the Mexican army, which was twice their size, in just 18 minutes. It was during the Battle of San Jacinto that Santa Anna surrendered and signed an armistice that gave Texas its independence.

Due to his heroism, it's not at all surprising that Sam Houston served as the first president of the Texas Republic. Eighty percent voted for him in the election. He was later re-elected.

When Texas eventually became part of the United States again, Houston was elected as one of the state's senators.

Houston's heroism is memorialized in Texas in many ways. For starters, the city of Houston, which was the original capital of the state, was named after Sam Houston.

There's also a 67-foot statue of Sam Houston that stands in Huntsville, Texas. Though there are larger statues in the United States (including the Statue of Liberty and Our Lady of the Rockies), the Sam Houston statue is the largest statue in America that's modeled after a real person.

The kicker to all of this? Though he may be Texas's hero, Sam Houston wasn't even *from* Texas! Houston was born in Rockbridge County, Virginia.

He later started his political career in Tennessee, where he was elected Governor. He resigned from office after his wife Eliza left him and made his infidelity and alcoholism public knowledge. He then went to live with a Cherokee tribe in Arkansas, where he became an honorary Cherokee and married a Cherokee woman.

Thirty years after resigning from his position as Governor of Tennessee, he was elected Governor of Texas (making him the only Governor to have ever been elected to serve in that capacity for two states).

Regardless of where he was born, Sam Houston was a pretty remarkable guy!

The Texas State Capital Was Named After "The Father of Texas"

While Houston was named after Sam Houston, the new capital of Texas was named after another important figure in Texas history. Austin, Texas, was named after Stephen F. Austin, "The Father of Texas."

So, who was the man that gave Texas's capital city its name? Why was he important?

Stephen F. Austin was the first to establish an Anglo-American colony in Texas when it was a province of Mexico. During his time, Texas grew into an independent republic.

The idea wasn't actually Stephen F. Austin's. It was his father, Moses Austin, who was the first to take steps towards establishing a colony in the region. Moses Austin traveled to San Antonio with a petition that would grant him land and received permission to establish a settlement of 300 families across 200,000 acres of land. However, Moses Austin died before he was able to accomplish his plans, leaving Stephen F. Austin to complete the settlement.

Stephen F. Austin was responsible for more than just establishing the settlement. He also oversaw immigration, established a law enforcement system, allocated land, and ensured the development of social infrastructure (e.g. roads, sawmills).

Without Stephen F. Austin, Texas wouldn't be what it is today.

There Was Once a Death at the Texas State Fair

The Texas State Fair is the largest fair in the United States. Although the fair doesn't formally document the number of attendees, it's estimated that about 3 million people visit the fair every year.

The Texas State Fair is most well-known for its 55-foot statue and greeter, Big Tex, the world's tallest cowboy. It also has the largest Ferris wheel in the entire Western Hemisphere! Some of the foods you'll find include corn dogs, Frito pies, and turkey legs. There's live entertainment, exhibits, and other fun attractions. It's one experience you won't want to miss out on.

But not every day has gone smoothly at the Texas State Fair. In 1979, there was an accident involving the Swiss Skyride gondola cars. One of the gondola cars got caught on a tower. A second car ended up crashing into it, which caused both cars to plummet 85 feet into the tent-covered game booths below.

The accident is one that never should have happened at all. It was caused by 90 mph winds.

91-year-old Fred Millard, who was a passenger in the first gondola car, died. His wife and young daughters were among 17 people injured in the accident. One woman was left paralyzed as a result of the accident. She died in 1986.

About $10 million was awarded to victims of the accident in court settlements.

The Swiss Skyride was immediately shut down following the incident. The ride has since been replaced, however. In 2007, a new and improved Texas Skyway gondola ride could be found at the fair. The new gondola ride has better safety features to prevent another accident from occurring.

You Can Watch a Movie Where Lee Harvey Oswald Was Arrested

Lee Harvey Oswald, who assassinated the late President John F. Kennedy, was arrested at the Texas Theater in Dallas, Texas.

What some may not know is that Lee Harvey Oswald wasn't originally arrested for killing the president. He was first arrested for shooting and killing Dallas police officer J. D. Tippit.

Oswald's arrest came about on November 22, 1963, when a shoe store manager named John Brewer noticed him loitering suspiciously outside his store. Brewer noted that Oswald fit the description of the suspect in the shooting of Officer Tippit. When Oswald continued up the street and slipped inside the Texas Theater without paying for a ticket, Brewer called a theater worker, who alerted authorities.

Fifteen Dallas police officers arrived at the scene. When they turned on the movie house lights, they found Lee Harvey Oswald sitting towards the back of the theater. The movie that had been airing at the time was *War is Hell.*

When Lee Harvey Oswald was questioned by authorities about Tippit's homicide, Captain J. W. Fritz recognized his name as one of the workers from the book depository who had been reported missing and was already being considered a suspect in JFK's assassination. The day after he was formally arraigned for murdering Officer Tippit, he was also charged with assassinating John F. Kennedy.

Today, the Texas Theater is a historical landmark that is commonly visited by tourists. It still airs movies and hosts special events. There's also a bar and lounge.

The Texas Theater was the first theater in Texas to have air conditioning. It was briefly owned by famous aviator and film producer, Howard Hughes.

Texas's Capitol Building is the Largest in the United States *and* It's Haunted

One might think that the largest Capitol building in the country is the nation's Capitol in Washington, D.C., but you'd be wrong. In fact, the Texas State Capitol stands seven feet higher than the nation's capitol building. It's the largest state Capitol in the United States!

Located in Austin, Texas, the Texas State Capitol was one of the top seven tallest buildings in the world when it was built. Built of limestone and granite, Texas's Capitol building has a statue of a lady with a sword on top. The 16-foot, 2,000-pound aluminum Goddess of Liberty statue sits on top of the Capitol building.

Aside from its size, there's also something else pretty well-known (and dare we say cool?) about the Texas State Capitol building. It's haunted. There have been numerous reports of ghost sightings in the Capitol building. Visitors have claimed to have had encounters with the ghosts of Sam Houston, Andrew Hamilton, and Edmond Jackson Davis. Some have even claimed to see the ghost of a "lady in red."

Bonnie and Clyde Are Buried in Texas

Surely, you've heard the story of Bonnie and Clyde, love-struck lovers and partners in crime. They're probably the most infamous outlaws of all time. There's no doubt this iconic couple has gone down in history. There have been movies made and songs written about them. But did you know that Bonnie and Clyde had roots in Texas?

Both Bonnie and Clyde were born in Texas. Clyde Barrow was born in Ellis County, Texas, in 1909. The following year, Bonnie Parker was born in Abilene, Texas.

Their story begins in West Dallas where the two met in 1930 at a mutual friend's house. Clyde had been caring for the friend, who had a broken arm, when Bonnie stopped by. At the time, Bonnie was just 19 years old and married to a man who was in jail. She remained married to him until the day she died. In fact, it's even been said that she died wearing her wedding ring.

Upon meeting, Bonnie and Clyde were instantly taken with one another. It was love at first sight. Many historians believe that the entire reason Bonnie remained by Clyde's side through their violent crime spree was because she loved him.

When she took Clyde to her mother's home to meet her mom, he was arrested for a robbery he had committed in Waco. When she visited him in jail, she smuggled in a gun that would help him escape. She hoped that Clyde would get on the straight and narrow, but instead she ended up joining him on his crime sprees.

The outlaws traveled the United States in stolen cars and committed both robberies and murders together. They received national attention when they robbed a National Guard armory, killing nine policemen and stealing an arsenal of weapons. The FBI and other law enforcement officers began to chase them.

In May of 1934, Bonnie and Clyde were killed in Bienville Parish, Louisiana. They were shot by four Texas officers and two Louisiana officers.

While Bonnie and Clyde are both buried in Dallas, Texas, their bodies are interred at two different cemeteries. Clyde is buried in a family plot with his brother, Marvin "Buck" Barrow, at Western Heights Cemetery. Bonnie is buried at Crown Memorial Park.

Want to spend the night where Bonnie and Clyde rested? If so, then one Texas landmark you may want to check out is the Fort Worth's Stockyards Hotel, which the partners in crime used as a hideout.

The room they stayed in is called "The Bonnie & Clyde Suite." It has a number of historic artifacts, including a poem Bonnie wrote for Clyde and her .38 revolver.

Two United States Presidents Were Born in Texas

Did you know that two United States presidents were born in Texas? What you might be surprised to learn is that they weren't George W. Bush or George H. W. Bush! Though the Bushes are well-known for establishing their political careers in Texas, both father and son were born in New England states.

So, which presidents *were* born in Texas?

Dwight Eisenhower was born in Denison, Texas, though he moved to Kansas when he was just a toddler. He later became the 34th President of the United States.

Lyndon B. Johnson, however, had strong roots in Texas. His family founded Johnson City, and he was born in nearby Stonewall, Texas. Johnson was a U.S. representative and later a U.S. senator in Texas before becoming the Vice President of the United States.

Ironically, Johnson became the President of the United States while he was in his home state. You see, Lyndon B. Johnson wasn't actually elected to be the President. He was John F. Kennedy's Vice President. It wasn't until John F. Kennedy was assassinated in Dallas by Lee Harvey Oswald on November 22, 1963, that Johnson became president.

Just two hours after JFK was assassinated, Lyndon B. Johnson was sworn into office aboard Air Force One while it was stationed at Dallas Love Field Airport.

A Popular Card Game Has Texas Origins

As its name suggests, Texas Hold'em was started in the Lone Star State. While it's unknown who exactly came up with the idea of Texas Hold'em, the game can be traced back to Robstown, Texas, in the early 1900s.

The game began to spread like wildfire throughout Texas. In 1967, a group of Texan card players took the game to Las Vegas. One of those card players was Crandell Addington, who is one of the co-founders of the World Series of Poker. Addington is also a member of the Poker Hall of Fame.

The game was originally called Hold'em before it was taken to Vegas. It was there that it received the name Texas Hold'em.

The Golden Nugget in Las Vegas was the first and only casino to offer Texas Hold'em. Unfortunately, the casino's poker room didn't receive many high-paying players. As a result, the game didn't become popular. It wasn't until top poker players were invited to play Hold'em at the Dunes Casino that it gained popularity with gamblers.

In 1969, Texas Hold'em was added to the Second Annual Gambling Fraternity Convention. The following year, this convention was renamed the World Series of Poker. No-limit Hold'em became the main event, and has remained the main event ever since.

Today, Texas Hold'em is one of the most popular types of poker.

RANDOM FACTS

1. The Alamo is Texas's most popular historic site. It gets more than 2 million visitors every year who come to see the buildings, which have been restored, and the monument honoring all of the fallen soldiers.

2. In 1836, Sam Houston defeated Stephen F. Austin in the presidential election. However, Austin was appointed as Secretary of State, a position that he held until he died later that year.

3. Sam Houston wasn't happy about Austin's location as capital. He believed that it was too remote, which would make it difficult to defend from the Mexican Army and the Native Americans.

4. Despite being a slave owner himself, Sam Houston was actually against slavery. He voted against making slavery more widespread in the United States and refused to swear allegiance to the Confederate States of America. This led to him being removed from his position as Governor of Texas.

5. Texas is unique in terms of how it came to be a part of the United States. It's the only state that did not become a part of the country by territorial annexation. Instead, it became a part of the United States by treaty. It took years of debate before it happened. The issue that caused the debate was slavery. Texas had a large population of slaves, with 30,000 of its 125,000 residents being slaves. People throughout the United States feared that adding a new slave state would interfere with Congress and other political issues.

6. Each year on March 2nd, Texans celebrate Texas Independence Day. It commemorates the state gaining its independence from Mexico. The day is also known as Texas Flag Day and Sam

Houston Day. To celebrate the state's independence, there are festivals which include live band performances, chili cook-offs, re-enactments, and more.

7. Six Flags amusement park, which was founded in 1961, was named after Texas's six flags! Though there are several locations throughout the country, the original park is located in Arlington, Texas. It is split into several different sections, with park attractions depicting the six flags that have flown over Texas, including Spanish and Mexican sections of the park.

8. There's a popular myth that Texas could secede from the United States of America at any time. This isn't true. However, the state of Texas *could* hypothetically change in the future. In Texas's 1845 annexation agreement, it was decided that the state could divide into five different states without approval of the U.S. government. Although no attempts have actually been made to divide Texas into five states, state lawmakers have toyed with the idea of dividing Texas into two states.

9. Texas has the highest maximum highway speed limit in all of America. There's a stretch of highway between Austin and San Antonio that allows you to drive at 85 mph. If you love to speed, then you just might love Texas.

10. Three of the top ten most populated cities in the United States are located in Texas. These cities include Houston (population of 2.3 million), San Antonio (of 1.49 million), and Dallas (of 1.3 million).

11. The Texas Rangers are the oldest statewide law enforcement agency in the United States. The force came into existence in 1823. The Texas Ranger Hall of Fame museum is located in Waco. Members of the Texas Rangers included Will Rogers, John Wayne, Chuck Norris, and former President George H. W. Bush.

12. As the saying goes, "Everything is bigger in Texas." Well, Texas itself is pretty big. It's the second-largest state in the

United States. The first-largest state is Alaska and the third-largest state is California. Encompassing 268,820 square miles, the state of Texas is two times the size of Germany!

13. Although you might think the saying "Don't mess with Texas" came about because of its state pride, it actually originated as a part of its anti-litter campaign. The state spent about $20 million annually to clean up trash along its highways. The slogan was designed to help with its anti-litter campaign. It gained so much popularity that Texans display it on bumper stickers, shirts, and anywhere else they want to show off their state pride today.

14. Like most states, there are still a number of odd laws perpetuated in Texas. It's illegal to sell your eye, milk another person's cow, take more than three sips of beer while standing, or shoot a buffalo from the second story of a hotel.

15. Texas has its own Eiffel Tower. The 65-foot tower was built in Paris, Texas, in 1995. It has been boasted as the "second-largest Eiffel Tower in the second-largest Paris."

16. There are more than 145 languages spoken in Texas. Aside from English, you'll hear everything from German and Vietnamese to Hindu and Tagalog spoken in this state!

17. Texas's state motto is "friendship." It was chosen due to the Caddo's meaning of the word Tejas.

18. Though Texas is a part of the United States, the state still owns all of its public lands. What does this mean? In order for the United States to build anything within the borders of Texas, it must first ask for permission. This includes public or state parks.

19. The Lone Star State has sued the United States more than 40 times in the past 100 years over everything from women's health to the environment. Most of those lawsuits occurred during the Obama Administration.

20. As of 2010, Texas had a population of more than 25.1 million people.

Test Yourself – Questions and Answers

1. What does the word Tejas mean?

   a. Friends
   b. Enemies
   c. Soldiers

2. Which United States President *wasn't* born in Texas?

   a. Lyndon B. Johnson
   b. George W. Bush
   c. Dwight Eisenhower

3. Why is Texas known as the Lone Star State? What was it nicknamed after?

   a. The country band called Lonestar
   b. A horse named Lone Star who won a lot of races in Texas
   c. The Lone Star flag of the Texas Republic

4. Who was the first President of the Texas Republic?

   a. Davy Crockett
   b. Lyndon B. Johnson
   c. Sam Houston

5. Which animal was brought to Texas in the 1850s by the United States Army to help assist soldiers traveling in the desert?

   a. Camels
   b. Kangaroos
   c. Mules

Answers

1. a.
2. b.
3. c.
4. c.
5. a.

CHAPTER TWO

TEXAS'S POP CULTURE

Texas is a state that's rich in pop culture. It's had a huge influence on one genre of music, in particular. Do you know which one? Do you know which famous Tejano singer has roots in Texas or where she's buried? Have you heard about the influential musician who was bullied while she was growing up in Texas? To discover the answers to these and other interesting facts, read on!

Country Music Started Out in Texas

Country music is the most listened to genre of music on radio stations today. Have you ever wondered how country music came to be?

Well, it all started back in the early 1900s with a Texas fiddler named Eck Robertson. Robertson grew up on a farm and started learning how to play the fiddle at the age of five. He later learned to play the banjo and guitar.

In 1904, a sixteen-year-old Robertson decided that he wanted to become a professional musician and began to travel and play his music. Two years later, Eck Robertson met his wife. Together, they performed at fiddling contests and silent-movie theaters.

Eck Robertson later met 74-year-old fiddler, Henry C. Gilliland. In 1922, the two traveled to New York City where they auditioned for and secured a recording contract with the Victor Talking Machine Company. They recorded the first four country songs every produced, but only two of them—"Turkey in the Straw" and "Arkansas Traveler"—ended up being released. Robertson was asked to return to the studio to record six more songs, this time without Gilliland.

Country music has come a long way since then, but we can thank Texas for its beginnings.

And the First Country Album to Go Platinum Came from Texan Musicians!

The first country album to go platinum was a collaboration of more than one artist. The album was called *Wanted! The Outlaws* and featured songs from Texas natives Waylon Jennings and Willie Nelson. It also featured Jessi Colter (Waylon Jennings's wife) and Thomas Paul "Tompall" Glaser.

The album, which was released in 1976 by RCA Records, was inclusive of songs that had already been released. It was the record label's attempt at getting music performed by Waylon Jennings to sell, as well as marketing music by Willie Nelson, who was outselling Jennings.

RCA Records also hoped to capitalize on outlaw country music, which was a new subgenre of country music. Outlaw was considered to be more progressive in terms of sound and emphasized the drug culture.

The country album was the first in history to gain platinum status when it reached one million sales.

Wanted! The Outlaws quickly rose to the top of country charts, hitting number one, and also earned a #10 spot on the pop charts.

Two hit singles came from the album. They were "Suspicious Minds" and "Good Hearted Woman."

The Richest Female Musician is From Texas, But She's Not a Country Singer

As of 2017, R&B/Pop singer Beyoncé Knowles-Carter was the highest-paid female musician by a landslide. That year alone, she made $105 million! Many may not know that Queen Bey was born and raised in Houston, Texas.

Beyoncé and Solange Knowles are often considered Texas's most famous sisters.

Beyoncé first began competing in the local talent shows. The singer says she sold her very first song at St. John's United Methodist Church in Houston.

In 2017, Beyoncé went back to her home state to help with Hurricane Harvey relief efforts. She, her mother Tina Knowles, and her former band member Michelle Williams all went to Houston to help distribute supplies to those in need. They handed out food and diapers to Hurricane Harvey victims. Through her organization BeyGOOD, the singer also donated cots, wheelchairs, feminine products, and more to those in need.

This wasn't the first time Beyoncé has made charitable contributions to her hometown. In 2017, she donated $7 million to help with Houston's homeless.

Although she's not a country singer, Beyoncé has mentioned that she wants to make a country music album at one point. Though she has yet to release a full country album, the singer *did* record a country track called "Daddy Lessons" for her *Lemonade* album. The song has received support from a number of artists within the country music community, including Dierks Bentley and Karen Fairchild from Little Big Town. It should be interesting to see if Beyoncé will revisit her country roots in her music in the future.

This Famous Singer Was Bullied While She Was Growing Up in Texas

Janis Joplin is often considered one of the most influential musicians of all-time. Countless singers have credited her influence over their own music. But did you know that Janis Joplin wasn't always that popular? In fact, she was bullied in Texas.

Growing up in Port Arthur, Texas, Janis Joplin was an excellent student with a bright future. She was involved in extracurricular activities in high school, such as Glee Club and the Future Teachers of America. But high school wasn't all rainbows and butterflies for Joplin.

Janis Joplin was bullied by former NFL coach Jimmy Johnson, with whom she went to high school. This led Joplin to become the rebel of the small town she grew up in. She colored her hair and spent a lot of time in blues bars.

After high school, Joplin headed off to Texas University. Unfortunately, college wasn't any better for her when it came to bullying. In fact, she dropped out after just one semester because the other students were so mean to her. She was voted "The Ugliest Man on Campus" by the Texas University fraternities. Though the singer went on to have great success, that label was said to have haunted her for the rest of her short life.

You Can Celebrate Selena's Life in Corpus Christi

By now, you've probably already heard of Grammy-winning Tejano musician Selena Quintanilla-Perez, who was murdered at a hotel in Corpus Christi, Texas. Today, she's considered a legend.

For those who don't already know the story, it goes like this: Selena, who was considered the Queen of the Tejano world, was just 23 years old when she was murdered on March 31, 1995. At the time of her death, Selena's fame had been on the rise. Between United States and international sales, she and her family, who performed her backup music, had sold more than 60 million albums. She was most well-known for her songs "Como la Flor", "Bidi Bidi Bom Bom", and "Dreaming of You."

Her life came to a tragic end after she confronted her friend and fan club president, Yolanda Saldivar, about stolen documents at a Days Inn in Corpus Christi. The documents would prove that Saldivar was stealing money from Selena. Saldivar refused to provide her with the documents. She told Selena that she had been raped. Selena drove her to the hospital, where doctors said Saldivar had been lying.

When Selena and Yolanda Saldivar returned to the hotel, they argued. Saldivar shot Selena in the back when she turned to leave the hotel room. Selena ran to the hotel lobby for help. She named Saldivar as the person who had shot her before she fell to the floor. Selena was pronounced dead upon arrival to the hospital.

Saldivar had gone to her car and pointed a gun at her own head as she was surrounded by police officers before surrendering.

Selena had become a household name throughout much of the world, but people in her home state really loved her. On the day of her death, Texas radio and television stations received many calls from distraught fans and listeners.

Yolanda Saldivar was sentenced to life in prison without the likelihood of being granted parole. Although a rumor starts every few years that Saldivar has died, it has been confirmed that she remains alive in the Mountain View Correctional Unit in Gatesville, Texas.

There was a movie called *Selena*, which starred Jennifer Lopez, about the life and death of the Tejano musician. The movie made $35 million at the box office and helped Lopez rise to fame.

Selena's legacy is still kept alive in Corpus Christi today. There are a number of ways you can celebrate the life of the Tejano singer when you're visiting the city.

For starters, there's a Selena Museum that was started by the musician's family. It's in the old music studio where the family used to create their records. You'll get a tour of the studio room, which was the same one used in the movie *Selena*. Other things you'll see at the museum include some of her iconic outfits, her Grammy award, her red Porsche, her decorative egg collection, a display of Selena Barbie dolls, and so much more. The museum is every Selena fan's dream.

There's also a memorial statue called the Mirador de la Flor, or Selena's Seawall. The monument is located at the corner of Shoreline Boulevard and Peoples Street T-Head. Hundreds of fans visit her memorial every week.

Selena is buried at Seaside Memorial Park in Corpus Christi. Some people believe that the gravesite may even be haunted by Selena's ghost! There have been reports of hearing the late musician singing near her grave. Some have even claimed to see what they believe to be the ghost of Selena walking along the Seawall.

Eeyore's Birthday is Celebrated in Austin

Are you a fan of *Winnie-the-Pooh*? If so, you might want to visit Austin, Texas, to celebrate Eeyore's birthday. Yes, that's right. The city celebrates the fictional donkey's birthday in the form of a festival, which usually takes place on the last Saturday of April at Pease Park.

This festival began in 1963 when the English Department students at the University of Texas at Austin chose the theme for their spring picnic. The reason they chose Eeyore's birthday as the theme for the picnic was that in A. A. Milne's *Winnie-the-Pooh* stories, Eeyore thinks his friends Winnie, Tigger, Piglet, Owl, and Rabbit have forgotten his birthday, when in reality they had planned a surprise birthday party for him.

The very first year of the party, the students had a picnic. They brought honey (because what would a *Winnie-the-Pooh* themed picnic be without some honey?), lemonade, beer, a maypole, and a live donkey draped in flowers.

The theme of the picnic was embraced by Austin's hippie community. Today, that Eeyore themed picnic has evolved into a huge festival. It's still celebrated by much of the hippie community, as well as the hipsters. Many of the original college alumni still attend the event with their families.

Sponsored by the Friends of the Forest Foundation, Eeyore's Birthday Party in Austin has a number of festivities. You'll find live music, food and drink vendors, and more. Proceeds go to support local charities.

The party begins at 11 a.m. and runs until dusk. There are typically costumes and costume contests, so don't be afraid to dress up. However, clothes tend to come off later at night, so parents with children might consider attending the festival earlier in the day.

To keep the spirit of Eeyore's birthday going, there's always a maypole and a live donkey in attendance at the festival every year!

Three *Disney* Child Stars Were Born in Texas

If you're a fan of *Disney*, it might surprise you to know that three of your favorite child actresses came from Texas.

Lizzie McGuire actress Hilary Duff and her older sister Haylie Duff both grew up in Texas. Their father owns a chain of Texas convenience stores, so Hilary grew up between Houston and San Antonio, where the stores are located.

The Duffs' mother encouraged both girls to pursue acting, singing, and ballet. They both performed at local theaters, as well as appearing in a San Antonio theater's production of *The Nutcracker*.

Hilary Duff's mom moved her and her sister to California in 1993 to pursue their acting careers. Hilary earned a few small roles before being cast in her first major film, *Casper Meets Wendy*.

In 2001, the *Lizzie McGuire* show premiered. Hilary Duff became a household name. She gained even more attention that year when media caught wind of her relationship with pop singer Aaron Carter.

Another *Disney* actress who started out in Texas? Selena Gomez! The actress was born in Grand Prairie, Texas. Selena Gomez's mother was also a former stage actress. Selena became interested in an acting career while watching her mother prepare for the stage. Her first role was in *Barney & Friends*, which is where she first met our third Texan who went on to become a *Disney* star—Demi Lovato.

Despite being born in Albuquerque, New Mexico, "Sorry Not Sorry" singer Demi Lovato grew up in Dallas. The star's mother was a former Dallas Cowboys Cheerleader. Lovato has credited her mother's stories about the difficulty of being a Dallas Cowboys Cheerleader, with teaching her the value of hard work.

Demi Lovato also has a half-sister named Madison Lee De La Garza, who played fellow Texan Eva Longoria's daughter in the show *Desperate Housewives*.

Barney & Friends Was Filmed in Dallas

Barney, the purple dinosaur, was an iconic character for millennial children. Did you know that *Barney & Friends* got its start in Dallas, TX?

The concept of the series was created by Dallas native Sheryl Leach, a former inner-city school teacher and marketing executive. Leach thought there was a market for preschool-aged children. She couldn't have been more accurate. The series had a seventeen-year run! It initially aired on PBS Kids in April of 1992 until production stopped in September of 2009.

During the time it aired, the series was filmed in the Dallas area. It makes sense why Selena Gomez and Demi Lovato were part of the cast of *Barney & Friends*.

The series might make a comeback. A series revival was initially discussed for 2017, but there hasn't been any word yet on when or if *Barney & Friends* is still set to return. We hope if it does return, it will still be filmed in Dallas.

Lots of Movies Have Been Filmed in Texas

Quite a few movies have been filmed in Texas. This is partly due to the nice weather, but it's also because the NASA Johnson Space Center is a popular filming location for many sci-fi movies.

Here's a list of a few of the many movies that have had scenes filmed in the Lone Star State:

- *Miss Congeniality*, starring Sandra Bullock, features some scenes that were filmed in San Antonio and Austin. There were scenes filmed on Congress Street in Austin and at two Austin hotels, the Driskill Hotel and the Hyatt Downtown.

- *Pearl Harbor* was filmed in Corpus Christi. A large part of the movie was filmed aboard the USS Lexington in the Corpus Christi Bay. The film stars Ben Affleck, Josh Hartnett, Alec Baldwin, and Cuba Gooding, Jr. Filming the movie on the USS Lexington proved to be controversial, with war veterans being infuriated over the ship being used to portray a Japanese ship.

- *What's Eating Gilbert Grape*, featuring Johnny Depp and Leonardo DiCaprio, was filmed in Manor, Texas. Gilbert works at a grocery store set in a fictional town in the movie. The actual grocery store in the film was Manor Grocery.

- *Armageddon* features scenes that were filmed at the Johnson Space Center. There were also scenes filmed in Denton, TX.

- *Transformers: Dark of the Moon* contains a scene that was shot at the Johnson Space Center.

- *Boyhood* was filmed in and around Houston. Some of the scenes were filmed on location at Minute Maid Park and the Houston Museum of Natural Science.

- *Terms of Endearment*, starring Shirley MacLaine and Jack Nicholson, features scenes that were shot throughout the Houston area. In the movie, the couple's lunch scene was filmed at Brennan's Restaurant in Midtown Houston. Scenes were also filmed on location at East Beach, Leon's Gourmet Grocer, the University of Nebraska, Lincoln General Hospital, and Lincoln Municipal Airport.

- *Space Cowboys*, starring Clint Eastwood, contains scenes that were filmed at the Johnson Space Center.

- *Apollo 13* is another movie that was filmed at the Johnson Space Center.

- *Any Given Sunday* contains scenes that were filmed at the Texas Stadium.

- *Boys Don't Cry*, starring Hilary Swank, was filmed in Texas, even though the actual story that the movie is based on took place in Nebraska. Scenes were filmed on location at Dad's Broadway Skateland in Mesquite, the Hunt County Courthouse in Greenville, and the McKinney Grain Company in McKinney. Scenes were also filmed throughout Crandall, Texas.

Other movies that were filmed in Texas include *The Rookie, The Tree of Life*, and *Any Given Sunday.*

A *Supernatural* Star Owns a Brewery in the Austin Area

Best known for his role as Dean Winchester in the hit show *Supernatural*, Jensen Ackles was born in Dallas, Texas.

Though he moved to Los Angeles to pursue acting, Ackles recently moved back to Texas with his wife and child.

Jensen Ackles and his brother-in-law recently decided to turn their hobby of brewing beer into a business. On January 10th, 2018, their craft brewery, Family Business Beer Co., opened in the Austin area.

It's unlikely that you'll actually see Ackles working at the brewery since he spends most of the year filming *Supernatural* in Vancouver, B.C. But hey, you never know!

The actor told KXAN-TV that you might also be able to spot him at ABGB, his favorite brewpub in Austin.

Ackles' friend and *Supernatural* co-star Jared Padalecki, who plays his brother Sam Winchester, also lives in the Austin area.

Late Actor Patrick Swayze Fell in Love with Horses in Texas

Though you might think he only had a love for dancing, *Dirty Dancing* actor Patrick Swayze also loved horses.

Swayze, who is also well-known for his role in the movie *Ghost*, was born and raised in Houston, Texas. The actor, who lived in the Oak Forest community of Houston until he was 20, was quite the equestrian. He even learned calf-roping!

His love of horses first began when he was a young boy. He visited Gleannloch Farms during this time, which is where he first fell in love with Arabian horses. He saw their horse named Morafic, which he later credited for the reason he fell in love with the Arabian breed.

You might be wondering how Swayze got into dancing when his horses were his real passion. His love for dance came from his mom, Patsy Swayze. She was a dancer herself, as well as a dance instructor and film choreographer. Patsy Swayze later choreographed movies such as *Urban Cowboy* and *Hope Floats*.

Patsy Swayze founded the Houston Jazz, of which she was the director. She also later opened the Swayze School of Dance, where Patrick was one of her students. It was there that he met the woman he would later go on to marry, Lisa Niemi, who also had a love for acting and was a fellow horse fanatic.

After his rise to fame, Patrick Swayze took a break from show business in order to breed Arabian horses with his wife. Due to their acting schedules, most of their horse shows were in Texas. They personally competed in the Dallas/Fort Worth big region IX show.

Patrick Swayze's favorite horse was a chestnut Arabian stallion named Tamsen.

Prior to losing his battle with pancreatic cancer in 2009, Swayze chose to live out his final months of life at his horse ranch with his wife. One of their stallions attended his memorial service.

A *Gossip Girl* Actress Was Born While Her Parents Were in Prison in Texas

Gossip Girl and *Roommate* actress Leighton Meester was born in Texas while both of her parents were in prison. Leighton's parents, along with her aunt and grandfather on her mom's side, were arrested for smuggling 1,200-pound marijuana shipments out of Jamaica.

Though it was originally rumored that Leighton was born in prison, she was born in a hospital. Leighton's mom had to serve 16 months in prison after she was born.

News of the story broke when *US Weekly* released an article about it. The cover read "She overcame!" And we would have to agree. Leighton's story is very inspiring. Despite her family's difficult past, the actress was still able to land her role as Blair Waldorf on *Gossip Girl* and become a household name.

Late Actress Debbie Reynolds Loved Growing Up in El Paso, But She Didn't Visit Often

Late actress Debbie Reynolds, who was famous for starring in films like *Singin' in the Rain, Tammy and the Bachelor*, and *Halloweentown*, said her El Paso upbringing helped shape her career in Hollywood.

The actress grew up in El Paso during the Great Depression. During that time, she would entertain her neighbors by singing and dancing for them. Reynolds loved performing and later went on to become one of Hollywood's most well-known actresses in the 1950s.

Although Debbie Reynolds said she loved growing up in El Paso and that she had a great childhood there, she didn't come back to visit often. She said that her visits made her sad since they were usually for funerals.

Reynolds did return to El Paso in 2010 to make an appearance at a screening of *Singin' in the Rain*. The film was aired at the Plaza Classic Film Festival. She spoke at the festival about her career and about growing up in El Paso. El Paso residents later praised her for her bravery in visiting again.

Debbie Reynolds died in 2016 in Los Angeles. She suffered from a stroke just one day after her daughter, *Star Wars* actress Carrie Fisher, passed away.

A Popular Country Band Was Named After the State

You probably figured out by now that the country band Lonestar was named after the Lone Star State. But do you know why?

Well, let's go back to the band's beginning. It may surprise you to know that Lonestar wasn't the band's first name. The band originally started out as Texassee. This name came about because all of the members of the group were from Texas. They also all somehow met each other while they were in Texas. However, it wasn't until band members Richie and Dean ran into one another in Nashville that they got the idea to start a band. After they had the idea, they called band members Michael and Keech to come out to Nashville.

In case you haven't already figured it out, Texassee was the result of Texas + Tennessee. Get it? Yeah, the record label thought the name was pretty lame, too.

When the band got a record deal, one of the conditions of the deal was that they would need to change their name. One of their songwriters told the producer of the album that they should choose a band name that would let people know they were all from Texas. That's how the name Lonestar was born.

The band has had several No. 1 singles, but they're most well-known for their songs "Amazed" and "I'm Already There."

Willie Nelson Has an Unusual Favorite Texas Childhood Pastime

We've heard of celebrities with some really unusual favorite pastimes. For example, Mike Tyson is said to have loved racing pigeons when he was younger, while Johnny Depp has a collection of Barbie dolls he plays with. But Texas country singer Willie Nelson's favorite pastime just might take the cake in terms of weirdness.

Nelson, who grew up in Abbott, loved to fight bumble bees when he was a kid. *Uh... what?*

Willie Nelson said he and his friends would go to fields where they would fight off swarms of bumblebees. They would get stung so much that their eyes would swell shut.

We can't imagine how this would be any fun, but apparently, his days of bumblebee fighting brings him fond memories.

Willie Nelson blames it on his small-town upbringing. He told *The New York Times*, "That shows how bored you can get in Abbott."

Apparently, he loved bumblebees so much that he mentions them in a line of his song, "Crazy Like Me."

We wonder if his favorite Texas adult pastime is walking down the street that's named after him. The city of Austin paid homage to the singer by naming a street downtown after him!

RANDOM FACTS

1. Though he was raised in Tennessee, R&B singer Usher was born in Dallas, Texas. He later went on to play in the 2001 movie titled *Texas Rangers*!

2. *Desperate Housewives* actress Eva Longoria's hometown is Corpus Christi. When she was in high school, she worked at a local Wendy's. In 2008, she returned to Wendy's to work the counter for a day.

3. Actor Matthew McConaughey was born in Uvalde, Texas, and grew up in Longview, Texas. He went to Longview High School, where he was voted "Most Handsome" during his senior year. Later, after his rise to fame, McConaughey was reported for a domestic disturbance in Austin. Responders found him naked and playing the bongo. The actor was believed to be high on herbal intoxicants.

4. Willie Nelson, Carol Burnett, and Carolyn Jones (of *The Addams Family*) were all born in Texas during the same month!

5. *Charlie's Angels* actress and former sex icon, Farrah Fawcett, was born in Corpus Christi. The actress attended the University of Texas and was voted one of the 10 most beautiful coeds. After Fawcett died of colon cancer in 2009, the friends she grew up with in Corpus Christi remembered her as "bubbly, smart, funny, athletic, and a loyal friend," according to the *Daily Herald*.

6. Texas-born Jessica Simpson may be from the country, but she hasn't always been down with her roots. Simpson once forgot the lyrics to a Dolly Parton song that she performed at a tribute event for the musician. However, Dolly forgave her and later sang on a track of Simpson's country album, *Do You Know*.

7. Selena Gomez was named after the late Selena Quintanilla-Perez. It's amazing how much the two have in common: both Texans, both with Mexican heritage, and both talented musicians.

8. Jared Padalecki and Jensen Ackles both spoke in favor of David's Law, which has since passed. The Texas law, which was named after a teen who committed suicide, criminalizes cyberbullying and requires schools to follow protocol.

9. Although *The Texas Chain Saw Massacre* is based on actual events, you may be surprised to learn that its inspiration doesn't come from Texas at all. The movie is actually based on Wisconsin serial killer Ed Gein.

10. *Gilmore Girls* and *Sisterhood of the Traveling Pants* actress Alexis Bledel is Tejano. She was born and raised in Houston, but her mom is from Mexico. The actress told *Latina Magazine* that while people usually mistake her as Irish, her family has embraced the Mexican culture. The actress told *Latina Magazine* that they speak Spanish in her parents' home and her mom "cooks amazing Mexican food."

11. Sandra Bullock, who lives in Texas, owns Walton's Fancy and Staple in Austin. It's an upscale restaurant, bakery, floral shop, and event planning business.

12. There was a TV show based on Dallas, Texas, and you've probably heard of it. *Dallas*, which aired from 1978 to 1991, was filmed in Frisco, Texas, which isn't too far away from Dallas. The show was filmed at the Cloyce Box Ranch.

13. *Teen Mom* star Farrah Abraham owns a frozen yogurt shop called FROCO FRESH & FROZEN in the Austin area.

14. Houston-born actress Jennifer Garner helped provide relief during Hurricane Harvey through the organization Save the Children, for which she's a trustee.

15. *Party of Five* and *I Know What You Did Last Summer* actress Jennifer Love Hewitt was born in Waco, Texas. She won "Texas

Our Little Miss Talent Winner," which led talent scouts to encourage her to pursue a career in acting. She later went on to star in the show *The Client List*, in which she plays a Texas woman who is struggling to make ends meet and turns to prostitution at a massage parlor. *The Client List* is loosely based on an actual prostitution scandal that happened in Odessa, Texas, in 2004.

16. Texan actor Jamie Foxx is a huge fan of the Dallas Cowboys. In fact, he originally hoped to play for the team. We wonder how different his career would have turned out.

17. Fred Gibson, who wrote the book *Old Yeller*, was a journalist in the late 1930s. He wrote for the *Corpus Christi Caller-Times*.

18. Country singer and Arlington native Maren Morris was given the title Chairwoman for the Texas Music Project, a non-profit organization that helped her become famous herself. The organization helps provide music education to disadvantaged groups. Texas Music Project sent Morris to a Grammy songwriting class in California.

19. *Fast and the Furious* actress Michelle Rodriguez grew up in San Antonio. She has fond memories of her mom's Spanish band playing in Brackenridge Park.

20. Musician Austin Mahone was born and raised in San Antonio. One of his first performances was at the Houston Rodeo in 2013, where he had the audience do the Harlem Shake. He performed with fellow Texan Demi Lovato. Mahone told *The Houston Chronicle* that he always gets Whataburger whenever he's back in Texas.

Test Yourself – Questions and Answers

1. Which famous singer was born and raised in Houston?

   a. Rihanna
   b. Britney Spears
   c. Beyoncé

2. Which of the following *Disney* childhood actresses did *not* play in *Barney & Friends*?

   a. Hilary Duff
   b. Selena Gomez
   c. Demi Lovato

3. Which city celebrates *Winnie-the-Pooh* character Eeyore's birthday?

   a. Corpus Christi
   b. Austin
   c. Dallas

4. Which actor from *Supernatural* recently opened a brewery in the Austin area?

   a. Jensen Ackles
   b. Jared Padalecki

5. Which Texas musician recorded a song with Dolly Parton?

   a. Maren Morris
   b. Jessica Simpson
   c. Beyoncé

Answers

1. c.
2. a.
3. b.
4. a.
5. b.

CHAPTER THREE

TEXAS INVENTIONS, IDEAS, AND MORE!

Have you ever wondered what businesses, products or inventions got started in Texas? Do you know which popular soda came from Texas? Which stores got their start in Texas? There are a number of things that may be a part of your daily life that originated from the Lone Star State. Some of them may even surprise you.

Dr Pepper

Most people either love it or hate it, but did you know that Dr Pepper originated in Waco, Texas? In fact, it's the oldest soft drink brand and the Dr Pepper Snapple Group is the oldest soft drink manufacturer in the United States!

Dr Pepper was invented by a pharmacist named Charles Alderton in 1885. He worked at Morrison's Old Corner Drug Store. While his job was to mix medications, Alderton also enjoyed creating new soft drink recipes at the drug store's soda fountain.

The first to taste-test Alderton's original recipe for Dr Pepper was Wade Morrison, the owner of the drug store. The owner liked the flavor of the drink as much as Alderton did, so they began offering it to store customers. Early customers began to call the drink "Waco" at first. They would ask for "a Waco" or "a shot of Waco."

Wade Morrison has been credited with naming Dr Pepper. However, there's a lot of controversy over why he chose the name.

According to the Dr Pepper Museum, which is located in Waco, there are 12 different theories.

The most popular theory is that it was named after an actual Dr. Pepper. It's been rumored that Pepper may have either given Morrison his first job or Morrison may have been in love with Pepper's daughter, though there's nothing on record that proves either theory.

Another possible theory is that it may have been given "Dr." to convince people that the soda was healthy. This was commonly used to trick people into buying products in the 1880s.

Despite the many theories that abound on how Dr Pepper got its name, no one knows for sure. It seems that it will forever remain a mystery!

Though the early spelling of the name was "Dr. Pepper", the period after "Dr" was later removed to make a stylistic statement. An early logo containing the period also made the logo difficult to read.

The recipe for Dr Pepper is a secret. However, a book of formulas and recipes that were believed to be from Morrison's Old Corner Drug Store was once discovered at an antique store in the Texas Panhandle. There was a recipe in the book called "D Peppers Pepsin Bitters", which people believed may have been an early recipe for Dr Pepper. Dr Pepper Snapple Group denied that this was a recipe for the soda. The company has also denied claims that Dr Pepper contains prune juice.

Slurpee's and Frozen Margaritas

The international convenience store chain 7-Eleven opened its first location in Dallas, Texas in 1927. In fact, this was the very first convenience store in America. When 7-Eleven first opened, it sold grocery store staples like eggs and milk, as well as blocks of ice. The following year, it also began to sell gasoline and other convenience items. In 1965, 7-Eleven began selling the Slurpee, which was first called the "ICEE."

The Slurpee later became the inspiration for the frozen margarita. The margarita itself had already been invented in Mexico, but the frozen margarita originated in Texas. The first frozen margarita machine, which can now be found at the Smithsonian, was invented in 1971. It was created by a restaurateur named Mariano Martinez who drew his inspiration from the Dallas 7-Eleven.

According to *The Dallas Morning News*, Martinez said, "I had a sleepless night and the next day, I stopped to get a cup of coffee at 7-Eleven and I saw that Slurpee machine. The entire concept hit me at one time."

The Underwire Bra

Bras come in so many shapes and sizes today. It's hard to think that, at one point, they didn't even have underwire bras. We can thank Texas for its invention.

Howard Hughes' son, Howard Hughes, Jr., was an inventor and filmmaker himself. The Houston native is credited with developing the first workable underwire bra.

Hughes' invention was first introduced to the world in the movie he made, *The Outlaw*. The bra was worn by Jane Russell. Russell wasn't impressed with the underwire bra. She claimed that it hurt so much that she ended up secretly taking it off and stuffing tissues in her regular bra.

Despite the actress's disappointment with the bra, the underwire bra still took off. It likely became popular due to two reasons: 1) The amount of publicity it received thanks to the movie, and 2) The discontinuance of metal rationing once World War II had ended.

Microchips

Today, we take our cell phones, computers, tablets, and other electronics for granted. You may not realize this, but you can actually thank a Dallas-based electronics company for your ability to use these items.

Texas Instruments, which is based in Dallas, designed the first microchip. It introduced its invention to the world in 1959 at the Radio Engineers' annual trade show in New York City.

The crazy part about it all was that no one realized what a huge invention this was at the time. No one had a clue that microchips would become the foundation of all the electronics we use today.

Whole Foods

Whole Foods is one of the most well-known high-end, natural-food supermarket chains in the country. With over 80,000 employees and more than 400 locations across the world, the store has been ranked as one of the top 100 places to work. And we get it. What other grocery store chain hires certified cheese professionals? (In order to qualify, one must receive their certification from the American Cheese Society, in case you're wondering).

You probably know that Whole Foods sells organic products to health-conscious customers. All of their meat is free of hormones and antibiotics. The store has a ban on foods containing high fructose corn syrup—along with 100 other ingredients!

But did you know that the first Whole Foods opened in Austin? It all started back in 1980 when four Austin grocers decided to band together to create the supermarket. Over time, the company began to add more locations in Texas, neighboring states, the rest of the United States, and now stores can even be found in other countries.

The Whole Foods store located in Austin remains the largest store in the entire chain. It encompasses 80,000 square feet of space, a rooftop ice skating rink, and a full bar that you can drink at, once you've finished grocery shopping. You can go grocery shopping, ice skating, and enjoy an alcoholic beverage all in one place on the same day.

Pace Picante Sauce

If you love salsa, you've probably heard of Pace Picante Sauce. The Pace Foods Company was started in 1947 by David Pace. Despite growing up in Louisiana, Pace ended up in San Antonio due to pilot-training school during World War II.

Pace began his business with syrups, jams, and jellies. However, he decided that the "real syrup of the Southwest" was Mexican picante sauce. Today, most of us refer to this as just "salsa."

David Pace tried a unique form of marketing his picante sauce. He would take it to restaurants with him and then leave it behind for other people to try.

Pace was known for creating a "No Heat" jalapeno, which he used in his mild products. It gives the salsa its flavor without delivering an overabundance of spice.

Pace Foods is located in Paris, Texas. Today, some of the specialty sauces they are known for, besides their picante sauce, include their Salsa Verde, Mexican Four Cheese Salsa con Queso, Pico de Gallo, Pineapple Mango Chipotle Salsa, and Black Bean & Roasted Corn Salsa.

In 1995, the company was bought out by the Campbell Soup Company.

Weed Eater

The Weed Eater was invented in Houston by George Ballas, the grandfather of professional dancer, Mark Ballas, of *Dancing with the Stars* fame.

The idea came to Ballas one day when he was working in the yard and took a break to wash the car. The spinning nylon bristles of an automatic car wash gave him the idea to design a similar product, which would protect the bark of the trees that he was weed trimming around.

He sought investors, but no one thought the invention was worth anything. Still, Ballas persisted and put his own money into his idea. It all turned out to be worth it in the end. In 1977, he sold his company for a whopping $80 million.

Dell Computers

Dell is one of the most well-known computer brands in existence today. You've probably even owned one at some point in time. Did you know that the company got its start in Austin?

Dell Computers was started by Michael Dell. He built the first Dell in his off-campus dorm room at the University of Texas at Austin in 1984. Michael Dell ended up dropping out of college during his freshman year to focus on his business. He did this after receiving just $1,000 from his family!

It all paid off in the end. In 2014, Michael Dell's net worth was estimated to be a whopping $18 billion.

The very first Dell computer sold for $795. During Dell's first year, the company grossed over $73 million.

Breast Implants

Have you ever wondered who the brains behind breast implants were? Well, the mystery has been solved. You can thank two doctors from Houston for changing the world of plastic surgery forever.

Doctors Frank Gerow and Thomas Cronin were the geniuses behind breast implants. It was after squeezing a blood bag that Gerow came up with the idea of a silicone breast.

Wondering who the first guinea pig was? Well, the very first implant was done on a dog named Esmerelda. Though Esmerelda ended up chewing at her stitches a couple of weeks later, requiring the breast implant to be removed, the operation was considered successful.

Fast forward to spring of 1962 when Timmie Jean Lindsey, a mother of six, underwent surgery to have silicone breast implants inserted at Jefferson Davis Hospital in Dallas, Texas.

While the doctors were pleased with the results of the surgery, they had no idea that their invention would be what it is today. Thomas Biggs, a junior plastic surgery resident at the time, told *BBC*, "Sure it was a little bit exciting, but if I'd had a mirror to the future I'd have been dumbstruck."

It's thought that breast implants gained so much traction because the 1950s brought about cultural changes that included a societal expectation of bigger breasts.

As of 2012, it was estimated that somewhere between 1.5-2.5 million women had received breast implants in the past decade.

Liquid Paper

Liquid paper, which is used to eliminate mistakes from papers, comes in many brands today. One of the most popular versions of the product is Wite-Out. Well, you can thank a woman from Texas for the invention.

In the 1950s, a typist named Bette Nesmith Graham came up with the idea behind Liquid Paper because she needed to figure out a way to prevent one typo from ruining an entire page of typing. Her invention included tempera paint, which she mixed in her kitchen.

Graham first started selling the product as "Mistake Out" from her home in 1956.

Her invention was so successful that Gillette bought it in 1979, for $47 million.

Fritos

There's a reason Texans love their Frito pie! Fritos originated from Texas.

You might think Fritos and corn chips were invented at the same time, but this couldn't be further from the truth. Corn chips originated in Mexico.

It was during the Depression that Charles Elmer Doolin, a confectioner from San Antonio, bought a bag of fried chips at a local gas station. Doolin decided to come up with his own recipe.

As it turns out, Doolin's recipe was a hit. Fritos made their way to restaurants throughout Dallas and even to Disneyland.

In 1959, Doolin teamed up with Herman Lay. Together, the two of them formed the Frito-Lay company. The company now produces Doritos, Cheetos, Tostitos, Ruffles, and other beloved snack foods. Frito-Lay's headquarters are in Plano, Texas.

You can get a Frito pie, which is a bag of Fritos with a scoop of chili and cheese, at the Texas State Fair!

Fajitas

Have you ever wondered who invented fajitas?

Since it's one of the most popular menu items at a Mexican restaurant, most people think that Mexico is to credit for the invention of fajitas. However, fajitas actually come from Texas — and the history of the recipe goes way back.

Fajitas were invented in the 1930s, in Texas's Rio Grande Valley. It's thought that ranch hands and cowboys were the ones who created this recipe since they were often paid in meat trimmings. A fajita involves grilling meat (usually steak), peppers, and onions and serving it on a flour or corn tortilla.

However, it wasn't until 1969 that fajitas began to gain popularity. It was during this time that a guy named Sonny Falcon opened a fajita stand in Kyle, Texas. Once they began to gain traction, Tex-Mex restaurants began to add fajitas to their menus, even before they gained popularity throughout the world!

Ruby Red Grapefruit

Did you know that ruby red grapefruit didn't naturally occur? Believe it or not, no one actually meant for this variation of grapefruit to happen at all.

In 1929, the first ruby red grapefruit was found on a small orchard in Rio Grande Valley, Texas. Prior to its discovery, pink and white grapefruits weren't very popular. Both were too sour. However, this new grapefruit variety was different from all of the others, with its red flesh and sweeter taste.

In fact, ruby red grapefruit was enjoyed so much by the locals that *millions* of dollars were spent trying to figure out how to breed redder, sweeter versions of this fruit. The Rio Red, the Star Ruby, and the March Ruby all came about as a result of this effort.

Five years later, the grapefruit industry in Texas was booming, all thanks to its new, sweeter fruit!

Shopping Centers

Shopping is an American tradition, but did you know that shopping centers actually originated from Texas?

The very first shopping center was born in Dallas. The Highland Park Village, which opened in 1931, consisted of luxury retailers that were all built by one owner. What was unique about the Highland Park Village was that it was the first planned shopping center in the United States.

According to the Highland Park Village's website, it was "the first planned shopping center in the United States with a unified architectural style and stores facing in toward an interior parking area."

Today, some of the retailers that can be found at Highland Park Village include Anthropologie, Ralph Lauren, Tory Burch, Dior, Fendi, Cartier, Jimmy Choo, Starbucks, and more.

Corn Dogs

Nowadays, corn dogs can be found at just about any state fair. You can even buy them in your frozen foods section at most supermarkets. But did you know that corn dogs were first introduced in Texas?

In fact, corn dogs are one of the most popular attractions in the Texas State Fair's history. The Fletcher's Corny Dog was first sold at the fair in 1942 by the Fletcher brothers, Neil and Carl. It's believed that the ease of eating the corn dogs off a stick was part of the reason why they gained so much popularity. Fletcher's Corny Dogs have been tasted by everyone from Julia Child to Oprah Winfrey!

Since 1942, their menu has expanded. They have added a turkey dog option and have experimented with jalapeno cheese corn dogs.

In the 1980s, Fletcher's made a (failed) attempt at expanding their corn dog business by opening franchise locations in Texas and a few other states. They have since decided that they will remain selling only at the Texas State Fair for now.

Bill Fletcher, one of the current owners of Fletcher's, says that the recipe is a family secret—and it's no wonder! Approximately 400,000 corn dogs are sold at the Texas State Fair each year.

RANDOM FACTS

1. Cookies 'n cream was first mass-produced by Blue Bell Creameries, which is headquartered in Brenham, Texas. The idea came about after one of the Blue Bell employees sampled the flavor at an ice cream parlor. Though Blue Bell doesn't claim to be the brains of the idea, they were the first to have the idea patented and were also the first to gain rights to use Oreos in their ice cream.

2. The balloon-expendable stent, which is used to unclog blocked vascular vessels during coronary surgery, was invented at the University of Texas Health Science Center. It was invented by Julio Palmaz, a doctor of vascular radiology. He received a patent in 1985, which was recognized as one of the "Ten Patents that Changed the World" of the century.

3. Despite what its name might lead you to believe, the popular franchise Texas Roadhouse did *not* start in Texas. It wasn't even started by a Texan. Texas Roadhouse is headquartered in Louisville, Kentucky—which is where its owner is also from. That being said, Texans are huge fans of Texas Roadhouse. There are more Texas Roadhouse store franchises in Texas than in any other state. Willie Nelson even owns a Texas Roadhouse franchise in Austin!

4. Automatic Teller Machines, or ATMs, were designed by Don Wetzel of a Dallas-based firm called Docutel. Although Wetzel didn't invent the first ATM, he's responsible for their ability to provide you with information about your account balance, deposit money, and so on.

5. The first full drive-in movie theater was opened in Comanche, Texas in 1921. The drive-in theater played silent films.

6. Ammonia-free hair color was invented in Texas, but it wasn't invented by a Texan. It was created by Farouk Shami, who had moved from Palestine to Houston. He ventured into the hair product business when he moved to Texas, but he had a severe allergy to ammonia. His company, BioSilk, has accommodated celebrity customers such as Courtney Cox and Madonna and now earns $1 billion a year.

7. Mary Kay Cosmetics was started in Dallas in 1963 by a woman named Mary Kay Ash. She started the company with just $5,000! Today, Mary Kay Cosmetics is the sixth-largest direct-sales company in the entire world.

8. 3-D printing was invented in the 1980s by a University of Texas alumnus, who founded the method selective laser sintering, or SLS. Today, 3-D printing is used to create everything from bionic ears to organs.

9. The TopsyTail, which was designed to create an inverted ponytail, was an invention that came straight out of Texas. Dallas inventor Tomima Edmark was the brains behind the TopsyTail, which was all the rage in the early '90s.

10. Chain restaurant Chili's was started in Dallas, Texas. Larry Levine opened the first Chili's Bar & Grill in Dallas in 1975.

11. Speaking of chili, did you know that chili itself originated from Texas? It was thought to be a staple of travelers in the 1850s. During those days, travelers would form bricks out of dried beef, suet, chili peppers, and salt, which they would later boil during their travels. It later evolved into the chili con carne that we know today. This fall season, comfort food was first sold in the late 1800s at the San Antonio Chili Stand. Since San Antonio was a tourist hotspot, the stand was instrumental in the future popularity of the dish in both the West and South. In 1977, chili was declared Texas's official state dish.

12. Whataburger is a burger chain that can be found in Southern states, ranging from Florida to Arizona. The first Whataburger

was opened in Corpus Christi in 1950 by Harmon Dobson. It has been said that Dobson's goal was to make a burger so good that you would say, "What a burger!" The first Whataburger to be opened with its iconic orange-and-white striped, A-frame building was in Odessa, TX. Today, there are over 800 locations.

13. In 1967, a group of engineers at Texas Instruments, Inc., were given eight years to design the first hand-held electronic calculator. A patent for the calculator was issued to the company in 1974.

14. Scoop Away Clean Clumping cat litter was invented by San Antonio inventor William Mallow. Mallow also helped out with perfecting the formula of Graham's Liquid Paper.

15. Though Gatorade was designed to help prevent dehydration in Florida Gators football team players, it was founded by Dr. Robert Cade, who was born and raised in San Antonio. Dr. Cade was a medicine and nephrology professor at the University of Florida. After he was approached by the assistant Gators coach, who inquired about the cause as to why his players weren't urinating when they played football, Cade developed the rehydration drink with help from a team of research doctors.

16. Elevator music got its start in Dallas. It all began in the Statler Hilton. The idea behind elevator music was that no one would have to talk to each other when they were in elevators.

17. Contrary to what you might think, German chocolate cake didn't actually come from Germany! The first known reference to German chocolate cake was in an issue of the *Dallas Morning Star* in 1957. The cake was named after Samuel German, who created the dark baking chocolate that was used in the original recipe.

18. Car radios were designed in the 1920s by Dallas inventor Henry Garrett. Now we know who we can blame for hearing the same songs over and over again.

19. Tito's Vodka was created by Bert Butler "Tito" Beveridge II, a Texas native. Sales of his vodka were slow when his company opened in 1997. However, sales gained major traction in 2001 after Tito's Vodka won the Double Gold Medal for vodka at the San Francisco World Spirits Competition. The vodka beat more than 70 high-priced brands.

20. The idea of serving nachos at sports stadiums started in 1976 at a Texas Rangers game. Frank Liberto came to the realization that diluting cheese sauce with water and jalapeno juice would be a cheap way to turn a profit. Other stadiums soon caught on to the idea and it's now one of America's favorite game-time snacks.

Test Yourself – Questions and Answers

1. Which convenience store got its start in Texas?

    a. Wawa
    b. Sheetz
    c. 7-Eleven

2. Which snack food did *not* originate from Texas?

    a. Stadium nachos
    b. Corn chips
    c. Fritos

3. Who originally invented fajitas?

    a. The Indians of Texas
    b. Sam Houston
    c. Cowboys and ranch hands

4. Which restaurant chain did *not* start out in Texas?

    a. Texas Roadhouse
    b. Chili's
    c. Whataburger

5. Which soda got its start at a drug store in Waco, Texas?

    a. Dr Pepper
    b. Root beer
    c. Mr. Pibb

Answers

1. c.
2. b.
3. c.
4. a.
5. a.

CHAPTER FOUR

TEXAS SPORTS: FOOTBALL, RODEO, AND MORE!

You probably know that Texans are crazy about their sports. In fact, it's been said that no state loves football the way Texas does. With not just one but *two* NFL teams, most people in Texas live and breathe football. But did you know that football isn't the official sport of Texas? Do you know which sport is? Read on to find out the answers to these questions and other interesting facts about sports in Texas!

Texas is Home to Many Professional Sports Teams

Did you know that of all the states, Texas has the second-highest number of professional sports teams? The only state with more professional sports teams than Texas is California.

Texas has two National Football League (NFL) teams: the Dallas Cowboys and the Houston Texans.

The state is home to three National Basketball Association (NBA) teams: The San Antonio Spurs, the Houston Rockets, and the Dallas Mavericks.

The state's Major League Baseball (MLB) teams include the Texas Rangers and the Houston Astros.

There are two Major League Soccer (MLS) teams in Texas. They are the FC Dallas and the Houston Dynamo.

The Dallas Stars are the only National Hockey League (NHL) team in the entire state.

That's a lot of sports teams! And it's not even counting the state's professional women's sports teams and its unprofessional sports teams.

Texas is also known for its college football teams, the University of Texas Longhorns and the Texas A&M University's Aggies.

The Dallas Cowboys Are Worth a Lot of Money, But Jerry Jones is *Not* the Richest NFL Team Owner

It may come as no surprise to you to learn that the Dallas Cowboys are worth *a lot* of money.

In fact, according to a 2015 article from *Forbes*, the Dallas Cowboys have been the top-earning NFL team for the past 18 years. In 2015, *Forbes* stated that the team was valued at $4 billion. In 2014 alone, the team earned $620 million in revenue.

So, why are the Dallas Cowboys the most valuable team in the NFL? Well, in 2014, the team had the highest number of people attend their games. They earned $120 million in premium-seating revenue. The Dallas Cowboys' stadium also earns money from non-NFL events. Those figures, though, don't include the amount of money Dallas Cowboys fans spend on memorabilia!

It's just another sign of how much Texans as a whole love football in comparison to those who live in other states.

You might be surprised to learn that Jerry Jones, the owner of the Dallas Cowboys, is *not* the richest NFL team owner. According to *Forbes*, Jerry Jones's net worth is a whopping $5 billion, but the richest is Paul Allen, who owns the Seattle Seahawks and has an estimated net worth of $17.8 billion. Jones ranks as the 5th richest NFL team owner.

Friday Night Lights Is Based on a Real High School Football Team in Texas

You've probably heard of the football-oriented TV show *Friday Night Lights*, starring Kyle Chandler and Connie Britton. Did you know the Emmy award-winning show is actually based on a real Texas high school football game?

The show is based on a 1990 non-fiction book called *Friday Night Lights: A Town, a Team, and a Dream* by H. G. Bissinger.

The TV show centers on the fictional town of Dillon, Texas, and its high school football team, the Dillon Panthers.

However, the book was written about Odessa, Texas's Permian High School Panthers football team of 1988. The reason Bissinger chose to write about the town of Odessa was that he set off in search of a town where high school football was the most important thing. He spent the football season in Odessa with the coaches, players, and their families to garner appropriate research for the book.

There was a lot of backlash from Odessa residents after H. G. Bissinger published *Friday Night Lights: A Town, a Team, and a Dream*. He was supposed to do a book signing after its publication, but he had to cancel it due to threats of bodily harm. The residents were upset that Bissinger talked about the racism and misplaced academic priorities in the football-obsessed town.

All that being said, H. G. Bissinger's portrayal was fairly accurate. For many Texans, there's nothing more important than high school football.

The Super Bowl Has Been Held in Houston

Due to the state's love of football, it should be no surprise that the Super Bowl has been hosted in Houston on more than one occasion!

The first time the Super Bowl was ever hosted in Houston was in 1974 at Rice Stadium. That year, the Minnesota Vikings beat the

Miami Dolphins. The score was 24-7. It was the second year in a row the Vikings had played in the Super Bowl.

In 2004, the Super Bowl was again hosted in Houston, this time at Reliant Stadium. The New England Patriots won against the Carolina Panthers by a score of 32-29.

The last time the Super Bowl was held in Houston was in 2017. That year, the Super Bowl was hosted at NRG Stadium. Houston seems to be a lucky city for the New England Patriots because they won the Super Bowl *again* that year. They defeated the Atlanta Falcons by 34-28.

The Super Bowl Came to Be Because of a Texan

Did you know the Super Bowl wouldn't be the Super Bowl if it weren't for a Texan?

Okay, so the Super Bowl itself wasn't actually created in Texas. However, the *name* of the Super Bowl was invented by a Texan.

The term "Super Bowl" was coined by Lamar Hunt, American Football League Founder, Kansas City Chiefs owner, and then Dallas resident.

Hunt mentioned the idea at an NFL owner's meeting. That was in the 1960s. The name wasn't actually official – as in printed on game tickets – until 1970. The Super Bowl had already been played three times before it officially received a name.

Hunt said that he was actually joking about the name, crediting his kids' Wham-O Superballs for the idea.

It's Not Easy to Become a Dallas Cowboys Cheerleader

Dallas is known for its gorgeous cheerleaders. If your dream is to become a Dallas Cowboys Cheerleader, you should know that it's not easy. In fact, the process of becoming and staying a cheerleader for this dream squad is pretty grueling!

There are a number of qualifications one must meet in order to become a Dallas Cowboys Cheerleader. While there are no height and weight requirements, cheerleaders need to look well-proportioned and should be "lean" enough to look good in the uniform.

During auditions, potential cheerleaders are quizzed on their knowledge of sports, nutrition, and the history of the Dallas Cowboys.

Judges will also make their selections based on the following: dance technique, figure, personality, high kicks, poise, enthusiasm, showmanship, and more.

Once a Dallas Cowboys Cheerleader has been selected, she will need to continue to work hard to maintain her position. Dallas Cowboys Cheerleaders practice 20 to 30 hours per week, with most cheerleaders having other jobs. Not only will cheerleaders need to remain fit, but they must also choose a look they plan to stick with for the entire season. All tattoos are required to be covered.

Demi Lovato once reportedly said during an interview that her mom, a former Dallas Cowboys Cheerleader, said the squad wasn't even allowed to get a drink of water—even when they were dying of thirst!

In addition to being able to meet physical and performance requirements, Dallas Cowboys Cheerleaders are also trained in etiquette and interview techniques. A lot of the girls from the team use their positions to help raise money for charities.

Famous Dallas Cowboys Cheerleaders

There are a number of Dallas Cowboys Cheerleaders who have gone on to become famous through other endeavors.

Perhaps one of the most well-known former Dallas Cowboys Cheerleaders is Melissa Rycroft. After she left the team, she appeared as a contestant on *The Bachelor*. After that, she competed on the 8th season of the show *Dancing with the Stars*, which she won.

Another one of the most well-known former Dallas Cowboys Cheerleaders is Erica Kiehl Jenkins, a member of the Pussycat Dolls.

Bonnie-Jill Laflin is another former Dallas Cowboys Cheerleader who rose to fame after she was a part of the team in the 90s. She went on to have a recurring role in both *Baywatch* and *Ally McBeal*. She also starred in Dierks Bentley's music video for "Come a Little Closer."

Jill Marie Jones is a former Dallas Cowboys Cheerleader who later went on to star in the hit show *Girlfriends*.

Texas Hosts Two Bowl Games

The Sun Bowl, which generally takes place at the end of December, is held in El Paso every year. It's a college football bowl game. It's one of the oldest bowl games in the country. The only bowl game that's older than the Sun Bowl is California's Rose Bowl.

The first Sun Bowl was held on New Year's Day in 1935. At that point, it was held between high school football teams. It wasn't until the following year that the bowl was held for college football teams.

Hyundai is the current sponsor of the Sun Bowl. It bought naming rights to the game, which it will sponsor until 2019. Until that point, the game is called the Hyundai Sun Bowl.

Texas also hosts the Cotton Bowl Classic, another college bowl game that has taken place annually since 1937. It's currently known as the Goodyear Cotton Bowl Classic due to sponsorship reasons. It's held at the Cowboys Stadium in Arlington.

Surprisingly, Football is *Not* Texas's State Sport

If you're a Dallas Cowboys fan, you might be surprised to learn that Texas's state sport is *not* football. This seems nearly impossible, considering how much Texans love their football.

So, what *is* the state sport? Rodeo, which became the official state sport in 1997!

You may be wondering how rodeo got to be so popular in the Lone Star State. Well, rodeo dates back as far as the 1500s, when the Spanish and Mexican settlers introduced horses and cattle to the Southwest.

The word "rodeo" originated from the word vaquero. It means "round-up". Many of the rodeo skills that cowboys compete with today are skills that assisted cowboys and ranch hands during their round-ups.

It wasn't until after the Civil War that rodeo really started to grow in popularity. With the influx of wild cattle in the Southwest and a market for them in the East, cattle drives were born. Cattle ranches began to grow in popularity and so did cowboys.

During this time period, cowboys would hold informal competitions during the cattle and steer round-ups. At that point in time, there were no prizes involved in these competitions. Cowboys participated in rodeo style events as a form of entertainment.

Those early rodeo competitions actually ended up hurting the sport as a whole. Since the cowboys were willing to do it for free, they weren't viewed seriously later on. They needed to break free of the image of doing it for entertainment in order for it to be taken seriously as a professional sport – especially a *paid* professional sport.

The first rodeo on record took place in Pecos, Texas, on the 4th of July in 1883. It was the first rodeo competition that involved cash prizes. Although rodeo events continued in Pecos, it wasn't until 1929 that the event began to run every year.

The first indoor rodeo event was held in Fort Worth in 1917!

The Rodeo Cowboys Association was founded in Houston in 1945.

A cowboy from Texas has been credited with developing steer wrestling. Bill Pickett came up with a method of bulldogging steers, which involved biting their upper lips and grabbing the steer's horns to throw it to the ground. He showed off his method at Texas fairs and rodeos before being contacted by an agent in 1904, who helped him tour the West.

Today, there are a number of standardized rodeo events. Aside from steer wrestling, there's also bareback riding, bull riding, calf roping, saddle bronc riding, and team roping. Bull riding is the most popular rodeo event.

The Texas Rodeo Cowboy Hall of Fame is located in the Fort Worth, Texas, historic district, Fort Worth Stockyards.

The Houston Rodeo is HUGE

The Houston Rodeo is a good example of the saying, "Everything is bigger in Texas." The Houston Livestock and Rodeo is the largest rodeo *in the entire world!*

Also known as RodeoHouston, the rodeo has been held at the NGR Stadium in Houston for 15 years. In 2017, a record-breaking 2.6 million people attended the rodeo, which is 20 days long.

The rodeo isn't the only thing you'll see. Prior to the rodeo show, there's a cattle roundup that takes place in Downtown Houston with a parade. You can also participate in the ConocoPhillips Rodeo Run, which consists of 5k and 10k walks and runs. Last, but certainly not least, there's the World's Championship Bar-B-Que Contest.

Aside from the rodeo competitions, you can expect to see a number of other events at RodeoHouston. Some of these events include livestock competitions and auctions, pig racing, shopping, and an international wine competition. There's also a carnival and shopping.

Although the rodeo gets a lot of criticism due to the potentially unfair treatment of animals, the Houston Rodeo takes good care of the animals. In fact, animals are examined by judges during the hours leading up to the competitions to make sure that they're healthy enough for each event. Afterwards, the animals are reexamined. If animals have been injured, they're treated.

Animals aren't the only thing you'll see at the Houston Rodeo. There are concerts held at the rodeo each year. Some of the many popular musicians who have performed at RodeoHouston in the past include Elvis Presley, Garth Brooks, Justin Bieber, Janet Jackson, Beyoncé, Selena, Ariana Grande, Bon Jovi, Kenny Chesney, Luke Bryan, and Bob Dylan.

The Richest Rodeo Cowboy of All Time is a Texas Native

Rodeo champion Trevor Brazile has been called the Michael Jordan of Rodeo and is known to be a "phenomenon with a rope." Brazile has won 23 titles worldwide.

Brazile is the richest cowboy in the history of the Professional Rodeo Cowboys Associations. As of 2015, he was the first rodeo cowboy to have ever earned $6 million.

Trevor Brazile was born and raised in Amarillo. His father, who was also a four-time rodeo finalist himself, was the one who encouraged Trevor to learn to rope from a young age. The skills his father taught Trevor helped him to excel in steer roping, tie-down roping, and team roping.

Brazile was later trained by Hall of Fame team roper Roy Cooper. It was through Cooper's training that Brazile developed the confidence and determination it took to turn him into the rodeo success he is today!

The "Rankest Bull of All Time" Died in Texas

The most famous bull of all time died in Texas. Bodacious, who weighed 1,800 pounds, has been called the "rankest bull of all time."

Bodacious was a part of the rodeo in 1993. He knocked out famous bull rider Cody Lambert. Many of the riders were determined to ride Bodacious because the bull could give them very high points. However, in order to earn the points, riders had to stay on the bull for eight seconds and that was a problem. Most riders couldn't stay on Bodacious for even a second!

After so many riders were injured by the bull, Bodacious retired after just two years in the rodeo.

In 1999, Bodacious was one of the few animals to have been inducted into the Professional Rodeo Cowboys Association Hall of Fame.

Bodacious died of kidney failure at Andrews Rodeo Company Ranch in Addielou, Texas, in May of 2000.

The Heisman Trophy Was Named After a Texas Coach...

The Heisman Trophy is an award that's given out each year to the most outstanding college football player in the United States whose performance demonstrates the "pursuit of excellence with integrity". It's presented prior to the postseason bowl games by the Heisman Trophy Trust.

The trophy was named after John Heisman, who was a coach and athletic director at Rice University in Houston. The award was renamed to honor Heisman following his death in 1936. Though it was originally only given to players "east of the Mississippi," it was expanded during this time to include players "west of the Mississippi" as well.

...and Players from Texas Have Won the Heisman Trophy!

Several Texas college football players have won the Heisman Trophy.

The Heisman Trophy was first given to a Texas player in 1957. The player was a Texas A&M Aggies halfback named John David Crow.

In 1977, the trophy was awarded to Texas Longhorns running back Earl Campbell.

A Texas Longhorns player named Ricky Williams was given the award in 1998.

In 2012, Texas A&M Aggies quarterback, Johnny Manziel, received the Heisman Trophy.

Of the four Texas college football players who won the Heisman Trophy, both John David Crow and Earl Campbell went on to be inducted into the College Football Hall of Fame.

George Foreman is From Texas

George Foreman is arguably the most well-known athlete from Texas. The former professional boxer is a two-time heavyweight champion, as well as an Olympic gold medalist. He competed between the years of 1969 and 1977 and then again between 1987 and 1997.

Foreman was born in Marshall, Texas. He grew up in Houston's Fifth Ward. George Foreman wrote in his autobiography, *By George: The Autobiography of George Foreman*, which he had a troubled childhood, even dropping out of high school. He took up amateur boxing, which led him to his future success.

While George Foreman had many achievements through boxing, it's not the only reason he's had so much success. Foreman is more well-known today for being the face of the George Foreman Grill. It's been estimated that Foreman made more than $200 million for endorsing it.

RANDOM FACTS

1. Of Texas's professional male sports teams, Dallas is home to five of them: the Dallas Cowboys, the Dallas Mavericks, FC Dallas, the Texas Rangers, and the Dallas Stars. It's also home to the women's NBA team, the Dallas Wings.

2. The Dallas Cowboys have played in the Super Bowl eight times, and they only lost three of those games. The Cowboys won during the years of 1971, 1977, 1992, 1993, and 1997.

3. The Dallas Cowboys are the only NFL team that had 20 consecutive winning seasons, which occurred between the years of 1966 and 1985.

4. The world's first covered, domed stadium can be found in Texas. The Astrodome, which is located in Houston, has been called the "Eighth Wonder of the World". The stadium, which opened in 1965, has hosted numerous sporting events, rodeos, and concerts. It was even used as a shelter for people who were evacuated due to Hurricane Katrina in 2005.

5. There are more than 1,300 football stadiums in Texas. This means there's enough room to seat over 4 million people! This is enough to seat all of the people living in the state of Oklahoma or the country of Panama.

6. The oldest high school football stadium is Lang Field, which belongs to St. Anthony's Catholic High School. It's the home stadium of the St. Anthony's Yellow Jackets.

7. Football player Earl Campbell has played for the Texas Longhorns, the Houston Oilers, and the John Tyler Lions. Combined, he ran 15,582 yards—or 8.8 miles—for the Texas football teams he's played for.

8. Former Dallas Cowboys quarterback Tony Romo has participated in many Dallas-area charity events, with organizations like the Make-A-Wish Foundation, the United Way, and the Society for the Prevention of Cruelty to Animals.

9. Tony Romo was mentioned in *Forbes's* 2007 list of America's Most Eligible Bachelors. He was also voted as the Sexiest Male Athlete in a list put out by Victoria's Secret in 2008.

10. Dallas Cowboys Hall of Famers Emmitt Smith and Michael Irvin had the most successful running back/wide receiver season of all time. In 1995, the two were the first and only running back and wide receiver who, together, ran 1,600+ yards in just one season.

11. Roy Rogers once visited the Houston Rodeo in 1956. He wore a fake mustache, glasses, and a fireman's uniform while he checked out the livestock exhibits because he was afraid of being mobbed by fans.

12. World champion road racing cyclist Lance Armstrong is from Plano, Texas. Though he's known today for cycling, he actually began his athletic career as a swimmer for the City of Plano Swim Club—and a talented one, at that! He finished 4th place in the state competition in the 1,500-meter freestyle.

13. The Texas Sports Hall of Fame Museum is located in Waco, Texas. Some of the things you can see at the museum include the Texas Hall of Fame Gallery, a Cotton Bowl Exhibit, the Southwest Conference Gallery, the Dave Campbell Library, and the Tom Landry Theater.

14. In 1947, Gene Autry was a part of the downtown Houston Rodeo parade.

15. Some of the earliest baseball cards in existence portray players from the Texas League. These baseball card sets, which were released in 1910, are called "Old Mill" and "Mello-Mint, The Texas Gum."

16. Carl Lewis, who won nine gold Olympic medals over the course of four Olympics, lived in Houston. The athlete was inducted into the Track and Field Coaches Association Hall of Fame in 2016.

17. Texas Motor Speedway is home to one of the biggest TV screens in the entire world. The screen, which is called "Big Hoss," is more than 20,600 square feet. When it was unveiled in 2014, it was the largest HD LED screen in the world. However, it has since been surpassed by a TV screen at the NFL Jacksonville Jaguar's EverBank Field.

18. Jack Johnson, who was the first black man to hold a Heavyweight Championship, came from Galveston. He held the title from 1908 to 1915.

19. Mia Hamm is a retired pro soccer player who won two Olympic gold medals and twice helped the United States win the FIFA Women's World Cup. Hamm grew up in Wichita Falls and has been inducted into the Texas Sports Hall of Fame.

20. Retired NBA legend Shaquille O'Neal went to high school in San Antonio! He helped his high school basketball team win the state championship. He still holds the Texas high school basketball team record of 791 rebounds.

Test Yourself – Questions and Answers

1. Which famous athlete was *not* born and raised in Texas?

   a. George Foreman
   b. Michael Jordan
   c. Shaquille O'Neal

2. What is Texas's official state sport?

   a. Football
   b. Baseball
   c. Rodeo

3. The Houston Livestock and Rodeo is the largest rodeo in:

   a. The entire world
   b. The United States
   c. The state of Texas

4. What was the name of the famous bull who died in Texas?

   a. Bootylicious
   b. Bodacious
   c. Bronx

5. The book *Friday Night Lights: A Town, a Team, and a Dream* by H. G. Bissinger was written about which high school football-obsessed town in Texas?

   a. Abilene
   b. El Paso
   c. Odessa

Answers

1. b.
2. c.
3. a.
4. b.
5. c.

CHAPTER FIVE

TEXAS'S UNSOLVED MYSTERIES, SUPERNATURAL, AND OTHER WEIRD FACTS

Just about every state has at least one unsolved mystery. Have you ever wondered what unsolved mysteries, murders or weird crimes have happened in Texas? Have you heard about the scandal that affected one town's high school in Texas? Do you know what creepy folklore haunts the state? What crimes in Texas have affected the entire United States? Read on to find out what scary, eerie or just otherwise weird or bizarre things have happened in Texas.

Jack the Ripper May Be Tied to Texas

You've probably heard of the London serial killer Jack the Ripper by now. But did you know that Jack the Ripper may somehow be linked to another serial killer who murdered people in Texas?

In the late 1800s, there was a serial killer in Austin who came to be known as "The Servant Girl Annihilator." The killer was responsible for eight axe murders in the city between the years of 1884 and 1885. The first few people who were murdered were servants, but later victims were not. Though the killings were referred to as the Servant Girl Murders, one of the girls' male partners was also a victim.

The murders only stopped after private investigators were brought in to solve the case. It was believed that the killer only stopped the murders out of fear of getting caught. Although there were a number of people questioned, none of them were actually tried for murders.

Three years later, the Jack the Ripper murders began to happen in the Whitechapel district of London.

It's a popular belief that the Servant Girl Annihilator and Jack the Ripper may have been the same person. There are two different theories about how this killer struck in both Austin and London. Was the killer from Texas, London, or somewhere else entirely?

The first theory involves a Malaysian cook named Maurice. The restaurant Maurice had worked at had been in the same neighborhood where most of the victims of the Servant Girl Murders had lived. Maurice told people he was going to London and he left in January 1886, just weeks after the murders had stopped in Austin. Some have theorized that he left Austin to prevent being caught for the Servant Girl Murders and set out to continue kills in a new place, leading him to go on to become Jack the Ripper. Was Maurice's departure merely a coincidence or did he end up in London?

There's another popular theory, which says that Jack the Ripper may have been visiting Austin at the time of the Servant Girl Murders. In her book *Jack the Ripper: The American Connection*, author Shirley Harrison tosses around this theory. She suggests that Liverpool-born James Maybrick, who is believed by many to be responsible for the Jack the Ripper killings based on his own controversial diary entries, was actually the Servant Girl Annihilator!

Harrison suggests that Maybrick was in Austin at the time of the Servant Girl Murders. He was later poisoned by his wife, who interestingly enough, was from the United States. Florence Maybrick was from Mobile, Alabama.

After she murdered her husband, there was never another homicide committed by either the Servant Girl Annihilator *or* Jack the Ripper ever again.

So, did Jack the Ripper really have a connection to Texas or was it merely just a coincidence? More than 100 years have passed and the world may never know.

Werewolf Sightings Have Been Reported in Texas

Are you a believer in the supernatural? If so, it might not surprise you to know that werewolf sightings have been reported in Texas. While werewolf sightings have been reported all over the country, there have been many more in Texas than other states.

Perhaps one of the most well-known werewolf reports comes out of Greggton, Texas, which is located near Longview. In a 1960 issue of *Fate Magazine*, a woman named Delburt Gregg detailed her encounter with a werewolf, which had taken place two years earlier.

Mrs. Gregg said she was home alone when she heard a scratching sound on the screen window in her bedroom during a thunderstorm. When lightning flashed, she saw what she called a "huge, shaggy, wolf-like creature" that glared at her with "baleful, glowing, slitted eyes."

Delburt Gregg said that as she ran to grab a flashlight, the wolf went to hide in her bushes. She waited for the animal to leave in hopes of seeing it again, but it never emerged from the bushes. Instead, she saw a man climb out of the bushes and walk down the street.

Another story comes out of Converse, Texas, though this one is a bit more controversial. It has been said that in the 1960s, a man sent his son hunting in the woods. The boy was stalked by the wolf and ran home. His father told him to go back. When the boy never came home later that night, a search party found a huge werewolf devouring his body. Though many are skeptical of the story, the "Wolf-Man of Converse" is still a legend in the town today.

In Kimble County, there's also a legend about an old Native American man who would take the form of a wolf to avoid being captured by cavalrymen. It was said that when he was cornered, he would turn into a wolf and attack, often injuring or even killing those who wanted to capture him.

Folklore or not, there are plenty of stories to tell by the campfire during your next trip to Texas!

The Amber Behind AMBER Alerts Was Murdered in Texas

Sure, you know about AMBER Alerts. Nowadays, you even get them sent to your smartphone. But do you know the story of how they began? Do you know about the girl who AMBER Alerts were named after?

Though AMBER stands for America's Missing: Broadcast Emergency Response, the Alert system was actually named after a real-life girl named Amber. She went missing in Texas in the '90s.

Amber Hagerman was a 9-year-old girl who was kidnapped and murdered in Arlington in 1996. She was kidnapped when she was riding her bike with her brother in a grocery store parking lot. A blue truck was spotted leaving the scene.

Four days after Amber Hagerman went missing, a dog walker discovered her body floating in a creek a few miles away from the grocery store. Amber's throat had been slit.

Sadly, it's been more than 20 years and Amber Hagerman's death still remains a mystery. Who killed Amber? Sadly, no one knows. There have been no suspects in her murder. All police have to go on is a description that was given by a man who witnessed the abduction from his yard. The case still remains open to this day and every lead is treated as though it was the first.

Despite the fact that there haven't been answers in Amber Hagerman's death, some positivity has come out of the tragedy. As of November 2017, the AMBER Alerts system has helped bring home 897 children.

Amber Hagerman's story has been turned into a *Lifetime* movie called *Amber's Story*.

The Texas Cheerleading Scandal Made National Headlines

You may have heard of the *Lifetime* movie called *Fab Five: The Texas Cheerleader Scandal* starring Jenna Dewan-Tatum and Ashley Benson, but did you know that it's actually based on a true story?

The real-life story took place in McKinney, Texas, when a group of spoiled cheerleaders known as the "fab five" made national headlines in 2005. Some have called them the Real Life *Mean Girls*. Others have referred to them as "girls gone wild." No matter how you look at it, these girls were downright rotten. They insulted teachers, skipped classes, and terrorized their coaches.

They gained attention when they posted racy photos wearing their cheerleading uniforms on Myspace. In the photos, the girls were wearing bikinis, showing off their underwear, and posing in a Condoms to Go shop while wearing their uniforms.

A teacher from their school even said the girls were more difficult to deal with than gang members.

Michaela Ward, the 4th cheerleading coach who the girls drove out in just one year, was the first coach to try to discipline the girls. Stories of what actually happened tended to be contradictive. The girls claimed that Ward tried to befriend them and stated that she didn't discipline them.

Regardless of what really happened, the girls publicly attacked the coach and claimed that she had made false allegations against them.

Michaela Ward told *Good Morning America* that the girls went as far as to send dirty text messages to Ward's husband and another coach.

Ward later sued the school for wrongful termination and defamation. She is still a cheerleading coach today.

So, how did these girls manage to get away with so much? The head ringleader's mother was the school principal, who undermined the coach for trying to discipline the cheerleaders. Ward said it wasn't only the principal to blame but the entire administration *and* parents who prevented the girls from being reprimanded.

One of the Most Famous Hate Crimes Took Place in Texas

One of the most famous, controversial, and horrendous hate crimes in all of American history took place in Jasper, Texas, on June 7th, 1998. It was on that day that James Byrd, Jr., an African-American man, was murdered by three white supremacists named Shawn Berry, Lawrence Russell Brewer, and John King.

The three men beat Byrd. They defecated and urinated on him before they chained his ankles to the back of a pickup truck and dragged him for about 1.5 miles. It was hitting a culvert that killed him by severing his head and arm. The autopsy report showed that Byrd lived through most of the trip and was conscious.

All three of Byrd's killers have been charged and convicted. Lawrence Russel Brewer was executed for the crime in 2011. Shawn Berry is currently on death row, awaiting appeals. Berry received a sentence of life in prison.

James Byrd, Jr.'s son, Ross Byrd, wasn't happy with all of these sentences. Ross Byrd has participated with *Murder Victims' Families for Reconciliation*, an organization that speaks out against the death penalty. Ross Byrd has actively campaigned to spare the lives of those who murdered his father. He told *Reuters*, "You can't fight murder with murder." Ross Byrd felt the killers should have spent their lives in prison.

James Byrd, Jr.'s death was one of the two hate crimes that led to the federal Matthew Shephard and James Byrd, Jr. Hate Crimes Act. The act, which is generally just referred to as the Matthew Shephard Act, was signed into law in 2009 by President Barack Obama.

A Serial Killer Struck in Texarkana in the 1940s

Have you heard of the movie *The Town That Dreaded Sundown*? The movie is loosely based on the Texarkana Moonlight Murders that happened between February and May of 1946.

The serial killer, who came to be known as "The Phantom Killer" or "The Phantom Slayer," attacked eight people in a matter of 10 weeks. Five of those victims died. Contrary to popular belief, the Phantom Killer didn't only strike during a full moon. The killer did only attack during nighttime hours, however, which was what led the deaths to be called the "Moonlight Murders."

The murders caused a huge wave of panic throughout the town of Texarkana. People went out and stocked up on guns, ammunition, locks, and other forms of protection. People locked themselves in their homes at night, while many people's fear led them to leave town completely. While the Texas Rangers investigated the case, local teens tried to lure the killer.

There was one prime suspect in the case. Youell Swinney's wife described in great detail that he was responsible for two of the homicides. Since Mrs. Swinney refused to testify against him and later recanted her story, Swinney was never convicted of the crimes. However, two of the lead investigators in the case believed that Swinney was guilty.

One of the things that threw investigators off was that Swinney's fingerprints didn't match any of those connected with the homicides. It made some of the investigators wonder if Swinney's wife's story was credible.

Even so, Youell Swinney was arrested and imprisoned for selling cars. Though Swinney made multiple comments about knowing that he was wanted for more than just auto theft, he never made a formal confession to the crimes.

What makes the case even more mysterious was anonymous phone calls that were received by family members of the victims in 1999 and 2000. The caller claimed to be the daughter of the Phantom Killer and apologized for what her father had done. Swinney was not a father to any daughters.

Were those phone calls from the real Phantom Killer's daughter or were they only prank calls? To date, the case remains an unsolved mystery!

Four Teens Girls Were Murdered in a Texas Yogurt Shop

Four girls between the ages of 13 and 17 were murdered in a yogurt shop in Austin in 1991.

On December 6th, 1991, there was a fire at I Can't Believe It's Yogurt! Once the fire had been put out, the firefighters discovered the bodies of four teen girls, three of which were stacked in a pile.

Their names were Amy Ayers, Jennifer Harbison, and sisters Sarah and Eliza Thomas. Eliza and Jennifer had been working the night shift when the other two girls stopped over to help close the yogurt shop.

When the girls were found, they were undressed and had been gagged and bound with their own clothes. They had all been shot in the head. The fire had burned their bodies. Detective Mike Huckabay compared the scene to things he had seen as a soldier in Vietnam.

Money had been stolen from the cash register, leading investigators to believe that the murders had started out as a robbery attempt that went awry.

The case proved to be difficult to solve. Since the killer had set the yogurt shop on fire, there was DNA from firefighters in the yogurt shop. Additionally, a lot of the evidence got washed away with water. Investigators have said that modern technological advances make it so the crime might have been easier to solve today, but things weren't so easy in 1991.

More than 50 people confessed to the yogurt shop murders. Police believe many of them to be mentally ill or seeking notoriety for the killings.

Kenneth Allen McDuff, a serial killer who was in the Austin area at the time of the homicides, was interviewed. However, authorities ruled him out as a suspect.

At one point, four suspects were charged with the murders. The suspects were Maurice Pierce, Robert Springsteen, Michael Scott, and Forest Welborn. Though they had been arrested eight days after the Yogurt Shop Murders, they weren't charged until eight years later.

Michael Scott and Robert Springsteen confessed to the murders, stating that it was a robbery that went wrong. Springsteen also confessed to raping one of the victims.

Charges were dropped against Welborn and Pierce. While investigators believed Pierce was the mastermind of the robbery/killings, there was no evidence that proved his involvement.

Both Scott and Springsteen went to trial. However, the charges against both Scott and Springsteen were dismissed in 2009. It was believed that they were coerced into making false confessions. There was no evidence against either suspect, and it was determined the trials were unfair.

The Austin Police Department had been planning for a retrial against the two when something surprising happened. New DNA evidence from an unknown man was found on one of the girl's bodies, throwing the entire case off.

As of 2016, the Austin Police Department is still continuing the investigation.

Austin Police Department Detective Jay Swann told *New York Post* that he still believes Springsteen and Scott were involved in the murders.

Swann also continues to believe that Maurice Pierce played a role in the murders. Maurice Pierce was killed in 2010, however. He stabbed a police officer during a traffic stop. The officer shot him.

The 1991 Yogurt Shop Murders have been the subject of three non-fiction novels: *Who Killed These Girls? Cold Case: The Yogurt Shop Murders* by Beverly Lowry, *See How Small* by Scott Blackwood, and *Murdered Innocents* by Corey Mitchell.

A Venomous Snake Once Went MIA in Austin

It was July of 2015 when a cobra went missing in Austin. Word of the snake being on the loose first got out when an 18-year-old man named Grant Thompson was discovered dead in his car.

Thompson worked at the Fish Bowl Pet Express, which his mother owned. When he was found, he had cobra bite marks on his arm, but the cobra was nowhere to be found.

Everyone in Austin was on the lookout for the snake, which ended up going viral during the hunt. Humorous tweets and memes of the cobra in tourist hotspots made their way around the Internet. Although jokes were cracked, the situation was really no laughing matter.

Grant Thompson's death was ruled a suicide, with autopsy reports showing that he didn't try to pull away from the snake. The venom led him to ultimately go into cardiac arrest. He also had a history of suicidal thoughts in the past.

After days spent searching for the snake, a driver found it located near the Lowe's Home Improvement store parking lot where Thompson's body was found.

We can imagine how much relief everyone in Austin felt once the snake was no longer on the loose!

An Alien May Have Died in Aurora, Texas

If you believe in the extraterrestrial, then the story of what happened on a farm near Aurora, Texas, may interest you.

In April of 1897, a UFO allegedly crashed into a windmill on a farm belonging to Judge J. S. Proctor. It was said that the pilot of the aircraft did not survive the accident and was buried at the Aurora Cemetery.

The incident was first reported in the *Dallas Morning News*. The article was written by S. E. Haydon, a resident of Aurora. Haydon claimed that the pilot of the aircraft was "not of this world," even going as far as to claim that an Army officer near Fort Worth had determined it was a "Martian." It was also reported that hieroglyphic-like words on metal were found in the wreckage.

Though it occurred 50 years beforehand, many people have compared the Aurora UFO incident to Roswell.

Although supernatural believers want to believe an alien did, in fact, die in Texas, others aren't so sure this is really the case. Many people believe the Aurora UFO incident was a hoax, including former mayor Barbara Brammer.

According to Brammer, the town had gone through a number of devastations during the months leading up to the incident. The local cotton crop had been destroyed, a tragic fire destroyed businesses, a spotted fever caused many fatalities, and a train never made it to town as planned. She believed that the incident was all a hoax to draw people to town.

In 1979, *Time* magazine conducted an interview with an 89-year-old woman, who was a resident at the time of the accident. The woman, who was named Etta Pegues, claimed that S. E. Haydon wrote the article as a joke and to "bring interest to Aurora." Pegues also claimed that there was no windmill on the farm where the accident allegedly occurred.

The Aurora UFO incident was featured in a 2005 episode of *UFO Files*. Two eyewitnesses of the town were interviewed. Though one did see smoke from the crash and both claimed their parents saw the wreckage, neither of the eyewitnesses saw the wreckage themselves. A grave marker with a UFO was found at the Aurora Cemetery, but the cemetery did not grant investigators access to the remains.

UFO Hunters also investigated the incident in a 2008 episode. While the investigators failed to find anything definitive at the cemetery, they were given access to the site of the crash. They did not find anything indicative of the accident. However, they did find evidence of a windmill on the property, which was contradictory to what Pegues said during the *Time* magazine interview.

Did an alien die in this small town in Texas? Did a UFO even crash here at all or was it all for attention?

Whether the Aurora UFO incident was true or merely a hoax, there has been no shortage of other reports of UFO sightings in Texas.

A Texas UFO tracking website claims that there were many sightings in 2017 alone. According to *Community Impact Newspaper*, the highest number of sightings in 2017 were reported in Central Texas.

In 2017, there were nine reports of UFO sightings in Austin and ten more in San Antonio. There was a total of 27 alien sightings reported in all of Central Texas in 2017 alone. These numbers originated from the National UFO Reporting Center.

If you're worried about an alien crashing in your backyard in Texas, try not to worry *too* much. The National UFO Reporting Center says that the number of reported UFO sightings in Texas is actually pretty low, given how geographically large the state is. You'd have to worry more in states like Pennsylvania, New York, Washington, California, and Ohio, which have the highest number of reported sightings.

The Fort Worth Zoo Is Believed to Be Haunted

Lions and tigers and *ghosts*? Oh, my! Many people have claimed to have experienced paranormal encounters at the Fort Worth Zoo. In fact, there are believed to be not just one, but *two* ghosts haunting the zoo.

The first ghost is believed to be that of Michael A. Bell. Bell was a former elephant trainer until his death in 1987. He was tragically crushed when he tried to move several elephants into a larger pen. Since his death, a number of zoogoers have reported seeing a man near the elephant and zebra area of the zoo, the same area the trainer was typically seen when he was alive.

If you're near the zoo café, you might spot another ghost. This one is a woman from the 19th century who is dressed all in white and carries a parasol. People have seen her slowly pacing in front of the café. No one knows what her identity might be, but people claim to see her often. In fact, she apparently looks so lifelike that people have reportedly mistaken her for a zoo employee or actress!

If you take any photos at the Fort Worth Zoo, you might want to see if you notice anything besides the animals.

The Mystery of Ripley's Believe it or Not! And Madame Tussaud's Palace of Wax

If you visit the Ripley's Believe it or Not and Madame Tussaud's Palace of Wax in Grand Prairie, you might not know about the mystery that surrounds it.

Over 30 years ago, there was a fire at the museum that caused 300 wax figures to melt. At the time, the wax collection was the largest in the country and was valued at $4 million. Bob Cox, one of the museum co-owners, claimed that "hobos seeking shelter" had set the fire, according to *D Magazine*.

It was believed that Bob Cox set the fire himself in order to collect insurance money. Cox, who had a long history of financial and gambling problems, was set to go to trial for arson. Patsy Wright, his ex-wife and former co-owner of the museum, was slated to testify against him. However, Wright died 10 days before the trial, which was scheduled to begin in November of 1987.

On the night of her death, Patsy Wright took Nyquil to fall asleep, as she so often did. But this time, someone had put a lethal dose of strychnine in her Nyquil.

When investigators tried to uncover who had poisoned Wright, they came up with a number of possible theories. However, the most obvious was that Cox had killed her so she couldn't testify against him.

To make things even stranger, a former receptionist at the museum had died unexpectedly in the early '80s. Lori Williams was just 26 years old when she suddenly fell ill and died 11 days later. A cause of death was never determined. She had told a friend that she believed her husband had been poisoning her but is it possible that Cox may have been behind her death as well?

The case appeared on an episode of *Unsolved Mysteries*, and not much has changed. Wright's murder remains an unsolved mystery to date.

Texas Has One of America's Most Haunted Hotels

Do you want to have a sleepover with some spirits? If so, then you might want to take a trip to Austin. The Driskill Hotel in Austin is believed to be one of the most haunted hotels in the entire United States! In fact, the hotel is so well-known for being haunted that the hit song "Ghost of a Texas Ladies Man", by Concrete Blonde, was written about it.

The grand staircase of the hotel is said to be haunted. In 1877, a girl who was chasing a ball accidentally fell down the stairs and died. People have reported hearing giggles and the sound of a ball bouncing on the stairs.

Some have also said that the hotel's founder, Colonel Jesse Driskill, has been known to haunt the place. Driskill was known for smoking cigars and workers have reported randomly smelling cigar smoke. Creepy, right? Well, it gets worse.

It's Room 525 that has been said to be most haunted. Two brides who were on their honeymoon both killed themselves in the bathtub of Room 525. These incidents allegedly took place twenty years apart. The "suicide brides" are said to haunt the room, causing flickering lights, random noises, knocking, and other disturbances that have seriously creeped out guests. Some have even claimed to see apparitions.

Are you still wondering if it's haunted? The best way to find out is to stay there for yourself.

A Stretch of Highway in Texas Was Known to Be Used as A Dumping Ground for Dead Bodies

There's a stretch of highway on I-45 South between the cities of Galveston and Houston where many bodies have been dumped. The highway has been nicknamed the "Highway of Hell." Others were found on a 25-acre patch of land, which is now known as "The Killing Fields."

It's been estimated that about 30 bodies have been found in the area since the 1970s, with the most recent body being discovered in 2016. That being said, it is believed that there are many bodies still out there that haven't yet been found.

Why are so many bodies found in the area? It's been considered the perfect area to get away with murder. The area is so remote that it's said you wouldn't be able to hear someone yelling and that there would be nowhere to run.

So, who's responsible for these deaths? It has long been believed that serial killers are responsible for the majority of these homicides. A lot of the victims shared similar physical features and most of the victims were between the ages of 10 and 25.

There have been several suspects over the years, including a few who have been convicted of some of the murders.

In 1998, a convicted murderer named Edward Harold Bell told police that he was responsible for 11 of the murders. Unfortunately, there wasn't enough evidence to convict him.

A second man was convicted of three of the murders. He's also a suspect, but hasn't been charged, for the murder a fourth victim, whose remains he led police to in 2015 when he was already serving 60 years for kidnapping charges.

A man named Kevin Edison Smith was convicted of murdering Krystal Jean Baker 16 years after her death. He has been sentenced to life in prison.

The majority of the murders are still considered unsolved today.

A movie called *Texas Killing Fields* was released in 2011. The movie is loosely based on the homicides. Although it caused a lot of controversies, particularly with the victims' families, the purpose of the film was to try to raise awareness about the murders and to encourage anyone who may have any information to come forward.

There Are Ghost Towns in Texas

If you're a ghost hunter, the sad news is we're not talking about towns that are haunted by dead people. But what could be eerier than an old abandoned town? If you've seen the movie *The Hills Have Eyes*, then you know just how creepy ghost towns can be!

If you want to explore some ghost towns, then you've come to the right state. Texas is home to 13 ghost towns. Which towns are worth exploring?

The two most well-known ghost towns in Texas are Terlingua and Lobo, which were mining and agricultural towns respectively. Both towns were abandoned when the cost of minerals and agriculture became too expensive after World War II.

Glenrio is another one of Texas's most popular ghost towns. The town, which is located along Route 66, was once hopping. By 1985, however, the town was abandoned. The movie *The Grapes of Wrath* was filmed in Glenrio.

Indianola was once expected to be a beach hotspot that would compete with Galveston. That all changed when two hurricanes hit the town in 1875 and 1886, causing destruction that led the town's residents abandonment of it.

Many of these ghost towns are worth seeing, especially if you've never been to a ghost town before.

Chupacabra Sightings Have Been Reported in Texas

Just mentioning the legendary chupacabra is enough to send farmers running to check their livestock and to spark a heated debate. Some people believe in it, while others aren't so sure. Whether it's real or merely folklore, there have been reports of chupacabra sightings in Texas.

What is a chupacabra, exactly? The animal, which is believed to only exist in folklore, was first reported in Puerto Rico. As a result, the creature's name has Spanish origins. The Spanish translation of "chupar" and "cabra" is "goat-sucker." The chupacabra was known to exist off the blood it drank from livestock, particularly goats.

In 2007, a woman named Phylis Canion spotted a bony, hairless creature with a canine-like body and bluish gray skin on her farm in Cuero, Texas. Later, she began to find that her chickens' necks had been torn open and that they had been drained of their blood. When a neighbor found the creature dead on his property, Canion brought it home. Since then, she and her husband have done numerous documentaries on the creature for networks like *National Geographic*, *Animal Planet*, *Discovery Channel*, and *History Channel*.

The weirdest part about it all was that this wasn't the first report of a chupacabra in Texas. There have been numerous reports of sightings, mostly in Eastern Texas. Ben Redford, a researcher for the

Center of Skeptical Inquiry and author of the book *Tracking the Chupacabra*, has even called the Lone Star State a "factory" for the legendary creature.

RANDOM FACTS

1. Five Texas towns made NeighborhoodScout's list of 100 most dangerous cities in America in 2017. The towns, from least to most dangerous, were Beaumont, Lubbock, Houston, Balch Springs, and Odessa.

2. A 19-year-old man in Galveston who bit a woman's neck claimed to be a 500-year-old vampire in 2011. When he was taken to jail, he begged police officers to restrain him out of fear of killing them because he needed to "feed."

3. The USS Lexington, which is located in Corpus Christi, is said to be one of the most haunted ships in the United States. People have claimed to feel the presence of spirits. It's thought that Charly, a former crew member, now haunts the ship and acts as a tour guide. There have also been reports of hearing the sound of screams, cries, and even the distant sound of weapons being fired. The USS Lexington has even been featured on the show *Ghost Hunters*.

4. In 1998, Texas got rid of the "last meal" it once offered to death row inmates. Inmates can blame it all on a man named Lawrence Brewer, who ordered a five-course meal that he later refused to eat. Some of the foods that Lawrence ordered included a triple bacon cheeseburger, two chicken-fried steaks, a meat lover's pizza, three fajitas, and a pound of barbeque. Now instead of the last meal, a death row inmate's final dish consists of the same items as the other inmates.

5. In a graveyard outside of Anson, Texas, it's said that if you park your car a certain way and flash your headlights three times on a clear night, a strange white light will slowly drift down the road towards your car. The local legend says that the light is actually

a woman who's searching for her lost sons. When they were sent to the woods one night, they were told to flash their lantern three times. By the time she got to them, they had been killed. When car headlights flash, it's thought that the woman flashes her lantern back in search of her lost children.

6. Despite the town's name, a murder has never been reported in Slaughter, Texas!

7. A goat was once elected as town mayor in Lajitas, Texas. The goat, whose name is Clay Henry, was elected in 1986. However, he may have had a drinking problem. Clay Henry loved to drink beer.

8. There were sightings of strange lights in Lubbock, Texas, in 1951. There were 20 to 30 flashing lights. The lights were as bright as stars but much larger. Some spectators thought the lights were UFOs. The US Air Force said the lights were "an easily explainable natural phenomenon," but they never explained what that phenomenon was.

9. In July of 1945, the first atomic bomb was detonated about 20 miles from El Paso, Texas. It was the same design as the atomic bomb that was detonated in Nagasaki. Today, the amount of radiation at the test site in Texas is 10 times higher than normal.

10. A man reported seeing Big Foot in Kountze, Texas, in 1977. He was having car trouble at night and saw a thin, dark figure that was covered in hair crossing the road near Old Hardin Cemetery.

11. If you do have the good (or bad) luck of seeing Big Foot, it is legal to kill him in Texas.

12. What was believed to be a sea creature washed upon the shore of Texas City during Hurricane Harvey. The long creature that washed ashore had some really frightening-looking teeth. Fortunately, the mystery has been solved! A Museum of

Natural History biologist and eel expert determined that the "sea creature" was actually a fangtooth snake-eel.

13. Ghost Road, or the "Light of Saratoga," is a strange phenomenon in Texas. It's a light that randomly appears and disappears at the end of Bragg Road in Hardin County. Though it's often attributed to swamp gas, there's a local legend that says a railroad worker was decapitated in a railroad accident and the light is his ghost's lantern lighting the way as he searches for his own head.

14. There have been reports of sightings of skin-walkers, or Navajo, who use magic to turn themselves into animals or other disguises. Most of these reports come from South Texas.

15. Marfa, Texas, is home to a strange phenomenon. The Marfa Lights are white to yellow lights that appear and disappear in the sky and then travel to another area of the sky. They happen at any time of the day and during any month of the year. Legends have attributed them to everything from UFOs to Native American spirits. Surely, there must be some scientific explanation?

16. Water Wonderland in Odessa, Texas, used to be a lively water park. It was shut down in 1980 after a series of civil lawsuits were filed over injuries at the park. Today, it's filled with graffiti, squatters, and rattlesnakes. Due to the sense of abandonment you'll get from seeing the old water park, it has been listed as one of the creepiest places in Texas.

17. The "Texas Seven" was a group of seven men who escaped from a maximum-security prison on December 30, 2000. They were in on charges that included murder. After they escaped prison, the men were featured on *America's Most Wanted*. After a tip was received, four of the men were located in an RV park in January of 2001. Two of the remaining men were caught a couple of days later. The seventh man committed suicide before he was found. The six who had been captured alive were given the death sentence for murder.

18. A lake monster is said to reside in Lake Granbury. It's been nicknamed "One Eye." As you can probably guess, the lake monster is said to only have one eye. It's unknown if the lake monster was only born with one eye or if one of its eyes was injured. One Eye is said to resemble the Loch Ness Monster, with a long neck and humped back. To make things creepier, early Spanish settlers and the Native Americans spoke of something "terrible" and "savage" that lurked in the water of the Brazos River, which flows into Lake Granbury.

19. In March of 2017, space debris from what's believed to be a spacecraft was found in Freeport, Texas.

20. Ever think of freezing your body after you die? As of 2016, the "Mecca of Cryogenics" was being built in Texas. Also nicknamed as the "Center for Immortality," the center is one day expected to hold 50,000 frozen people who hope to return from the dead.

Test Yourself – Questions and Answers

1. What was the name of the girl whose disappearance led to the AMBER Alerts system?

   a. Amber Hagerman
   b. Amber Portwood
   c. Amber Rose

2. Which Texas man's death led to a law that was signed into legislation to fight against hate crimes?

   a. Matthew Shephard
   b. James Byrd, Jr.
   c. Michael Scott

3. What is the name of the patch of land where dead bodies have been found near I-45?

   a. The Killing Fields
   b. The Highway of Hell
   c. The Patch of Death

4. Which Texas hotel is one of the most haunted hotels in the United States?

   a. Stockyards Hotel
   b. Omni Austin Hotel Downtown
   c. The Driskill Hotel

5. Which Texas city ranks highest in the top 100 dangerous cities in America?

   a. Houston
   b. Beaumont
   c. Odessa

Answers

1. a.
2. b.
3. a.
4. c.
5. c.

CHAPTER SIX

TEXAS'S WILDLIFE, SCIENCE, AND OTHER COOL FACTS!

Have you ever wondered what types of weird animals you might see in Texas? Do you know which animal population was intentionally reduced in Texas? Have you ever wondered if Texas is hurting or helping our environment? You'll find the answers to these and other questions in this chapter!

Texas Hosts the Largest Rattlesnake Round-up in the USA

Texas hosts the largest and oldest rattlesnake round-up in the country.

The first Rattlesnake Round-Up was held in Sweetwater, Texas, in 1958. The purpose of the event was to kill as many rattlesnakes as possible in order to help lower the number of rattlesnakes in the town and surrounding areas.

The Rattlesnake Round-Up has been held in Sweetwater every year since. However, what was once meant to help a small town has now become an event that draws people from all over!

According to the *San Angelo Standard-Times*, the round-up saw a record-breaking 24,626 pounds of rattlesnakes in 2016. In 2017, more than 8,000 pounds of rattlesnake were killed at the event and over 40,000 people were in attendance. The event consists of a cook-off, a pageant, and more. It also brings more than a whopping $8 million to the local economy.

The round-up has a process they follow when they kill the snakes. They record the weights and genders of the snakes before skinning, beheading, and milking the snakes of their venom. The venom gets made into anti-venom and is sold to pharmaceutical companies. The rattlesnake meat is then deep-fried and served at the festival.

If you have a fear of snakes, we don't recommend attending this event. Just looking at photos from the Rattlesnake Round-Up are enough to give you the heebie-jeebies.

You Can See Dinosaur Tracks in Texas

Have you ever wanted to see some real-life dinosaur tracks? Well, you can in Texas.

Glen Rose, Texas, is considered "The Dinosaur Capital of Texas." Some even consider it to be the "Dinosaur Capital of the World," although others disagree. Regardless of its title, there's no doubt that this Texas town is a hotspot for those with a love for paleontology.

The first dinosaur tracks were discovered in Glen Rose in 1908 after a flood occurred. It was on the limestone floor of the Paluxy River that the tracks were spotted. Another one of the tracks was also found embedded in the bandstand of the Glen Rose town square, where it can still be found today.

The tracks were made up of large footprints with three toes. It's believed that the tracks belonged to the *Acrocanthosaurus*, which was slightly smaller but similar in shape to a *Tyrannosaurus Rex*.

Later in 1934, more dinosaur prints were discovered. These were larger. Although they were originally mistaken as Woolly Mammoth tracks, the prints are believed to have belonged to Sauropods. Later, a paleontologist discovered sauropod prints the size of small bathtubs!

Today, you can visit Dinosaur Valley State Park, which is located a few miles west of Glen Rose. The park spans 1,500 acres of land and has exhibits of some of the best dinosaur footprints in the entire world. It also exhibits the most well-preserved sauropod footprints that can be found *anywhere*.

As you can imagine, Dinosaur Valley State Park is a huge tourist spot. It's something you won't want to miss out on if you ever visit Texas. The park offers camping, bike riding, and other activities to visitors.

Texas's Bats Add Value to the State's Economy

If you love bats, then you might want to head to Texas. More species of bats can be found in Texas than any other state in the country. While 27 species of bats can be found in the state, it's rare to see them all.

The most common species in the state are the Mexican free-tailed bat. There's such a high population throughout the state that Texas even recognizes the Mexican free-tailed bat as its state flying mammal. Another one of the most common species of bats in the Lone Star State is the Brazilian free-tailed bat.

The evening bat and big brown bats can be found in East and Southeast Texas forests and woodlands. The red bat can also be found in these areas.

Bracken Cave, which is located in Comal County, Texas, houses the largest bat colony in the entire world! From the months of March to October, somewhere between 20-40 million Mexican free-tailed bats call the cave their home.

The South Congress Bridge in Austin also provides sanctuary to the largest urban bat colony. Austin isn't the only city in Texas where you'll see lots of bats, though. Thousands of bats take refuge under the Waugh Drive Bridge in Houston.

Although they may be creepy to some, bats are actually thought to be extremely useful to Texas farmers. The high population of bats helps to keep the pests that could potentially destroy farms under control.

You might be surprised to learn that bats also offer an economic advantage to the state. Guano, also known as bat poop, is rich in nitrogen and phosphorous. Guano makes a powerful plant fertilizer, and it's also used to make gunpowder.

The mineral is so useful, that in the late 19th century, the U.S. government offered free land to any farmers who found guano reserves and shared them with other American citizens.

Before Texas's oil reserves were discovered, guano was the No. 1 mineral exported by the state.

The bat colony in Bracken Cave produces an estimated 85-100 tons of guano every year. It's estimated that the bat's droppings are nearly 60 feet deep in the cave. They have accumulated there for thousands of years.

So, how is guano extracted from the cave, you wonder? Workers shovel the guano into a hopper, which is attached to a pipe that acts as a vacuum. An industrial vacuum is also used to remove guano from any hard-to-reach areas of the cave.

Over the course of 21 days, it's estimated that about 184,000 pounds, or 4,200 bags, of guano are removed from Bracken Cave.

It's not the safest practice since the ammonia fumes from guano can be dangerous to humans. Workers are required to wear gas masks when they enter the cave to remove the guano.

Unfortunately, Texas's bats are currently at risk. With the discovery of a deadly fungus called white-nose syndrome threatening to destroy America's bat population, scientists are worried that bats—and guano—may be in grave danger.

The United States' Deadliest Disaster Happened in Texas

There is no doubt that Texas is known for its natural disasters, but did you know that the deadliest disaster to *ever* hit the United States took place in Galveston, Texas?

The Great Galveston Hurricane, which is known to locals as the Great Storm of 1900, took place on the island of Galveston on September 8th, 1900. The hurricane was a Category 4 with 145 mph windfalls.

The death toll estimates range between 6,000-12,000, with most reports claiming there were 8,000 casualties. For comparison's sake, 1,800 people died during Hurricane Katrina. The number of fatalities during Hurricane Harvey was estimated to be around 88.

To put things into perspective, there were so many deaths during the great Galveston Hurricane that it was impossible to bury them all. Many of the dead bodies were dumped at sea. When bodies washed back to shore, many of them were burned in funeral pyres on the beaches.

The high death toll in Galveston can be blamed on several factors. For starters, weather officials didn't take the storm seriously. They thought Galveston had already experienced so many storms that the 1900 hurricane wouldn't be a big deal. Additionally, the storm caused major damage to the city and railways, which meant there was a shortage of food and water.

After the storm, the city of Galveston went through major changes to prevent another hurricane from causing so much damage. The Galveston Seawall was built for protection and the city was elevated by as much as 17 feet using dredged sand.

The Great Galveston Hurricane was the second-costliest hurricane to date. The amount of money spent rebuilding the city was estimated to be around $20 million in 1900, which is the equivalent of $516 million as of 2009. The only hurricane that was costlier than the 1900 Galveston Hurricane was Hurricane Katrina.

Prior to the hurricane, Galveston was the second-richest city in the United States, second only to Newport, RI.

One of America's Most Dangerous Diving Spots is in Texas

Are you a thrill seeker who's always on the lookout for new risks to take? Well, look no further. Jacob's Well is known as one of America's most dangerous diving spots. Though it's hard to find the exact number of people who have died there, it's estimated that the number is about a dozen.

Located near Wimberley, Jacob's Well appears to be safe on the surface. It looks like nothing more than a safe swimming hole. It's what lies *beneath* the surface that's dangerous. There are tight, curved caves underneath the water. Divers have gotten stuck in the caves and suffocated to death.

Despite the numerous deaths that have taken place at Jacob's Well, it's still a popular spot for adventure seekers. In fact, people have traveled from all over to dive at this swimming hole. But it's not for the fainthearted and we wouldn't recommend diving there.

Apparently, even professional divers have died at Jacob's Well. Scuba divers have found it difficult to make it through some of the tight openings with their tanks, having to take them off in order to pass through.

There's no need to avoid Jacob's Well completely! Though it's not a safe place to go diving, it is considered a safe spot for swimmers.

All Astronauts Start Their Training in Texas

One of the biggest tourist spots in all of Texas is the Space Center Houston, which is located in the NASA Johnson Space Center in Houston. You may remember that many movies were filmed at the Johnson Space Center, but did you know that astronauts actually go there for training?

In fact, the Space Center is the first place where *all* astronauts go for their training. Over the past 40 years, more than 3,000 people have begun training for their careers at Space Center Houston.

Space Center Houston is also home to the most popular vacation and summer space camps for kids. People book up to *years* in advance to ensure that their children will have a spot!

So, what can you expect as a tourist to the Space Center? Well, for starters, you'll have to take the NASA Tram Tour before you'll be able to enter the space center. Since the Space Center keeps the facility at 60 degrees regardless of the time of year, you'll want to pack a sweater or jacket.

Some of the most exciting things you can experience as a tourist at the Space Center include a tour of the Saturn V at Rocket Park, an interactive exhibit of Mars, and lunch with a NASA astronaut. That being said, there are so many exhibits and artifacts to be seen here that any NASA fan will be sure to enjoy.

The Largest Ranch in the Country is Located in Texas

Texas is known for its ranches, so it may come as no surprise that the largest ranch in the United States can be found in the Lone Star State. However, it might surprise you to learn just *how* big it is.

King Ranch is set on more than 800,000 acres, making it larger than the state of Rhode Island. According to *The New York Times*, 982 Central Parks could fit inside King Ranch. It's the second-largest ranch in the entire world, second only to Alexandria Station in South Australia!

The ranch was founded by Captain Richard King in 1853. The property was full of creeks and situated in the Wild Horse Desert of South Texas. Located in South Texas, King Ranch spreads into six different counties.

Since it was started, King Ranch has hosted some of the first cattle drives, developed two breeds of cattle (Santa Cruz and Santa Gertrudis), and has bred champion Thoroughbreds and fine Quarter Horses.

King Ranch has long been viewed as a symbol of Texas's power, wealth, and pride.

Today, King Ranch continues to operate as a ranch. It also farms cotton, citrus, sugar cane, grain, and other agricultural goods. Recreational hunting is also enjoyed on the ranch.

There are a number of books that have been written about the King Ranch. Edna Ferber's *Giant*, which was later turned into a movie, is based on King Ranch.

Lords of the Land by Matt Braun is loosely based on King Ranch.

The fictional ranch in James Michener's *Centennial* is also said to be based on King Ranch.

People Go Trophy Hunting in Texas

If you think you need to travel to Africa to go trophy hunting, you'd be wrong. All you need to do is head over to the Lone Star State!

It's surprising for some to know that trophy hunting is a common practice in the United States. Trophy hunting, as a whole, has been extremely controversial, especially since the death of Cecil the Lion in Zimbabwe. However, there are around 1,000 trophy-hunting facilities in the United States and 50% of them are in Texas.

A little-known fact about trophy hunting is that the money spent on trophies goes to protect endangered species. In fact, ranch owners say that certain species would be extinct entirely if it weren't for trophy hunting!

So, what types of animals can you go hunting for in Texas? What types of prices can you expect to pay? Prices vary according to the ranch. Some ranches may offer packages in which they'll transport you to the hunting areas and may even supply you with alcoholic beverages after your hunt.

Zebras are the most popular animal people go to Texas to hunt. The price for a zebra starts around $5,750. You can hunt the nearly-extinct scimitar-horned onyx for prices ranging anywhere from

$2,000-$19,000. Wildebeest, antelope, and axis deer are just a few of other types of exotic species that you can hunt if you're willing.

You're probably wondering when this happened. Since when does Texas have exotic animals? It all started back in 1930 when a herd of antelopes arrived on King Ranch. 1988 estimates showed that there were 67 exotic species residing in Texas with 90,400 kept at ranches and more than 70,000 free-ranging. In 2016, it was believed that those numbers had more than *tripled*.

The majority of the exotic animals in the state are said to be found in the Texas Hill Country region.

Texas is Hurting the Environment

Have you ever thought about what impact Texas has on the environment?

Texas is the United States' leading oil refinery state. As of 2012, it was estimated that the state's oil production accounted for nearly a third of all oil production in the United States.

In fact, if it were its own country, it would be the 6th leading nation in oil production. The state has 10 billion barrels of oil reserves and is home to 27 oil refineries, including Exxon and AT&T, Inc. As of 2015, Texas was producing 3.6 million barrels *a day*. That's a lot of oil!

Since it is the largest oil producer in the country, which also means Texas has the highest carbon dioxide emissions in the country as well. This is bad news since carbon dioxide emissions are one of the problems that currently contribute to climate change.

To make matters even worse, Texas is also the leading producer of cattle in the country. As a result, greenhouse gas emissions, or carbon dioxide, released during the agriculture process is higher in Texas than any other state. Research has also found that the methane released from cow belches is another factor that's contributing to global warming.

Most of Texas's Prairie Dog Population Was Killed Off

When you think of prairie dogs, Texas might come to mind. Years ago, black-tailed prairie dogs ran rampant in Texas. They could be seen just about anywhere in West Texas.

Prairie dogs live in colonies called "prairie dog towns." According to *Texas Monthly*, the largest prairie dog town to have existed in Texas was made up of 400 million prairie dogs—or half of the entire rat population living in Manhattan!

While they may look cute at the zoo, prairie dogs have long been considered a pest. The millions of prairie dogs that were living in Texas caused so much destruction to the crops and grass in the state, that it infuriated farmers and ranchers. As a result, they began to poison the prairie dogs in an attempt to get rid of as many of them as possible. Now, it's been estimated by the Texas Parks & Wildlife Foundation that only about one percent of the former prairie dog population remains in the state.

If you want to see some prairie dogs while you're in Texas, don't fret. The critters can still be seen in the Lone Star State. Efforts have been made to try to preserve the prairie dog, and they can be seen at local zoos.

One of the best places to see prairie dogs in Texas is at Prairie Dog Town in Mackenzie Park in Lubbock. The prairie dog colony was established in 1935 by K. N. Clapp. Clapp feared that the government's poisoning program would lead to the extinction of the prairie dog. He and a friend trapped two pairs of prairie dogs in the park, hoping that they would breed with one another. His vision turned out to be successful. The prairie dogs began to breed and many can be seen there today. In fact, Prairie Dog Town is a tourist hotspot.

Texas is a Really Windy State

Did you know that Texas has more wind farms than any other state in the country? As of 2017, wind energy was the second most popular form of electric in the state. Wind energy is even more common than coal-powered energy in Texas.

Not that this should come as any shock. Texas is known to be a windy state. Corpus Christi, in particular, has received a lot of attention for its high-wind speeds. Its windiness makes it one of the best cities in all of North America for sailing, kiteboarding, windsurfing, and kite flying. Corpus Christi has been host to the Windsurfing World Championships.

You Might Spot a Rare Wild Cat in Texas

There's a pretty good chance of seeing a wild cat in the Lone Star State. The bobcat is frequently spotted throughout the state, but some of the other wild cats tend to be much rarer. That being said, there are still many reports of seeing these cats.

The mountain lion, which is otherwise known as a cougar or puma, used to be found throughout the entire state of Texas. However, this has changed because mountain lions tend to avoid areas with large populations of people. The influx of urbanization caused mountain lions to be driven out of the habitats they once lived in. Nowadays, cougars are generally only found in the mountains of the Trans-Pecos area and in the brushland area of the Rio Grande Plain.

The jaguar is believed to be extinct in Texas. It's believed that the last jaguar in the state was shot and killed in 1946 in San Benito. In 2016, it was said that the last jaguar in the entire United States was living in Arizona. However, this doesn't stop people from reporting sightings of the elusive animal. Could some of them still be out there somewhere?

It's believed that some jaguar sightings might actually be sightings of the ocelot, or leopard cat, due to the similarities in their markings. Others argue that it would be nearly impossible to mistake the two, given the difference in their sizes. While the jaguar weighs between 120 and 210 pounds, the ocelot only weighs between 18 and 44 pounds.

Still, the ocelot *is* out there. Though the ocelot is endangered and facing near extinction, it was estimated in 2017 that there were about 80 ocelots remaining in the Lone Star State. They are found mostly along the state border.

The jaguarundi is another type of wild cat that you might spot in the state. The cat can be identified by its long body, long tail, short legs, and rounded ears. The jaguarundi can be a number of different colors, ranging from blackish and gray/brown to the color of a fox to chestnut colored.

Jaguarundi are also considered rare and are usually spotted in South Texas. Though they are currently on the list of endangered species, the U.S. Fish and Wildlife Service has hopes of increasing the population to 500 by 2050. The jaguarundi is endangered due to loss of habitat caused by urbanization, so the Fish and Wildlife Service's goal is to reintroduce the wild cat to its native Rio Grande Valley.

The Second Largest Canyon is in Texas

The largest canyon in the United States is, without argument, the Grand Canyon. The second-largest canyon in the country is located not too far from Amarillo, Texas.

The Palo Duro Canyon spans 120 miles through the Panhandle. It's anywhere from 6-20 miles wide and reaches depths of more than 800 feet.

The Palo Duro Canyon State Park is the second-largest state park in the country. Visitors can go hiking, biking, and horseback riding across 30 miles of the canyon. While you can camp at the state park, many people choose to stay in the stone and timber cabins.

The New York Times has called the Palo Duro Canyon "the other Grand Canyon." However, there's a world of difference between the two canyons. The Palo Duro Canyon is known for its trees. In fact, the Spanish meaning of "Palo Duro" is "hardwood."

Some of the animals that can be regularly found in the canyon include mule deer, roadrunners, coyotes, and bobcats. It's also home to the endangered Texas horned lizard, as well as other types of lizards and snakes.

The Palo Duro Canyon has a long history. The Comanche Indian tribe sought refuge in the Palo Duro Canyon. It was one of the last places they lived before being forced onto Oklahoman reservations. In fact, one of the most brutal battles of the Red River War took place in the canyon, during which the United States Army shot more than 1,000 horses in an unexpected attack against the Comanche Indians. Not too long after, the Palo Duro Canyon became the first commercial cattle ranch in history. The state park was established in 1934.

The canyon inspired Georgia O'Keefe's oil painting, "Red Landscape," which you can view at the Plains Panhandle Historical Museum.

Texas Has Two Official State Animals

The armadillo is Texas's official small mammal. The nine-banded armadillo, which is the only species of armadillo that can be found in the United States, was chosen to represent the state in 1995. A distant cousin of the sloth, armadillos coincidentally chose to migrate to Texas around the same time it became a state!

According to State Symbols USA, the armadillo has traits that are representative of true Texas, such as "a deep respect and need for the land, the ability to change and adapt, and a fierce undying love for freedom."

The Longhorn is Texas's official state large mammal. The animal was chosen due to its history in Texas. It was estimated that 10 million Longhorns were herded into Texas following the Civil War.

Longhorns neared extinction in Texas in the 1920s, but thanks to efforts made by the Texas Forest Service to preserve them in state parks, the animal still exists in the state today.

Before the Longhorn was chosen as Texas's official large mammal, it was already being used as a logo for businesses all throughout Texas.

El Paso is Nicknamed "Sun City"

El Paso is nicknamed "Sun City" because—you guessed it—it's really sunny there! In fact, according to the National Weather Service, El Paso is sunny 302 days a year or 83% of daytime hours. Although it's not the sunniest city in America, it's sunny enough to earn its nickname.

There are a number of events that take place in the city that involve its nickname. For example, El Paso hosts the Sun Bowl each year. It also hosts the Sun City Music Festival and the Sun City Craft Beer Fest.

RANDOM FACTS

1. Texas has more whitetail deer than any other state in the country. In 2017, it was estimated that there were about 3.6 million deer in the state. In addition, Texas is also known to produce the largest whitetail deer in the United States. This is because of the protein in the shrubbery that's eaten by the deer in the Lone Star State.

2. There is a town called Earth, Texas. It's the only town in the world that shares a name with the planet we live on. It's unknown how the town got its name.

3. Texans have been known to eat armadillos. Barbequed armadillos and armadillo chili are two popular foods that can be found at festivals throughout the state. But you might want to think twice before eating it! Research has found that handling armadillos and armadillo consumption are both linked to leprosy. Texas ships its armadillos to research facilities that study the animals to find a cure for the disease.

4. One of the worst droughts to have ever been recorded in American history took place in Texas. The drought has been called one of the "worst natural disasters in history." The majority of the counties in the state were declared disaster areas. The drought lasted for seven years, beginning in 1950 and ending in 1957. The drought caused the crops to die and led to an overabundance of dust, which got into people's homes. Farmers were forced to feed their cattle prickly pear cactuses. Though droughts in the state have been called worse than the Texas drought of the 1950s, none have lasted as long.

5. Dallas is the largest city in the country that isn't situated on a body of navigable water.

6. El Paso is located at the intersection of three states, two in the United States and one in Mexico: Texas, New Mexico, and

Chihuahua. It's the only major city located in Texas that falls into the Mountain Time Zone.

7. Amarillo, Texas, was named after a certain type of yellow grass that grows there. The city was previously called Oneida.

8. The prickly pear cactus is the official state plant of Texas. The prickly pear fruit, which is known as tuna, is commonly used in Texan cuisine. Texas prickly pear cactus jelly is a popular recipe. Native Americans are attributed for finding pharmaceutical uses of the prickly pear cactus. They believed it could treat everything from sunburn to chest congestion.

9. The Fort Worth Zoo, which was opened in 1909, has been rated as one of the top zoos in the entire country. At the time of its opening, the zoo only had a lion, a coyote, a peacock, two bear cubs, an alligator, and some rabbits. There are 7,000 species that can be found at the zoo today.

10. Texas is the state with the highest number of tornadoes in the entire country. The yearly average is just under 140 tornadoes. Between the years of 1951 and 2011, more than 8,000 tornadoes were recorded.

11. Despite having the highest number of tornadoes in the country, the biggest natural disaster threat to people living in Central Texas is flooding. Not only is Texas located in Tornado Alley, but Central Texas has also earned the nickname of Flood Alley.

12. The world's largest supply of helium can be found within 250 miles of Amarillo. In fact, 90% of the recoverable helium in the world can be found underground in Amarillo. Helium isn't a renewable source and is used in many industries.

13. Caddo Lake is considered to be the only natural lake in Texas! However, the Caddo Lake that is seen today is not the lake that was naturally created. Dams have been built to raise the surface of the original body of water. Texas is home to 15 rivers and 3,700 streams.

14. Even though it's often thought of for its deserts, Texas's deserts make up less than 10% of the state. In fact, Big Bend has the only deserts in the state. The majority of Texas is made up of plains, hills, woods, and coastal swamp.

15. It might sound like something straight out of a dystopian movie, but Houston has an underground tunnel system. Located 20 feet below ground, the tunnel runs for 7 miles and spans across 95 blocks. You can find restaurants, stores, and more in Houston's downtown tunnels.

16. The official state shell of Texas is the Lightning Whelk. According to State Symbols USA, the shell was chosen as the state shell due to its beauty, how frequently it is found in the state, and because it's only found along the West Coast of the Gulf of Mexico.

17. Dallas has been called "The Crossroads" because it is considered to be an intersection between Los Angeles, New York, Chicago, and Mexico City.

18. There's a replica of the Stonehenge that has been constructed in Ingram, Texas. Though it's not an archaeological phenomenon like the original, Stonehenge II is still a pretty thing to see.

19. Hamilton Pool, which is located near Austin, is one of the most remarkable sights of nature to be observed in Texas. It's a natural spring that's situated in limestone bedrock. Its water comes from an underground river. There's a deep overhang in one of the walls of the cavern that's of much interest to visitors. Over 100 years ago, the Hamilton Pool was completely covered by a dome that later collapsed. The Hamilton Pool is one of Texas's many tourist attractions.

20. Texas had the most damaging thunderstorm of all-time. In May of 1995, hailstones bigger than cricket balls fell in Fort Worth and Tarrant County. The hailstones that fell during that storm were up to 4" in diameter. The storm cost a whopping $2 billion in damage and injured about 100 people.

Test Yourself – Questions and Answers

1. What year did the Galveston Hurricane happen?

   a. 1991
   b. 1990
   c. 1900

2. Which town is "The Dinosaur Capital of Texas"?

   a. Rose Glen
   b. Glen Gardner
   c. Austin

3. What are the two state animals of Texas?

   a. Armadillo and zebra
   b. Armadillo and Longhorn
   c. Longhorn and prairie dog

4. What is the name of the only naturally occurring lake in Texas?

   a. Caddo Lake
   b. Texas Lake
   c. Houston Lake

5. What animal is most commonly hunted by trophy hunters in Texas?

   a. Antelope
   b. Wildebeest
   c. Zebras

Answers

1. c.
2. b.
3. b.
4. a.
5. c.

DON'T FORGET YOUR
FREE BOOKS

MORE BOOKS BY BILL O'NEILL

I hope you enjoyed this book and learned
something new. Please feel free to check out
some of my previous books on <u>Amazon.</u>

THE GREAT BOOK OF CALIFORNIA

The Crazy History of California with Amazing Random Facts & Trivia

**A Trivia Nerds Guide
to the History of the
United States Vol.3**

BILL O'NEILL

DON'T FORGET YOUR FREE BOOKS

GET THEM FOR FREE ON WWW.TRIVIABILL.COM

CONTENTS

INTRODUCTION

How much do you know about the state of California?

Sure, you know it's home to Hollywood. You know the state has a lot of natural disasters, ranging from earthquakes to wildfires. But what else do you *really* know about the state?

You might know California has a huge population, but do you know how it got some of its population?

Have you ever wondered how California was named? Do you know how it came to be nicknamed the Golden State?

Do you know which celebrities have held government positions in California?

You know all about Hollywood. At least, you *think* you do. Do you know who drove the film industry to California in the first place? Do you know how much it costs to get your name on the Hollywood Walk of Fame?

Did you know Beverly Hills wasn't always a community where the rich and famous lived? Do you know what it was before the glitz and glamour took over?

Do you know which popular toy originated from the state or which popular frozen treat was invented in California by accident?

Do you know which famous fast-food chain opened its first location in California?

Do you know about the celebrity sex icon whose death remains a mystery to this day?

Did you know California was once the murdering grounds for one of America's most famous serial killers? Do you know about the mysterious hotel death that went viral?

If you have ever wondered about the answers to these or other questions, then you're in luck! This book is filled with stories and facts about the state of California.

This isn't just any book about California. It will highlight some of the facts that have helped form the Golden State into what it is today. You'll learn facts about the state you've probably never even considered before. Once you're done reading, you'll know everything there is to know about California.

The state of California is rich in both its history and culture. While we'll try to stick to a timeline as we explore some of the state's most significant historical facts, we'll also jump around some.

This book is broken up into easy to follow chapters that will help you learn more about the Golden State. Once you have completed each chapter, you can test your knowledge with trivia questions!

Some of the facts you'll read about in this book are surprising. Others are sad, and some may even give you goosebumps. But the one thing all of these facts have in common, is that they're all fascinating. Once you've finished reading this book, you'll be an expert on the state of California.

The book will answer the following questions:

How did California get its name?

Why is it nicknamed the Golden State?

Why did filmmakers choose to open studios in Hollywood?

Which genres of music started out in California?

Which California-born celebrity sex icon's death remains a mystery?

Which fast-food chain got its start in California?

And so much more!

CHAPTER ONE

CALIFORNIA'S HISTORY AND RANDOM FACTS

California was the 31st state to join the United States. It's famous for the California Gold Rush, but did you know there was another rush that took place in the state? Do you know how the state got its name? Do you know what the official state animal is and why it's now extinct in the state? Do you know how California got its state nickname? Read on to find out the answers to these and other questions!

California Was Given Its Name by Mistake

Did you know California was mistakenly named?

When the Spanish first visited the area in 1533, they named the area "California," with lower California (now located in Mexico) being known as "Baja California" and upper California being called "Alta California." But what gave them the idea to name the region this in the first place?

The name "California" stemmed from a Spanish fictional romance novel called *Las Serges de Esplandian* by Garcia Ordonez de Montalvo, which was published in 1510. In the book, Montalvo described a mythical island paradise called Califia, where there were lots of pearls and gold.

Califia was a fictional place, but when early Spanish settlers found California in 1535, they believed they had actually found Califia.

The area, they thought, resembled Califia, since they mistakenly believed the peninsula was an island. In addition, they found pearls.

The earliest maps of California depicted the peninsula to be an island. Francisco de Ulloa would later discover the early explorers' mistakes, but it was already too late. Since the name California had already been applied to the maps, the name stuck.

Spanish Missions Had Devastating Effects on California's Native Americans

The Spanish began a California missions program in 1769. A total of 21 missions were built throughout California. The purpose of these missions was to convert Native Americans to Catholicism, as well as expand Spanish territory throughout the state.

Native Americans were provided with both religious and cultural instruction. They would then be baptized. Afterward, men would generally go to work in the fields and women were put to work in the kitchen.

Once the Native Americans in one area had been converted to Catholicism, the mission would be converted into a church. The missionaries would then move on to the next location where they would begin converting more Native Americans.

The missions program was stopped in 1833, not long after Mexico won its independence from Spain. During this time, the territory of California was still under Mexican rule. It was already too late, however. The Spanish missions already had devastating effects on the Native American population.

The Spanish missionaries brought diseases with them that the Native Americans weren't immune to. Before the California missions program began in 1794, it's been estimated that there were 300,000 Native Americans residing in the state—and only about 20,000 by 1834.

In addition, many of the Native Americans' cultures and traditions were lost during the process. Some have compared the California missions to slave or concentration camps. Prostitution is said to have occurred during those times.

In 1865, Abraham Lincoln granted the Catholic Church some of the buildings that were originally used as missions. Many of these structures can still be found today.

California Was Once a Country of Its Own

Did you know that California was actually its own country at one point?

During the 1840s, settlers moved to California from the east using the Oregon Trail and the California Trail. Once they arrived, the settlers began to rebel against Mexican rule.

In 1846, John Fremont led settlers to revolt against the Mexican government. They declared California an independent country, which they called both the California Republic and, less formally, the Bear Republic. They flew a flag they made, which consisted of a lone star and a hand-drawn grizzly bear, over the country.

The Bear Republic was short-lived, lasting for less than a month. The rebels didn't realize the United States had already declared war on Mexico. The Bear Republic gave up its independence and pledged its allegiance to the United States.

When the Mexican-American War ended in 1848, the United States managed to claim the territory of California. The Treaty of Guadalupe Hidalgo marked the end of the war. The United States paid Mexico $15 million in war damages. In exchange, Mexico gave the USA half of its territory, which included California (along with Arizona, Texas, and New Mexico, as well as parts of Colorado, Nevada, and Utah).

In 1850, California officially became a part of the Union.

In recent years, there have been talks about California becoming a country of its own again due to the state having views more liberal than most of the U.S. Is it possible for this to happen? According to *Constitution Daily,* a new constitutional amendment *could* make it possible for California to secede from the union and give the United States its own "Brexit." California would need to receive permission from the other 49 states. Will this ever actually happen? Time will tell!

You Can Thank the Gold Rush for California's Population

California is the state with the highest population in the USA. In fact, approximately one out of every eight United States residents lives in California. As of 2008, the state was estimated to be home to nearly 40 million people, which is more than the number of people living in the entire country of Canada. But did you know the Gold Rush is the reason California's population grew to begin with?

In 1848, James Marshall discovered gold at Sutter's Mill in Coloma, California. As a result, tens of thousands of people set out to California in hopes of getting rich. Between the years of 1848 and 1855, more than 300,000 people migrated to California. They came from the eastern United States, as well as other countries. It was the largest mass migration to ever take place in the history of the United States.

The California Gold Rush is also what helped turn San Francisco into the city it is today. What had started out as a small fishing village of 200 people became the now well-known city of San Francisco when it gained 35,000 new residents. Today, the city has an estimated population of nearly 900,000.

And it's no wonder! Between the years of 1850 and 1859, more than 28 million ounces of gold was extracted from California.

Although it was what first sparked interest in the state, the gold rush wasn't the only thing that drew people to the Golden State. When the California Gold Rush ended, people didn't stop migrating to California. In 1869, the First Transcontinental Railroad helped increase travel to the state. In addition, California became a major state for farming crops like grapes, almonds, tomatoes, and more. People saw it as a place for farms and wineries to thrive.

California Also Had a Silver Rush

California is generally associated with the gold rush and Nevada is known for its silver rush. But did you know that California had a silver rush of its own?

Calico in San Bernardino County is the town most often associated with California's silver rush. The town was established in 1881 when the largest amount of silver was found in California. Calico was home to about 500 mines. During the 12 years that people worked in the mines, more than $20 million in silver came out of Calico.

When the price of silver ended up dropping by more than half its value, the residents of Calico left the town. By 1904, Calico was a ghost town. By the 1950s, the town was purchased by Walter Knott, who founded Knott's Berry Farm. Knott preserved what was left of the town to turn it into a tourist attraction. He later donated Calico to San Bernardino County.

Today, Calico is a historical landmark and makes up part of a regional park. It's now known as "California's Silver Rush Ghost Town." It's a popular tourist attraction, visited by people from all over the world!

The Discovery of Oil Helped Shape Los Angeles Into the City it is Today

With an estimated population of more than 3.9 million, Los Angeles is one of the most populated cities in America today. Did you know it was once just a small town? In fact, in 1820, Los Angeles was only home to 620 residents.

It wasn't until oil was discovered in 1892 near today's Dodger Stadium that Los Angeles began to gain recognition. Over time, more oil was discovered throughout the city. In fact, by 1923, Los Angeles was producing 25% of the world's petroleum.

After oil was discovered, Los Angeles's population began to increase. By the 1900 census, it had grown to 100,000 people. By 1960, there were more than 2 million people residing in the city.

Even to this day, Los Angeles remains a large producer of oil. There are still over 3,000 oil and gas wells in the city that are active today. The majority of these wells are located in residential communities and retailer developments. One oil well located on the property of Beverly Hills High School produces 400 barrels daily and earns about $300,000 a year.

The Golden State Wasn't California's First State Nickname

California was nicknamed the Golden State due to both the gold rush and its golden poppies, which bloom in spring throughout the state. It's also been said that the sun may play a role in its current nickname. But did you know that California wasn't always known as the Golden State? It actually had another nickname first!

California was originally nicknamed the Grizzly Bear State due to its high population of grizzly bears in the early 1800s. It's been estimated that there were tens of thousands of the bears in the state during those times. When the human population increased, its grizzly bear population was killed off. The last grizzly bear in the state was killed in the early 1920s.

Today, the grizzly bear is the official state animal of California. It's the only state with an official state animal that no longer exists in the state.

Although the idea of featuring a grizzly bear on the California state flag came about when the rebels gained control, the grizzly bear on the current state flag is Monarch. Monarch was a 1,200-pound wild grizzly bear from California who was captured by a reporter named Allen Kelley. Monarch lived out the rest of his life as a star attraction at

Woodward's Garden in San Francisco and later at the Golden Gate Park.

The Bubonic Plague Epidemic in the U.S. First Broke Out in San Francisco's Chinatown

In the early 1900s, the bubonic plague began to make its way through the United States. Did you know the disease started out in California?

In 1899, a ship that sailed from Hong Kong to San Francisco was carrying two passengers with the bubonic plague. The plague was expected to be quarantined when the ship arrived on Angel Island. However, two stowaways managed to escape the ship. Both were found dead in the Bay area, and their bodies tested positive for the plague.

While the bubonic plague didn't immediately strike the city, it's believed that rats aboard the ship were probably responsible for the outbreak.

In March of 1900, a Chinese man's deceased body tested positive for the plague. An anti-Chinese movement took place, causing Chinatown to be quarantined. The quarantine was eventually lifted because it was bad for business, but people in Chinatown were subject to home inspections. There was a lot of resistance throughout the community, with people locking their doors or hiding dead bodies.

When two more bubonic plague victims were found dead, the San Francisco City Board of Health announced the plague's presence in the city. With President McKinley's permission, anti-plague initiatives were taken. By 1903, 122 people in San Francisco and surrounding areas had died.

In 1905, researchers confirmed that the bubonic plague was spread when fleas from infected rats bit humans.

The bubonic plague began to spread again following the 1906 San Francisco Earthquake. There was a large rat and flea infestation when people were living in the refugee camps following the disaster. This time, the bubonic plague spread even more rampantly before it ended in 1909.

The Deadliest Earthquake in the U.S. Took Place in California in 1906

You probably already know that California is known for its earthquakes. It's been estimated that there are approximately 10,000 earthquakes each year, but only about 15 to 20 of those reach a magnitude higher than 4.0. Unfortunately, thousands of lives have been lost in the Golden State as a result of earthquakes, however. In fact, the 1906 San Francisco Earthquake was the deadliest earthquake in U.S. history.

The earthquake, with a moment magnitude believed to be 7.9, struck at 5:12 a.m. on April 18th, 1906. Tremors were felt in surrounding areas. This caused devastating fires to break out in San Francisco. The fires lasted several days. They caused more damage than the earthquake itself. More than 80% of San Francisco was destroyed in the disaster.

Only 375 deaths were reported in San Francisco and throughout the bay area at the time. However, there were hundreds of fatalities in Chinatown that went undocumented. Although no one knows for certain how many people died during the 1906 San Francisco Earthquake, it's been estimated that there were up to 3,000 fatalities.

The number of lives lost in the disaster was the highest of any natural disaster in the history of California. The death toll also ranks high on the lists of disasters to have ever taken place in an American city.

In addition to the lives lost, between 227,000 and 300,000 people (out of about 410,000 affected) were left without homes. Refugee camps were set up in Golden Gate Park, the Panhandle, the Presidio, and across beaches. The camps remained there for more than two years.

The 1906 earthquake makes history for another reason, too. It's the first significant natural disaster that was ever documented in photographs and video recordings.

California Sterilized More People Through Its State-Run Eugenics Program Than Any Other U.S. State

Are you ready to hear about one of the most tragic things that have ever occurred in the history of California?

You may have heard of state-run eugenics programs, in which people were involuntarily sterilized. The idea was to prevent selected people from having children to eliminate society of people considered "defective." Thirty-two U.S. states had sterilization programs, but California's was, by far, the largest.

In 1909, California passed a sterilization law. It was the third state to do so. The law gave superintendents at state-run institutions permission to involuntarily sterilize patients who were found to be too "unfit" or "feebleminded." Males were given vasectomies against their will, while women were given salpingectomies (or fallopian tube removal).

Most of these sterilizations took place at state-run mental institutions, but they also took place in state prisons. People who were chosen to be sterilized were chosen due to a number of possible reasons. Patients could be sterilized for being mentally ill, handicapped, sexually deviant, homosexual, and criminals, to name a few of the many reasons.

Superintendents got to make the decisions, and there was no way for the young men and women who were sterilized to appeal their decisions. Most of them didn't even find out they were going to be sterilized until it was actually happening. Some were never even told by the facilities they were in what had happened.

The sterilization program was racially charged. In recent times, researchers have discovered that people with Spanish surnames were 2.5 times as likely to be sterilized than those without. Mexican immigrants were especially affected due to stereotyping. Mexican men were considered to be criminals, while Mexican women were believed to be hypersexual and would have too many children if they weren't sterilized.

Coercion was also used in some sterilization cases. Patients were sometimes given the option to leave the state-run institution they were at if they agreed to be sterilized.

It's been estimated that about 20,000 people were involuntarily sterilized in California between the years of 1909 and 1979. This makes up about one-third of all people involuntarily sterilized in the United States.

California's eugenics program was so large and considered to be so effective that the Nazi party in Germany even used it as a model for their own sterilization program.

In 1979, former California senator Art Torres, wrote the legislation outlawing sterilization.

Although sterilization is believed to be a thing of the past, it's been estimated that nearly 150 women were sterilized in state prisons between 2006 and 2010.

California's Wine Industry Took a Huge Hit During the Prohibition

Today, California is known for its wine industry. The Golden State grows over 3 million tons of wine grapes every year. The state produces approximately 90% of all wine in the United States, with 17 million gallons being produced annually. But did you know California's wine industry was once impacted by the Prohibition? In fact, the impact of the law devastated wineries.

Before we go into how the Prohibition affected California's wine industry, let's start from the very beginning.

California's wine industry dates all the way back to 1796 when Spanish Franciscan Missionaries planted vineyards in order to have wine for communion. The first variety of grapes planted in the earliest vineyards was known as the Mission grape and remained the most common variety until the 1880s.

In the early 1830s, vineyards were planted in Southern California. Jean-Louis Vignes and William Wolfskill, two of the earliest major wine producers, planted their first vineyards in Los Angeles.

As people began to migrate to California during the gold rush, the demand for wine increased. Vineyards began to increase throughout the state. They were planted throughout Northern California in Napa County, El Dorado County, Sonoma County, and Sutter County (which are home to some of the most famous California vineyards today).

By the 1900s, the booming California wine industry was recognized throughout the entire world. The state was exporting wine to England, Australia, Central America, and Asia.

There were more than 700 wineries in California by the time the Prohibition was passed in 1919. One of the loopholes of the Prohibition allowed people to produce up to "200 gallons of non-intoxicating cider and fruit juice" in their homes. People began making wine in their homes, causing grape sales—and prices—to soar. Vineyards began to produce low-quality grapes that were easier to ship.

By the end of the prohibition in 1933, less than 100 wineries throughout the entire United States had managed to stay afloat. It took more than 50 years for California's wine industry to return to the way it was prior to the Prohibition.

Today, California is known for producing some of the best wines in the entire world!

California Was the First State to Ban Marijuana

You probably already know that California was the first state to legalize medical marijuana. The law, which was passed in 1996, encouraged other states to eventually follow suit. Today, the use of marijuana for both medicinal and recreational purposes is legal in California. But did you know that California didn't always have such a liberal stance on marijuana? In fact, California was the first state to ban marijuana back in 1913.

In 1907, the Poison Act, which declared cannabis to be a poison, was passed in California. In 1913, an amendment to the act made possession illegal in the state. Possession would result in a misdemeanor. By 1925, possession could earn you up to six years in prison.

While California passed a medical marijuana program in 1996, it didn't take effect until 2005 when it started out in just three counties. Patients would obtain medical marijuana ID cards with the recommendation of a doctor. About 200,000 patients took advantage of the program, which drew controversy over people potentially abusing it. There were also issues with the medical marijuana program being legal at the state level but not the federal level.

In 2016, California voters voted to legalize marijuana for recreational purposes. There are still limits, however. It's illegal to smoke or ingest marijuana in public. It's also illegal to operate a vehicle or machinery while under the influence of marijuana.

The Film Industry Moved to Hollywood to Escape Thomas Edison

You know that Hollywood is at the forefront of the film industry and has been for a long time, but have you ever wondered why? Did you know famous inventor Thomas Edison is the reason the film industry came to be located in Hollywood?

As one of the greatest inventors of all time, Thomas Edison invented many of the camera and projector technologies of the time. This meant that Edison also held many patents of the products that were needed to make films or operate movie theaters. His patents gave him the power to control the film industry through his company, Motion Pictures Patents Company, located in New Jersey. It's been said that Edison took advantage of that power, becoming what many considered to be a control freak. His company was often suing filmmakers to stop their productions.

Filmmakers began to move to California so they would no longer be at Thomas Edison's mercy. It was harder for Edison to prevent filmmakers from using his patents because traveling across the country was difficult and expensive.

The first Hollywood studio to film a movie in the area was the Nestor Motion Picture Company. The movie was filmed in 1911 at the H.J. Whitley home. H.J. Whitley, known as the "Father of Hollywood," was a real estate developer who had founded the town. Whitley was responsible for building the Hollywood Hotel and the Hollywood sign.

H.J. Whitley later convinced other film companies to set up studios in Hollywood. These included Warner Bros., Paramount, RKO, and Columbia.

The rest is history!

Walt Disney Got His Inspiration for Disneyland at a Los Angeles Park

Walt Disney's daughters, Sharon and Diane, were riding the merry-go-round at Griffith Park in Los Angeles when he came up with the idea of an amusement park that could be enjoyed by adults and their children. The idea evolved when fans asked to visit the Walt Disney Studios, which he knew didn't have much to offer them.

Opening the park was easier said than done, however. Walt Disney found it difficult to find investors for the park. Most people, including his brother Roy Disney, thought the project would only end in ruin. Walt ended up creating a show called *Disneyland*, which aired on the ABC network. In exchange, the network funded the park. ABC was responsible for one-third of the $17 million it took to build the park. Walt ended up going to other extreme means to find funds, such as borrowing against his life insurance and selling his vacation properties.

Walt originally planned to open the park in Burbank, California, but Harrison Price from Stanford Research Institute advised him to build the park in Anaheim instead. Walt acquired a 160-acre plot of land that originally housed orange groves and walnut trees.

Walt originally planned to call his theme park Disneylandia, but ABC recommended that he go with Disneyland instead. When excavation of the site began, Walt decided to go with ABC's name recommendation.

The park opened in 1955, which had a huge impact on Anaheim. The city, which was originally a rural farming community, experienced rapid growth with the opening of Disneyland. Hotels and residential communities made their way to the area. Anaheim also became an industrial hub. Electronics, aircraft parts, and canned fruit also began to be produced in the area.

Several Actors Have Gone into Politics in California

Did you know that three actors have held political positions in California?

Ronald Reagan served as the 40th President of the United States between the years of 1981 and 1989. Prior to winning the presidential election, he was the Governor of California from 1967 to 1974. But before he even started a career in politics, Ronald Reagan was a popular actor. Many people have attributed his popularity in the film industry and his good looks as the reason he was ever elected into politics at all. Ronald Reagan starred in movies like *Cattle Queen of Montana*, *Hellcats of the Navy*, and *The Girl from Jones Beach*.

Clint Eastwood is well-known for his career in the film industry, but did you know he had a brief stint in politics? The actor rose to fame after he starred in *The Man with No Name* and the *Dirty Harry* films. He later went on to direct numerous films, including *Million*

Dollar Baby. But did you know that between 1986 and 1988, Clint Eastwood served as the mayor of Carmel-by-the-Sea in California?

Actor Arnold Schwarzenegger served as the Governor of California between 2003 and 2011. Prior to his political career, Schwarzenegger was best-known for his role in *The Terminator* film series. Though Schwarzenegger has talked about a possible presidential run in the future, his plans seem to have been derailed by accusations of sexual misconduct and a messy divorce from Maria Shriver.

RANDOM FACTS

1. The capital of the Golden State has changed more than once. When California first joined the union, the capital was San Jose. The capital was later moved to Vallejo and then Benicia before Sacramento was chosen as the state capital in 1854. Sacramento had an ideal geographical location for the state's capital. Since it's not located near an ocean, the chances of an invasion were low. Sacramento was also a popular destination for new settlers due to the gold rush.

2. California's state motto is, "Eureka!" The motto came about during the gold rush. It's been said that "Eureka!"—which means "I have found it!" in Greek—was said by Greek mathematician Archimedes when he found a method to determine the purity of gold.

3. Before it was named San Francisco, the city was known as something else first. It was originally called Yerba Buena, meaning "good herb" in Spanish.

4. Three of the 10 most populated cities in the United States are located in California. They are (in order): Los Angeles, San Diego, and San Jose. San Francisco, Fresno, Sacramento, Long Beach, and Oakland all fall into the top 50 most populated cities in America, according to moving.com.

5. The majority of California's residents are minorities. More than half of its population is made up of Asians, Hispanics, Native Americans, and other minority groups. More than 25% of California's residents were born outside of America. San Francisco is home to the second largest Chinatown outside of Asia and the largest Japantown in the United States.

6. Beverly Hills is one of the most famous neighborhoods in Los Angeles. Today, it's best known for its high-value real estate

and Hollywood movie star residents, both past, and present. But before it became known for its stardom and glamour, Beverly Hills started out as a lima bean ranch. Back in the 1800s, the land was owned and used to grow lima beans by business partners Andrew H. Henker and Henry Hammel. When it became a housing development in 1906, it was named after Beverly Farms and the hills of Beverly, Massachusetts. The first house was built in Beverly Hills in 1907. The development was planned to be an all-white community. People in Beverly Hills weren't allowed to sell or rent their homes to Jews.

7. During the stock market crash of 1929, thousands of banks in the United States failed. In 1933, there were only 11,000 banks remaining in the country. All of San Francisco's banks survived the stock market crash. In fact, the economy was so good in the region that construction of the Golden Gate Bridge began at that time.

8. Angel Island is thought of as the "Ellis Island of the West." It was used between 1910 and 1940. Unlike the more relaxed Ellis Island, immigrants were detained for days to months before they were allowed entry into the country. While the majority of the 1-3% who were rejected from entering into the country through Angel Island were Chinese, it's been estimated that 175,000 Asian immigrants entered the United States through the immigration station. Today, Angel Island is a state park and national historical landmark.

9. Like other U.S. states, California has a number of strange laws. Throughout the entire state, a vehicle may not surpass 60 mph without a driver. In Fresno, it's illegal to annoy a lizard in a public park. In Los Angeles County, you cannot throw a frisbee without a lifeguard's permission. In Dana Point, it's illegal to use your own bathroom while the window's open. In San Francisco, you're not allowed to store things in your garage. In Pacific Grove, it's illegal to "mess with, molest, or hunt" butterflies. California's odd laws don't stop at humans, either.

Animals cannot mate within 1,500 feet of a place of worship, tavern or school.

10. When it was first founded, Los Angeles was originally known as "El Pueblo de Nuestra Senora Reina de los Angeles sobre le Rio Porciuncula." The Spanish meaning of this is "the town of our lady queen of the angels on the Porciuncula River." Today, Los Angeles is simply known as "The City of Angels."

11. The largest county in the United States can be found in California. San Bernardino County takes up nearly 3 million acres of space. It encompasses more land than four U.S. states combined (New Jersey, Rhode Island, Connecticut, and Delaware).

12. The Great Flood of California took place between Christmas Eve of 1861 through the end of January of 1862. It rained almost continually during these time periods. The Central Valley turned into an inland sea, nearly 25% of the state's property was destroyed, and the state went bankrupt.

13. Wildfire season in California takes place between early summer and October. In Southern California, however, wildfire season is considered to be year-round due to chronically worse drought conditions in the region.

14. While Ladies Nights are a popular pastime throughout much of the United States, they're illegal in California. The reason? Gender discrimination.

15. Former United States President Richard Nixon is from Yorba Linda, California. He grew up in Whittier, California. After his older brother died of tuberculosis while attending Whittier High School, his parents sent him to Fullerton Union High School, which was an hour away. He attended Whittier College before eventually going to Duke University School of Law. Nixon was elected to the U.S. House of Representatives and served as the Senator of California before serving as Vice President and eventually as the 36th President of the United States.

16. Blue Diamond, which is located in Sacramento, is the world-leading almond producer. The plant produces over 12 million pounds of almonds per year.

17. "The Country Store" in Baker, California has sold more winning lottery tickets than any other store in the state.

18. La Jolla, California was originally named "La Joya" by early Spanish settlers. This translates into "the jewel." It's also been said that La Jolla was called "the land of holes" by the local Kumeyaay due to the city's sea caves. Rumor has it that pirates once used those sea caves to smuggle in contraband and other goods.

19. During the California Gold Rush, treasure hunters would sail into the San Francisco harbor and leave their ships abandoned. These ships were later used to build houses and businesses in the region.

20. The second largest natural disaster in the history of California was the collapse of the St. Francis Dam. Within two years of being built, the dam ruptured, causing water to engulf entire towns. It's been estimated that somewhere between 400 and 600 lives were lost in the natural disaster.

Test Yourself – Questions and Answers

1. The name California stemmed from what mythical island in a 1950 Spanish romance novel?

    a. Fornia
    b. Cali
    c. Califia

2. California's population boom wiped out which animal?

    a. Black bears
    b. Grizzly bears
    c. Cougars

3. The film industry moved to Hollywood to escape which famous person?

    a. Thomas Edison

    b. Albert Einstein

    c. Walt Disney

4. Beverly Hills originally started out as a ____.

    a. Avocado farm
    b. Lima bean ranch
    c. Almond grove

5. Which actor has not held a political position in California?

    a. Arnold Schwarzenegger
    b. Clint Eastwood
    c. Robert DeNiro

Answers

1. c.
2. b.
3. a.
4. b.
5. c.

CHAPTER TWO

CALIFORNIA'S POP CULTURE

California is a state that's rich in pop culture, which is no surprise since it's home to Hollywood. Have you ever wondered what famous people got their start in California? Which famous children's author lived in the state? What genre of music originated from the Golden State? What famous late iconic actress came from California? Read on to find out the answers to these and other random facts about California's pop culture!

How Hollywood Got Its Name

While it is a place, the term "Hollywood" is used to refer to anyone or anything regarding show business today. Have you ever wondered how Hollywood got its name?

H.J. Whitley, the Father of Hollywood and developer of the town, was the one who gave it its name.

There have been several different theories about why he chose the name. Some believe he picked the name due to a bush found in the area that closely resembles holly.

According to Whitley's diary, however, there was another reason he chose the name. One day, he came across an Asian man who was pulling wood in a wagon. The man told him, "I holly wood" to explain he was hauling wood. This inspired Whitley to name the town Hollywood— "holly" in honor of England and "wood" for his own Scottish origin.

Regardless of how the town was named, it's hard to imagine the world without Hollywood today!

The Rise and Fall of West Coast Hip Hop

West Coast hip hop originated in Los Angeles in the mid-1970s. Alonzo Williams from Compton, California began to DJ parties using the name the "Wreckin' Cru." Both he and another DJ named Rodger Clayton who deejayed under Uncle Jamm's Army began to host large parties at nightclubs.

Unlike East Coast hip hop, West Coast hip hop had stronger electronic music influences and was faster paced. West coast hip hop focused more on DJing than rapping. Breakdancing was invented as a result of West Coast hip hop, which also set it apart from East Coast hip hop.

Perhaps one of the most well-known albums to come out of the genre was *Straight Outta Compton*, which was put out by the group N.W.A in 1988. The members of the group included Dr. Dre, Ice Cube, Eazy-E, and MC Ren. In the 1990s, all of the members later went on to become platinum-selling solo artists.

Tupac Shakur's first album, titled *2Pacalypse Now*, came out in 1991. It quickly rose to popularity due to its focus on social injustice and police brutality. Tupac received a lot of critical acclaim for his music, which drew attention to West Coast hip hop.

The following year, Death Row Records put out Dr. Dre's first album, and his single "Nuthin' but a 'G' Thang" hit No. 2 on the *Billboard* Hot 100. The record company also saw success with Snoop Doggy Dogg's *Doggystyle* and 2Pac's *All Eyez on Me*.

There's no doubt that scandal in the hip hop industry helped increase West Coast hip hop's popularity. An East-West Coast feud between Puff Daddy and The Notorious B.I.G. of Bad Boy Records and Death Row Records and Tupac had been going on throughout the 1990s. The feud garnered a lot of publicity when Tupac Shakur was shot in 1994 while Biggie Smalls and Puff Daddy had been recording. Tupac accused Puff Daddy and Biggie Smalls of setting him up.

The hip hop industry as a whole was forever changed when Tupac was murdered in a drive-by shooting in 1996. Around the same time, Suge Knight, founder of Death Row Records, went to prison. The loss of the record company's founder and biggest musician led to the death of Death Row Records.

The East-West Coast feud ended when the Notorious B.I.G. was killed in a drive-by shooting. It was around this time that the popularity of the West Coast hip hop scene fell. Fans began to listen to the new East Coast hip hop artists, such as 50 Cent.

Other Music Genres Got Their Start in California

Surf music got its start in Southern California. It's a genre of rock music that's often associated with surf culture. Surf music came to be in the late 1950s and really blew up in the early 1960s. There were two different types of surf music: instrumental and vocal. Dick Dale was the most popular instrumental surf music artist, while the Beach Boys led the vocal side of the genre.

Third wave ska is another genre that started out in California. Third wave ska was popular with the punk culture scene during the late 1980s and became commercially successful in the 1990s. Some of the most popular bands included the Mighty Mighty Bostones, Reel Big Fish, Goldfinger, and Less Than Jake. The genre gained popularity when the band called the Donkey Show picked up steam in San Diego and went on to tour the rest of the state.

There were a number of other genres of music that grew in popularity thanks to bands who came out of California.

Heavy metal grew in popularity with the rise of Los Angeles-based band Metallica.

Pop punk also gained a large following thanks to the band Green Day, which originated from East Bay, California.

A Library in San Diego Honors Dr. Seuss's Legacy

Theodore Seuss Geisel, better known for his pseudonym "Dr. Seuss", lived in La Jolla, California.

Geisel and his wife Helen moved to La Jolla after World War II ended. During the war, Geisel drew political cartoons and later drew posters to directly support the U.S. war effort. It wasn't until Geisel moved to La Jolla that he began to write the famous children's books many of us have come to love.

While living in La Jolla, Geisel wrote *Green Eggs and Ham*, *The Cat in the Hat*, *Horton Hears a Who!*, *How the Grinch Stole Christmas!*, and other fan favorites.

Geisel died in 1991, but San Diego still honors Dr. Seuss's legacy. You can visit the University of California, San Diego's Geisel Library, which is home to the largest collection of original manuscripts, photos, drawings, and other artifacts. While the artifacts are preserved for most of the year, there's a Dr. Seuss exhibit held during the author's birth month (March) and during the summer months. There's also a Dr. Seuss and *Cat in the Hat* statue outside of the Geisel Library.

In Scripps Park in La Jolla, you can see the Monterrey Cypress tree that inspired Dr. Seuss's Lorax trees. Geisel was able to view the tree from the observatory at his home in La Jolla.

A 1990s Cult Classic Movie Centered on Beverly Hills

A 1990s film with a strong cult following took place in Beverly Hills. The movie *Clueless*, which was released in 1995, centered on a teenager named Cher growing up in the upscale community.

Cher was played by California native actress Alicia Silverstone, but she wasn't the first choice for the film. Sarah Michelle Gellar and Reese Witherspoon were both considered for the role.

Cher's house in the movie is supposed to be located at 901 Drury Lane in Beverly Hills. While this is an actual address, the mansion featured in the movie is actually located in the Valley. Her best friend Dionne's house was actually located in Beverly Hills, however.

Beverly Hills High School was used as inspiration for Bronson Alcott High, the fictional high school featured in the movie. Coincidentally, both Alicia Silverstone and Bronson Alcott (who played Travis in the film) both attended Beverly Hills High. Amy Heckerling, who wrote and directed *Clueless*, sat in on actual classes at Beverly Hills High to ensure the authenticity of the script. Herb Hall, who was a drama teacher at Beverly Hills High School, actually starred as the principal in *Clueless*.

The interior school scenes were filmed at Grant High School in Los Angeles. The exterior school scenes were filmed at Occidental College, which is also located in LA.

The Electric Fountain in Beverly Hills, Westside Pavilion Shopping Center in Los Angeles, and The Witch's House in Beverly Hills are also featured in the movie.

The movie brought about some new terminology that became popular for a time period during the '90s. Some of these terms included "betty," "baldwin," "as if," "whatever," "keeping it real," and "clueless."

This Celebrity Sex Icon Was Once the Second Choice for Queen at a California Festival

Norma Jean Mortensen "Marilyn Monroe" is one of the most well-known celebrity sex icons of all time. It's hard to imagine Marilyn Monroe being the second choice for anything, but she was.

Back in 1947, Los Angeles-born Norma Jean was crowned the first Artichoke Queen at the Artichoke Festival in Castroville, California. Norma was just 22 years old at the time, and she had not yet risen to fame.

Due to her lack of name recognition at the time, Norma wasn't the first pick for Artichoke Queen. However, the first choice wasn't available and Norma was.

Norma later went on to become "Marilyn Monroe," a stage name that she picked in collaboration with 20th Century Fox executive Ben Lyon. Lyon chose Marilyn because it reminded him of his sister and Norma chose her mother's maiden name, Monroe.

She starred in films like *Gentleman Prefer Blondes* and *How to Marry a Millionaire* and also became a singer and model. Additionally, Monroe had a widely publicized relationship with Joe DiMaggio, who was one of the most famous athletes at the time.

Castroville, which is known as the Artichoke Capital of the World, also went on to be successful. The town accounts for nearly 80% of artichoke production in the United States. Castroville's Artichoke Festival still runs today!

Lots of Songs Have Been Written About California

So many songs have been written about California that it would be nearly impossible to name them all. Some songs have been written about the people and places of California, while others have been written about Hollywood and a California state of mind.

Here are some of the most popular songs about California:

- "A Girl in California" by Merle Haggard
- "Beverly Hills" by Weezer
- "Blue Jay Way" by the Beatles
- "California Gurls" by Katy Perry featuring Snoop Dogg
- "California Love" by 2Pac featuring Dr. Dre
- "California Sun" by the Ramones
- "Cowboy" by Kid Rock
- "Free Fallin'" by Tom Petty
- "Hollywood" by Jay-Z featuring Beyoncé
- "I Left My Heart in San Francisco" by Tony Bennett
- "Malibu" by Miley Cyrus

- "Queen of California" by John Mayer
- "Santa Monica" by Everclear
- "Say Goodbye to Hollywood" by Billy Joel
- "Save Me, San Francisco" by Train
- "Surfin' U.S.A." by the Beach Boys
- "The Ghosts of Beverly Drive" by Death Cab for Cutie
- "Valley Girl" by Frank Zappa
- "We Built This City" by Starship
- "Welcome to the Jungle" by Guns N' Roses

These are just a few of the *many* songs about the Golden State!

Celebrity-Owned Restaurants in California

Thanks to Hollywood's presence in California, it's no surprise that a number of celebrities own restaurants in the Golden State. Here's a list of some of the restaurants owned by celebs throughout California:

- **Tagine:** Located in Beverly Hills, this Moroccan restaurant is co-owned by actor Ryan Gosling. Gosling and two of his chef friends opened the restaurant in LA because there was nothing else like it. The restaurant is known for menu items such as its black tiger shrimp, chicken bastilla, and lamb couscous.

- **Au Fudge:** Actress Jessica Biel may be best-known for her role as Mary in the '90s show *7th Heaven* and her marriage to former *NSYNC frontrunner Justin Timberlake, but she co-owns this restaurant located in Los Angeles. The restaurant has a Creative Space for kids, complete with an indoor treehouse and au pairs for hire, so parents can kick back and relax while they enjoy their meal. Some of the menu items include truffle grilled cheese, shrimp and grits, and Mrs. Timberlake's personal favorite: vegan Caesar salad.

- **Maria Maria:** With locations in Walnut Creek and Danville, Maria Maria is co-owned by Carlos Santana. Named after his song, the restaurant serves Mexican cuisine and offers live music.

- **Nobu:** With locations in both Malibu and West Hollywood, these restaurants are co-owned by Robert DeNiro. You'll find Japanese fusion food on the menu, such as Kaba ribeye and fresh sushi and sashimi. The restaurant is known for its homemade pistachio milk.

- **Ago:** Another one of Robert DeNiro's restaurants, this West Hollywood restaurant serves classic Italian food. DeNiro co-owns the restaurant with fellow actor, Christopher Walken, director Ridley Scott, and Miramax's executive producers Bob & Harvey Weinstein, and chef Agostino Sciandri (who the restaurant is named after). The famous restaurant was in an iconic lunch scene in the movie *Pulp Fiction*. Ago is well-known for its Tuscan-style flare and its extensive wine list.

- **Café Gratitude:** Located in San Diego's Little Italy, this plant-based restaurant is co-owned by musician Jason Mraz. The 100% organic vegan/vegetarian café serves items like asparagus risotto, grilled polenta, fresh juices, homemade soda, and wine. The focus of the restaurant is non-processed food.

- **Juniper & Ivy:** Celebrity chef Richard Blais owns this San Diego restaurant. Some of the items you can expect to find on the menu include Korean fried quail, baby beets, and grilled swordfish.

- **Mission Ranch Hotel and Restaurant:** Located in Carmel, this hotel and restaurant are owned by Clint Eastwood. Serving up American cuisine, the restaurant at Mission Ranch is considered one of the top dining experiences on the Monterrey Peninsula.

These are just some of the celebrity-owned restaurants in California!

The United States Hippie Culture Started Out in California

The hippie culture originated from the Lebensreform movement in Germany in the late 1800s and early 1900s. People involved with this movement recognized the importance of body and mind, the harmful effects of industrialization, and took up an appreciation for nature.

German settlers began to introduce their beliefs to the United States. Many of them moved to Southern California because its warm climate allowed them to practice an alternative lifestyle. Many of these settlers opened health food stores.

One of the groups was called the "Nature Boys." They adopted a back-to-nature lifestyle in California, in which they raised organic food. One of the group's members wrote a song called "Nature Boy," which Nat King Cole recorded. The song brought attention to their alternative lifestyle and sparked interest throughout the United States.

The Beat Generation subculture grew popular throughout San Francisco in the 1960s. The people involved with this subculture were originally called beatniks, but they later became known as "freaks" and then eventually "hippies."

A *Friends* Actress Got Her Role Thanks to a Los Angeles Gas Station

If you're a diehard Jennifer Aniston fan, you might already know that the actress was born in Sherman Oaks, California. But did you know she landed her *Friends* role thanks to a California gas station? Well, *sort of*.

Prior to her role in *Friends*, Jennifer Aniston starred in a series of failed TV shows. These included *Molloy*, *Ferris Bueller*, *The Edge*, and

Muddling Through. After playing in four shows that all ended up being canceled, Aniston was feeling a little hopeless, to say the least.

Jennifer Aniston was at a gas station in Los Angeles when she approached Warren Littlefield, the former head of *NBC*. She was looking for words of encouragement and reassurance—which Littlefield gave her, but he gave her something else, too.

Warren Littlefield helped Aniston land her role in *Friends*.

While the show's producers originally wanted Aniston to audition for Monica Gellar, that fell through because Courteney Cox was already considered to be a good fit for the role. So instead, Jennifer landed the role of Rachel Green—the role that became Aniston's career breakthrough.

It's hard to imagine how different the cast of *Friends* would have been if Jennifer Aniston hadn't approached Warren Littlefield at that gas station.

Many Talk Shows are Filmed in California

If you've ever wanted to be a guest at a talk show, then California's one of the states you should be in! There are a number of talk shows that are filmed in California. These include:

- *The Ellen DeGeneres Show*: You can hang out with Ellen at Warner Bros. Studios in Burbank, California. The show is recorded Monday through Thursday at 4 p.m.

- *Jimmy Kimmel Live!*: You can attend a live taping at El Captian Theater in Los Angeles Monday through Thursday at 4 p.m.

- *The Late Late Show*: Attend a live recording of James Cordon's show Monday through Thursday at 4 p.m. The Carpool Karaoke King's show is filmed at CBS Television City in Los Angeles.

- *Conan*: You can catch a live recording Conan O'Brien's talk show at Warner Bros. Studio at 3:30 p.m. Monday through Thursday.

- *Real Time with Bill Maher*: Attend a live taping of the political talk show. Located at CBS Television City in Los Angeles, the show is recorded on Fridays at 5:30 p.m. Audience members must be 16+ due to mature content.

Shirley Temple's Career Started Out in California, but it Wasn't Always Glamorous

Today she's remembered for her adorable curly hair and her roles in *Heidi*, *Curly Top*, *The Little Colonel*, and *Bright Eyes*. But did you know Hollywood's child starlet Shirley Temple got her start in California?

Shirley Temple was born in Santa Monica, California in 1928. When she was about three years old, her mother enrolled her in Ethel Meglin's Dance School in Hollywood. It was there that Temple was first noticed by a casting director, who gave Shirley her first contract.

It wasn't until Shirley Temple was five that she received a contract with Fox Films Corporation. Although this is where she got her big break and began to rise to fame, there was a lot of controversy over the abuse Shirley and other childhood stars endured from this production company. Children were forced to work under slave-like conditions.

Children were forced to rehearse for two weeks without pay and then were forced to film the movie within two days' time.

The production company had a punishment box, which contained an ice block. Children who "misbehaved" were forced into the box to cool off—a torture Shirley Temple was forced to endure. She was also forced to work after a painful operation on her eardrum and dance after a foot injury.

And then there was the issue of pay. At the time, Shirley Temple was only getting paid $150 a week and being forced to do commercials for free to underwrite the company's production costs. In 1934, Shirley's parents took Fox Film Corporation to court. The actress's income was increased to $1,000 per week with $15,000 for every movie she starred in. It's been estimated that this is the equivalent to $1.8 million today.

By 1939, Shirley Temple's acting career began to fail. She had been offered the role of Dorothy in *The Wizard of Oz*, but it ended up going to Judy Garland when Fox refused to loan her to MGM for the movie.

Fox soon realized that her childhood appeal had begun to fade and allowed her parents to buy her contract from them. After a series of flops at the box office, Temple retired from acting.

Temple went on to marry John Agar, with whom she had a child. Their marriage ended in a messy divorce due to his drinking problems and infidelity.

She later met and fell in love with Charles Alden Black, who had never seen one of her movies. Together, they had a son and daughter.

Later in life, Shirley Temple Black became heavily involved in California's Republican Party. She served as a U.S. Ambassador to Ghana and Czechoslovakia.

Temple passed away in 2014.

Tyra Banks Was Teased While Growing Up in California

Tyra Banks was born in Inglewood, California and attended John Burroughs Middle School and Immaculate Heart High School in Los Angeles. It may come as a surprise to some since Banks' career is essentially built around her beauty, but the former model and creator of *America's Next Top Model* was teased in school.

According to various sources, Tyra has said she grew three inches and lost 30 pounds in three months when she was 11 years old. The former model said she looked frail and sick, even though she wasn't. Banks said she would "stuff food" down her throat in an effort to gain weight, but nothing helped. Her classmates made fun of her 98-pound, "too skinny" figure. They would call her names like "Giraffe" and "Lightbulb Head." Tyra felt insecure and alone, but she managed to rise above her peers' taunting thanks to her mentors and role models.

To help girls overcome the issues she experienced growing up, Tyra has started an organization called the TZONE Foundation in Los Angeles. The non-profit organization helps young girls build self-esteem, addresses gender stereotypes, encourages a love of one's body and beauty, and also encourages female entrepreneurship.

You Can Check Out the Tanner's House from *Full House*

If you're a fan of *Full House* and the Netflix spin-off show *Fuller House*, then you already know the show is set in San Francisco. Did you know you can check out the house that's featured in the show?

The house featured in the show is Painted Ladies, a row of Victorian-style homes on Broderick Street, across from Alamo Square Park in San Francisco's Lower Pacific Heights. The exact address of the Tanner's house in *Full House* is 1709 Broderick Street.

There's good news and bad news.

First, the bad news. The house from *Full House* on Broderick Street was *only* used for the exterior shots in the opening credits of the show. There's been a lot of confusion about this issue amongst fans of the show. The interior of 1709 Broderick Street is *not* the same interior you see in the show. In fact, the house looks completely different on the inside!

The interior shots of the Tanner house were shot at Warner Bros. Studios in Los Angeles. Stage 24 at the Warner Bros. studio is currently being used to film *Fuller House* today.

Now, onto the good news. The *Full House* creator purchased the house at 1709 Broderick Street in 2016 for $4 million. He bought the house with intentions of restoring it to the way it looked in in 1987, which included painting the door red again. You can rest assured knowing that the Tanner's home has been restored to its former glory. Want proof? The same house is featured in the opening credits of *Fuller House*.

Even though you can't go inside, you can still take pictures of it—which more than 200 fans do when they stop by to check it out each day.

Maroon 5 Started Out as a Garage Band in California

Did you know the band Maroon 5 started out in California?

Maroon 5 frontrunner Adam Levine went to Brentwood School in Los Angeles. It's there that he met Jesse Carmichael, Mickey Madden, and Ryan Dusick. Together, they formed a garage band called Kara's Flowers. Their first show was at the nightclub Whisky a Go Go in West Hollywood.

An independent producer took notice of Kara's Flowers when they were performing on the beach in Maui, who they went on to record an 11-track album with. Kara's Flowers later scored a deal with Reprise Records and released their first album, *The Fourth World*, in 1997. Unfortunately, the album only sold 5,000 copies and Reprise dropped Kara's Flowers from the label.

After Kara's Flowers broke up, Adam Levine and Jesse Carmichael went to Five Towns College in Long Island, New York. They later dropped out and reformed a band with Mickey Madden and Ryan Dusick. They decided to change their style and experimented with different music genres before deciding on groove-style music.

They were eventually signed to Octone Records and, at the advice of the label, gained a 5th member, James Valentine.

While he worked as a writer's assistant for the TV show *Judging Amy*, he wrote a bunch of songs about his ex-girlfriend, Jane

Herman. These songs were the songs Maroon 5 recorded on their debut album, *Songs About Jane*. The album sold 10 million copies, and the band won a Grammy the following year for the song "This Love."

It's crazy to think that Maroon 5 wouldn't be the band they are today if those four guys hadn't met up at Brentwood High!

RANDOM FACTS

1. Tally's Electric Theater in Los Angeles was the first motion picture theater to open in the United States in 1902. The theater, which later came to be renamed The Lyric Theater, charged customers ten cents a ticket.

2. The band No Doubt is from Anaheim, California. The band launched female lead vocalist Gwen Stefani's music career, but there was originally supposed to be a male lead vocalist. John Spence, who formed the band with Gwen's brother Eric Stefani, was going to be the lead vocalist with Gwen as a backup. Spence committed suicide just days before No Doubt was going to be performing for record industry employees. The band moved forward with Gwen eventually taking the position of lead vocals. They gained a large following throughout California, playing with The Untouchables, Fishbone, and even the Red Hot Chili Peppers. Tony Ferguson of Interscope Records gave them a multi-album contract because he was impressed by their large fan following, who were frequently stage-diving at their shows.

3. Actress Blake Lively attended Burbank High School. She was senior class president, on the cheerleading squad, and a member of the choir. Her breakthrough role, *The Sisterhood of the Traveling Pants*, was filmed during the summer between her junior and senior years.

4. George Lucas, the creator of *Star Wars*, is a California native. He was born in Modesto, California and currently resides in Marin County.

5. Independent films are popular in California. San Francisco hosts more than 50 film festivals every year. The city is home to everything from the Disposable Film Festival to the Greek Film

Festival. The San Francisco International Film Festival is the oldest film festival in the United States.

6. You can see the house that was used for the exterior scenes in *Mrs. Doubtfire* starring Robin Williams at 2640 Steiner Street in San Francisco. The interior of the house was filmed at a warehouse in the Bay Area.

7. While he's most well-known for his poetry focusing on New England, Robert Frost was born in San Francisco.

8. Actress Cameron Diaz grew up in Long Beach, California. She went to Los Cerritos Elementary School and graduated from Long Beach Polytechnic High School, which she attended with another famous alumnus — rapper Snoop Dogg!

9. Actor Leonardo DiCaprio was born in LA. He attended the Los Angeles Center for Enriched Studies. The actor dropped out of high school during his junior year before earning his role on the show *Growing Pains* in 1992.

10. *Beverly Hills, 90210* was a TV show that aired for 10 years. The show focused on a fictional high school called West Beverly High School. Tori Spelling rose to fame as a result of the show. It's been rumored that Los Angeles-born Tori Spelling auditioned under a fake name so the casting directors didn't know she was the daughter of Aaron Spelling, who co-produced the show. Even Tori has admitted that she thinks her father's involvement helped her land the role, however.

11. The show *Baywatch*, which focuses on the Los Angeles County Lifeguards, was filmed on location in LA County. As a result, 40 bottles of sunscreen were used each month to keep the cast members' skin protected from the sun.

12. Actress Drew Barrymore was born in Culver City, California. She was born into the Barrymore acting family. Her father John Barrymore and all of her paternal grandparents and great-grandparents were stars. John Barrymore was considered to be the most acclaimed actor of his generation.

13. Actor Will Ferrell grew up in Irvine, California. He went to University High School where he was an athlete. Ferrell played soccer and basketball, and he was a kicker for the varsity football team. The *Elf* and *Step Brothers* actor credits growing up in a quiet, suburban neighborhood for his sense of humor because he was always looking for things to make fun of to break up the boredom.

14. Late English actor Alan Rickman lived in California. Best-known for his role as Severus Snape in the *Harry Potter* series, Rickman once failed the California state driving test because he drove too cautiously through a green light.

15. Actress Kaley Cuoco, who's most known for her roles in *8 Simple Rules* and *The Big Bang Theory*, is from Camarillo, California. While growing up in Southern California, Cuoco was a regionally ranked amateur tennis player. Cuoco gave up the sport when she was 16 years old.

16. The reality TV shows *Laguna Beach: The Real Orange County* and *The Hills*, which were set in Laguna Beach and Los Angeles, respectively, were all the rage when they aired in the 2000s. But did you know cast members Brody Jenner and Spencer Pratt starred in another less popular reality TV show called *Princes of Malibu*? The show focused primarily on Brody and his younger brother Brandon.

17. Actor Zac Efron is a California native. He went to Arroyo Grande High School and the Pacific Conversancy of the Performing Arts before landing his breakthrough role in Disney's *High School Musical*.

18. Jack London, the author of American classic novels *White Fang* and *Call of the Wild*, was born in San Francisco. He attended Oakland High School. Today, you can visit Jack London State Historic Park, which is made up of his home and Jack and his wife's graves.

19. Ellen DeGeneres hosted her high school reunion at her talk show. She flew 60 of the alumni from her graduating class to the studio where they celebrated their 30-year reunion.

20. One of the most well-known holiday songs was written in California. "Let it Snow" was written in Hollywood during a heatwave in July of 1945. The songs' writers, Sammy Cahn and Jule Styne, wrote it because they were dreaming about cooler temperatures.

Test Yourself – Questions and Answers

1. Which genre of music did *not* get its start in California?

   a. Surf music
   b. West Coast hip hop
   c. Jazz

2. Marilyn Monroe was crowned Queen at which festival?

   a. The Artichoke Festival
   b. The Almond Festival
   c. The Avocado Festival

3. Dr. Seuss got his inspiration for the Lorax tree from a type of tree that can be found at Scripps Park in La Jolla. The type of tree is a _____?

   a. Cherry Blossom Tree
   b. Cedar of Lebanon
   c. Monterrey Cypress Tree

4. Which celebrities attended high school together?

   a. Zac Efron and Blake Lively
   b. Cameron Diaz and Snoop Dogg
   c. Leonardo DiCaprio and Adam Levine

5. Which celebrity owns a restaurant named after one of his songs?

   a. Carlos Santana
   b. Adam Levine
   c. Jason Mraz

Answers

1. c.

2. a.

3. c.

4. b.

5. a.

CHAPTER THREE

FACTS ABOUTCALIFORNIA'S ATTRACTIONS

If you're thinking about planning a trip to the Golden State, there are a number of attractions you might want to check out while you're there. But how much do you really know about them? Do you know about one of Disneyland's most morbid early attractions? Do you know what the actual color of the Golden Gate Bridge is? (One hint: it's *not* gold!) Do you know about the famous tree that can be found in the state? Do you know how much it costs to get your name on the Hollywood Walk of Fame? Read on to find out the answers to these questions and other random facts about California's most famous attractions.

You Can See a Rainbow at Night at Yosemite National Park

If you've ever wanted to visit Yosemite National Park, then you probably know it has some really cool attractions. The park is so beautiful, that it even inspired the idea of national parks in general when Abraham Lincoln signed the Yosemite Land Grant back in 1864 to preserve the region—even though Yosemite National Park didn't actually come to be until 26 years after that, making it the third national park to be formed.

The park is home to over 400 species of animals and is most famous for Yosemite Falls, the tallest waterfalls in the entire world.

Yosemite National Park is also known for its ancient giant sequoia trees and its granite rock formations, which cast a fire-like glow at sunset.

But did you know that Yosemite National Park is home to another beautiful natural phenomenon? It's one of the few places in the entire country where you can see a rainbow at night. Yosemite's nighttime rainbows, which are called lunar rainbows or moonbows, happen during the spring and early summer. Lunar rainbows occur when the sky is clear and the moon is full enough to cast its light over the waterfalls.

Having a Star on the Hollywood Walk of Fame Comes at a Hefty Price

Have you ever wondered how much one of those stars on the Hollywood Walk of Fame cost? They come with a whopping $40,000 price tag! Wondering who pays for them?

In order to receive a star on the Hollywood Walk of Fame, one must be nominated first. Whoever fills out the application must list who will pay for the star. The star in question needs to agree to the nomination *and* they must attend the star's unveiling. The only celebrity who didn't attend the unveiling of her star was Barbra Streisand.

The first celebrity to receive a star on the Hollywood Walk of Fame was filmmaker Stanley Kramer in 1960. Since then, everyone from Mickey Mouse to Muhammad Ali has gone on to receive a star—or more than one star. Celebs can have stars in up to five categories, though the only celebrity who actually has five stars is Gene Autry.

The San Diego Zoo Was Home to the First Panda Cubs in America

Did you know that the San Diego Zoo is one of only four zoos in the entire United States that's home to giant pandas? In fact, the first two panda cubs to be born and survive until adulthood were born at the San Diego Zoo!

Bai Yun is a female panda who was loaned to the San Diego Zoo from China in an effort to help reduce the country's dwindling panda population. Part of the agreement was that all pandas Bai Yun delivered were to return to China after they reached their third birthdays.

In 1999, Bai Yun delivered her first panda cub at the San Diego Zoo. The baby panda was a female named Hua Mei, which translates to "China/United States." Hua Mei was conceived via artificial insemination. Her father was Shi Shi, a panda who had already been at the zoo.

In 2003, Bai Yun gave birth to another panda cub at the San Diego Zoo. The male cub was conceived naturally. He was named Mei Sheng, which means "born in the United States." His father was Gao Gao, another panda who was born in China and transported to the San Diego Zoo to father Bai Yun's offspring.

Since then, Bai Yun has given birth to four more cubs, all of which were conceived naturally. Even more, the zoo has been able to learn so much about giant pandas thanks to her.

Bai Yun can still be seen at the San Diego Zoo today, though she is now past the age of reproduction. Her last cub, Xiao Liwu, was born in 2012.

Disneyland's Opening Day Was a Disaster

Did you know that the opening day of Disneyland was actually a disaster?

Walt Disney may have spent *two decades* planning Disneyland, but he was anxious for the park to open just one year and one day after construction had started. The opening of the park was rushed, with painting and hammering going on until the park's opening was aired live on ABC—which 70 million Americans had tuned in to watch.

The live special, which was co-hosted by then-actor Ronald Reagan, gave Americans a look at the park. They got to see Magic Kingdom's four realms: Fantasyland, Tomorrowland, Adventureland, and Frontierland. What viewers didn't know was that behind the scenes, a total disaster was taking place.

Since visitors were only to be granted into the park on opening day via invitation-only, only 15,000 park visitors were expected to arrive. So, imagine the surprise when over 28,000 visitors made it through the gates, thanks to counterfeit tickets.

There were seven miles of traffic into the park, causing more traffic than ever on the Santa Ana Freeway. More lanes eventually needed to be added to keep traffic under control.

Visitors were disappointed to find that Tomorrowland wasn't yet ready. Some of the park's rides, such as Peter Pan and Dumbo the Flying Elephant, also weren't open.

The weeds around the Canal Boats of the Ride attraction hadn't been removed prior to opening day. Walt Disney had workers place exotic plant names in Latin next to them so that guests would think it was an arboretum.

Due to the 100-degree temperature, the asphalt on the Main Street, USA, melted into a sticky tar. The tar ended up getting stuck on women's high heels.

The plumbers Walt Disney hired had gone on strike, which meant the drinking fountains weren't working. The refreshment stands ran out of both food and beverages, causing many thirsty, sweaty people to leave the park.

Meanwhile, the Mark Twain's riverboat ride had been filled to capacity and caused water to wash over onto the deck.

Walt Disney promised that the park would be better equipped, noting that it might take a month before everything would be running smoothly.

Despite the park's disappointing opening day, people still wanted to go to Disneyland. Within seven weeks, the park saw more than one million visitors. By 2015, 750 million people had been to Disneyland.

And a Disneyland Ride Once Contained Some Creepy Props

Disneyland may boast itself as the "Happiest Place on Earth," but when one of Disneyland's most famous attractions opened back in 1967, it may have been one of the creepiest. Some of the ride's props were a little morbid, to say the least.

At the time of its opening, the Pirates of the Caribbean ride contained skeletons. As in, *human* skeletons. The skeletons came from UCLA Medical Center. They were later returned and buried, though it's been rumored that one human skull is still part of the ride today.

You might also be surprised to learn that Walt Disney's original concept for the Pirates of Caribbean was nothing like the ride is today. He originally wanted it to be an exhibit people would walk through, rather than an actual ride. However, Walt decided a boat ride made more sense, so he decided to make the ride similar to It's a Small World. The Haunted Mansion was also originally planned as a walk-through attraction.

Balboa Park is Bigger Than Central Park

Central Park is the most well-known park in the country, but did you know Balboa Park in San Diego actually encompasses more space? Central Park is set on 842 acres of land, while Balboa Park is made up of 1,200 acres.

So, what exactly can you find at Balboa Park? The San Diego Zoo, for starters. The park is home to a carousel that was built in 1910, 15 museums, the Marie Hitchcock Puppet Theater, restaurants, and so much more. The first IMAX Dome Theater is also located in Balboa Park.

There's also Palm Canyon, where you'll find 450 palm trees and a historic path, which connects with a canyon and leads to Old Cactus Garden.

In addition to being larger than Central Park, many consider Balboa Park to be far more laid-back.

The Golden Gate Bridge Isn't Actually Gold

The Golden Gate Bridge is an American icon, partly due to its appearance in the opening credits of *Full House*. It might come as no surprise that the Golden Gate Bridge isn't actually gold. The bridge has a redder appearance. So, what is the color exactly?

The bridge's color is actually called "International Orange." For touch-ups, the bridge's paint is currently supplied by Sherwin-Williams. The shade wasn't originally considered for the bridge.

Carbon gray, aluminum, and black were all early color options. The U.S. Navy wanted the bridge to be painted black with yellow stripes to make it visible on foggy nights.

But the bridge's architect, Irving Morrow, didn't want any of those colors. He thought black and aluminum both didn't capture the essence of the bridge.

His inspiration came from the red primary steel beams at Eastern factories were coated in. He felt International Orange was unusual to find in engineering. The color made the Golden Gate Bridge stand out from the sky and water, and it's also visible in the fog.

You might be wondering why the bridge is called the Golden Gate Bridge when it's not even gold in color. The bridge is actually named after the Golden Gate Strait, which lays between the Pacific Ocean and the San Francisco Bay. The strait was named by John C. Fremont, an explorer who thought the strait was a natural beauty. Contrary to popular belief, the Golden Gate Strait was *not* named due to the California Gold Rush. Fremont named the Golden Gate Strait two years prior to the discovery of gold in California.

Knott's Berry Farm Claims to be America's First Theme Park

Knott's Berry Farm in Buena Park, California claims to be America's first theme park. While some historians disagree, there's no doubt that Knott's Berry Farm *does* have a long history.

The amusement park is on the site of a former berry farm, which was started by Walter Knott and his family back in 1920. The Knott family sold berries, jams, and pies from the farm's stand. In the 1930s, they began to serve fried chicken dinners from their tea room. Their fried chicken became a popular tourist attraction, so they began to build shops for restaurant goers to spend time in while they waited to be seated.

In the 1950s, Walter Knott opened a county fair on the property. It was then that the idea of a theme park came about.

By 1968, the Knott family was charging an admission of 25 cents. The then-famous Calico Log Ride was added to the park the following year.

The park added Camp Snoopy. Snoopy has been the park's mascot since 1983.

In the 1990s, the Knott family sold the theme park to the Cedar Fair Entertainment Company (who also own the famous theme park, Cedar Point in Ohio). The company added a few large roller coasters and other thrill rides.

In 2009, the park became Nickelodeon University—though many still call it Knott's Berry Farm.

As of 2015, Knott's Berry Farm became the 12th most visited theme park in the United States.

One of the Most Famous Trees in the World is Located in California

Did you know one of the world's famous trees can be found in California?

Located in Sequoia National Park, the General Sherman tree is the largest living tree in the entire world. The giant sequoia is also one of the oldest trees in the world. It's believed to be anywhere from 2,300 to 2,700 years old.

The General Sherman tree is, without a doubt, one of Sequoia National Park's biggest tourist attractions.

It may surprise you to learn that the General Sherman is *not* the tallest tree on earth. It's also not the widest. It's considered to be the biggest tree in the world based on its volume.

The tree is 275 feet tall and 25 feet in diameter and has an estimated bole volume of 52,513 cubic feet.

In 1978, a branch fell from the General Sherman that was 6 feet in diameter and 140 feet in length, which is larger than most of the trees throughout the United States.

SeaWorld Almost Didn't Happen

The first SeaWorld location opened in San Diego in 1964. The theme park was home to the very first Shamu, an orca whale who was captured by fishermen a year after the park opened. But did you know SeaWorld almost didn't happen at all?

The park was created by first UCLA graduates. Their original idea, however, was to open an underwater restaurant that had marine life shows. Instead, they decided to create a theme park that would compete with Marineland of the Pacific, a marine life-themed park that was popular at the time.

When SeaWorld opened in 1964, it was home to sea lions and dolphins. The TV show *Flipper* came out the same year, which sparked an interest in dolphins and helped SeaWorld get popular.

Death Valley is the Hottest, Driest Place in the USA

You've probably heard of Death Valley National Park, but did you know it's the hottest, driest place in the entire country?

Death Valley reaches temperatures higher than 120 degrees Fahrenheit in the summer. In addition, the region only sees about two inches of rain annually. In 1929, Death Valley didn't get any rain at all.

You might be surprised to learn that, in spite of the hot summer temperatures and lack of water, there is still life in the region. There are more than 1,000 plant species and more than 350 species of animals. Bighorn sheep and mountain lions are among the animals you might spot at Death Valley National Park.

If you want to visit Death Valley National Park without fighting the heat, then you might consider visiting in February when the average temperature is 72 degrees Fahrenheit. There's also an average .52 inches of rainfall in Death Valley during February.

The Hollywood Sign is Almost as Secure as Fort Knox

Remember in the movie *Friends with Benefits* when Justin Timberlake and Mila Kunis climb on top of the Hollywood sign? The likelihood of that actually happening in real life is pretty slim, considering the Hollywood sign has nearly as much security as Fort Knox.

To prevent the sign from being vandalized, the Department of Homeland Security helped develop a security system that involves razor wire, infrared technology, motions sensors, alarms, and helicopter patrols. The sign is monitored 24 hours a day.

It might surprise you to learn that the Hollywood sign, which became a historical landmark in 1973, wasn't built due to Hollywood's movie industry. It was originally designed as a billboard to advertise the real estate development that H.J. Whitley was actively promoting at the time. The Hollywood Sign cost a lot of money to build. At the time, it cost $21,000 to build—which has been estimated to be worth more than $250,000 today.

There are Hundreds of Wineries in Napa Valley

Napa Valley is every wine lover's dream. You'll find about 450 wineries and about 815 brands of wine in the area. That's a lot of wine! How do you even know which ones to visit?

In 2017, Igor Sill ranked the 10 best wineries in Napa Valley as follows:

1. V. Sattui
2. Darioush Winery
3. Castello di Amorosa
4. Spottswoode
5. Inglenook Winery
6. Artesa Vineyards
7. Domaine Carneros
8. Luna Vineyards
9. Opus One
10. Stag's Leap Wine Cellars

Igor Sill created this list based on Yelp and TripAdvisor reviews, as well as his own experiences.

There's a Castle in California

If you want to see a castle, the Golden State might not be the first place that comes to mind. But California is home to a castle, which was built between the years of 1919 and 1947.

Hearst Castle was built as a home for William Randolph Hearst, who published the largest chain of newspapers in the late 19th Century.

William Randolph Hearst commissioned Julia Morgan to design the castle, which cost $6.5 million to build over the course of 28 years.

The castle has 56 bedrooms, 61 bathrooms, indoor and outdoor gardens, a movie theater, an airfield, and 127 acres of gardens—just to name a few of its features. At one point, it housed the world's largest private zoo. There were once lions, tigers, grizzly bears, jaguars, cougars, monkeys, and even an elephant. Hearst sold his animals off when he had financial difficulties and after his death in 1951, most of the animals that remained were donated to local zoos. Today, there are still zebras that roam the land.

William Randolph Hearst entertained many famous people at his castle. Many of his parties were hosted by actress Marion Davies, who Hearst is believed to have had an affair with. Clark Gable, Cary Grant, and many other celebs attended his parties.

With its palm trees, the exterior of Hearst Castle wouldn't make you think it resembles that of a European castle, but quite the contrary. The interior of Hearst Castle bares such a close resemblance to European castles that the dining hall was used as a model for set designers for the dining hall of Hogwarts in the *Harry Potter* movies.

Hearst Castle is open to visitors today.

The Origins of Alcatraz Island's Name May Surprise You

From 1934 to 1963, Alcatraz served as a "supermax" high-security prison on Alcatraz Island, which is located off the coast of San Francisco. It housed some of the most ruthless, hardened criminals during its time. Today, it's a popular historical attraction, likely due to its most famous inmate, Al Capone, AKA "Scarface."

It might surprise you to learn that Alcatraz Island's name has absolutely nothing to do with its prison. According to the Bureau of Prisons, the meaning of Alcatraz is "strange birds" or pelicans. The island was named in 1775 by Lt. Juan Manuel de Ayala, a Spanish explorer who was the first to map San Francisco Bay.

The name of the island is fitting. Alcatraz Island is known to be a great place to go birdwatching. Western Gulls are the most common bird that can be found on the island. You'll also find cormorants, snow egrets, black-crown night herons, and orange-footed pigeon guillemots.

From February to September, parts of Alcatraz Island are closed off to visitors to allow birds to nest.

RANDOM FACTS

1. California is home to more national parks than any other state in the country. Nine of the 59 national parks are located in the Golden State. These include Yosemite National Park, Sequoia National Park, Redwood National Park, Joshua Tree National Park, Kings Canyon National Park, Lassen Volcanic National Park, Channel Islands National Park, Pinnacles National Park, and Death Valley National Park.

2. Universal Studios Hollywood had more than 8 million visitors in 2016, making it the 15th most visited theme park in the world and the 9th in North America.

3. Channel Islands National Park is made up of five of the eight Channel Islands off California's coast. The largest island in the park is Santa Cruz Island, which is almost three times the size of Manhattan! Santa Catalina Island, generally known as Catalina Island, is another one of the Channel Islands. The island is most known for its beautiful beaches, Arabian horses, and golf carts, which are driven instead of cars due to the 20-year waiting list to own a car on the island. Buffalo Milk is a famous Catalina Island cocktail. It's made of crème de cacao, Kahlua, crème de Banana, and vodka, which are poured over ice and topped with half-and-half, whipped cream, and a sprinkle of nutmeg.

4. The California State Railroad Museum is located in Sacramento. The museum, which is the largest of its kind in the United States, contains 19 steam locomotives and exhibits honoring California's railroad legacy.

5. On Highway 99 in Madera County, there's a place where a palm tree and a pine tree can be found side-by-side. This location marks the border of Northern California and Southern California.

6. The Ronald Reagan Presidential Library and Museum is located in Simi Valley. When you're there, you can step aboard Air Force One, the plane which flew Ronald Reagan over 600,000 miles during his presidency.

7. At the top of Mount Diablo, you can see 40 out of the 58 counties in California. They are most visible on a clear day, especially after a winter storm.

8. Klamath Wildlife Refuge is home to the largest population of bald eagles in the entire country. Bald eagles can only be found there during winter, however.

9. Since 1937, more than 1,600 people have jumped to their deaths from the Golden Gate Bridge. About 26 people have survived the jump.

10. Caswell Memorial State Park is home to the riparian brush rabbit, which is one of the most endangered species of animals in the entire world. It's believed that only a handful of these rabbits remain in the wild.

11. Pier 39 gets 11 million visitors a year. The pier offers bayside views with sea lion sightings, shops, food, entertainment, and its popular 2-story carousel, which came from Italy in 2008.

12. The Golden Gate Park is rich in California history. It was home to 40,000 refugees following the 1906 San Francisco Earthquake, served the first fortune cookie in the United States, and was once home to Monarch the Grizzly. Another one of the coolest aspects of the park? Is Shakespeare Garden, which only features the plants and flowers William Shakespeare mentioned throughout his works.

13. Pacific Park on the Santa Monica Pier is the only amusement park in the entire world that has a solar-powered Ferris wheel!

14. Legoland in Carlsbad, California was the first Legoland to open in the United States. The first two parks were opened in

Denmark and England. Out of the six Legoland theme parks, Legoland California is one of only three that offers a water park.

15. The Presidio of San Francisco was once a U.S. Army military fort. Today, it's a popular park in the city and home to numerous attractions, including the Walt Disney Family Museum.

16. Lake Tahoe has been around for more than 2 million years. The lake, which is considered ancient, is one of the top 20 oldest lakes in the world. Lake Tahoe is also the 2nd deepest lake in America. With a depth of 1,645 feet, the water would still measure 41 inches if you poured it onto an area the size of California. The lake contains 39 trillion gallons of water. This is enough to supply everyone living in America with 50 gallons of water every day for five years.

17. The Redwood National and State Parks are considered a temperate rainforest. The Coast Redwood trees they contain, which are also known as Giant Sequoias, are the tallest trees in the world. Coast Redwoods grow the best in temperate climate conditions with little to no seasonal temperature changes, dense dripping fog, and moist, well-drained soil.

18. When the Children's Pool at La Jolla Beach was built in 1913, it was designed to be a place for children to learn how to swim. Today, the Children's Pool is a well-known haven for harbor seals and sea lions. The San Diego City Council shuts down the area December 15th through May 15th for the pupping season to keep the animals protected from beachgoers.

19. Joshua Tree National Park is located at an ecological crossroads. The park intersects the high Mojave Desert and the low Colorado Desert. The Joshua trees, which the park is named after, thrive in the sandy plains of the Mojave Desert. The Mojave Desert takes up the Western side of the park, while the Colorado Desert takes up the Eastern side.

20. 17-Mile Drive in Pebble Beach, California, inspired author Robert Louis Stevenson to write the book *Treasure Island* back in 1883. The idea for the novel, which has had a number of film adaptations, came to Stevenson when he was hiking the site of the now-famous Spyglass Hill Golf Course.

Test Yourself – Questions and Answers

1. At which of California's national parks can you see a rainbow at night?

   a. Sequoia National Park
   b. Yosemite National Park
   c. Kings Canyon National Park

2. Which of Disneyland's early attractions contained real human skeletons from UCLA Medical Center?

   a. Pirates of the Caribbean
   b. The Haunted Mansion
   c. Mark Twain's river ride

3. The General Sherman Tree at Sequoia National Park is the largest tree in the world based on which of the following?

   a. Height
   b. Width
   c. Volume

4. The dining hall in Hogwarts in the *Harry Potter* movies was modeled after a dining hall at which of the following?

   a. Magic Kingdom
   b. Hearst Castle
   c. Alcatraz Federal Penitentiary

5. What is the meaning of "Alcatraz"?

   a. "strange birds"
   b. "beautiful birds"
   c. "seabirds"

Answers

1. b.

2. a.

3. c.

4. b.

5. a.

CHAPTER FOUR

CALIFORNIA'S INVENTIONS, IDEAS, AND MORE!

Have you ever considered what inventions have come out of California? A number of popular foods, products, and other inventions that you might use on a daily basis have originated in the Golden State. Do you know which popular snack food started out at a theme park? Do you know what frozen treat was invented by accident? Do you know which successful fast-food chain's first location opened in California? Read on to learn more about some of the things that started out in California.

Doritos

Today, they're one of America's favorite junk foods. Did you know that Doritos got their start in Anaheim? The popular snack food started out at Disneyland, to be specific!

Elmer Doolin, the co-founder of Frito-Lay, opened a restaurant that was located in Disneyland's Frontierland in 1955. Doolin's restaurant was called Casa de Fritos, which is called Rancho Del Zocalo today. The restaurant purchased its tortillas and taco shells from Alex Foods, a food distributor in Anaheim.

Doritos were inspired by Mexico's traditional totopo and chilaquiles. The restaurant began to cut up and fry extra tortilla shells, which it added seasonings to. Doolin originally had Alex Foods produce Doritos, but when the demand for the tortilla chips got too overwhelming, production was moved to the Frito-Lay plant in Tulsa.

The chips were sold under the name Doritos, which means "little golden things."

When Doritos hit the market in 1966, they were an instant success!

Barbie Dolls

If you loved playing with your Barbie dolls as a kid, you can thank Ruth Handler, who was a resident of Los Angeles when she invented the doll in the late 1950s.

Ruth Handler was watching her daughter Barbara play with paper dolls when she got the inspiration behind the dolls. She noticed that Barbara was assigning adult roles to her paper dolls, even though the dolls were infants.

Ruth Handler told her husband, Elliot Handler, about it. Elliot Handler co-owned a toy company called Mattel, which he ran out of an El Segundo garage at the time. Elliot loved the idea.

In 1956, Handler went to Europe with her children where she found an adult doll called Bild Lilli. The doll was based on a comic strip and kids loved dressing her in outfits. Ruth bought three of the dolls and brought them back to Los Angeles, where she redesigned them with the help of an engineer named Jack Ryan.

The doll, which Ruth decided to name Barbie after her daughter, first debuted at the American International Toy Store in 1959.

During the first year of production, 300,000 dolls were sold.

The company behind the Bild Lilli doll sued Mattel for copyright infringement in 1961. Mattel settled out of court and purchased the patent rights to the Bild-Lilli doll.

The same year, Mattel put out a male doll that would be Barbie's boyfriend Ken—who was named after the Handlers' son, Kenneth.

Rocky Road Ice Cream

Have you ever wondered who to credit for this delicious ice cream flavor? While it's unclear who actually invented Rocky Road ice cream, one thing is for sure: it *did* come from Oakland, California.

Fentons Creamery, a historic ice cream parlor, claims to be the original creator of the ice cream flavor. Fentons Creamery's candy maker George Farren allegedly created a rocky road-style candy bar, which he blended into chocolate ice cream. It's been said this inspired his friends to make their own version of the ice cream with one change: they used almonds in place of walnuts.

Those friends who were inspired by Farren's creation were none other than William Dreyer and Joseph Edy, who founded Dreyer's Ice Cream in Oakland back in 1929. The popular ice cream brand still markets the flavor as "The Original Rocky Road"—even though the original recipe probably wasn't theirs.

Regardless of who created it first, Dreyer and Edy are the ones who named the ice cream flavor. The ice cream was created during the Great Depression. Its name was intended to give people hope during the "rocky" times.

Fentons Creamery still serves Rocky Road ice cream today.

Blue Jeans

You can thank California for those blue jeans you're wearing! Levi Strauss, of the now famous Levi's jeans company, is credited with designing the first pair of blue jeans. You might be surprised to learn that the idea wasn't actually his.

Levi Strauss, a German immigrant, opened Levi Strauss & Co. in San Francisco. His brother owned a dry goods store in New York City and the San Francisco location was a second branch of the business.

One of his frequent customers was a tailor named Jacob Davis. In 1870, a woodcutter asked Davis to make him a pair of strong working pants. Davis added copper rivets to the button fly and pocket corners to give the pants extra reinforcement.

The pants Davis designed for the woodcutter were a huge hit and other customers wanted the same type of pants. Soon, there was so much demand for his invention that Davis couldn't keep up. He asked Levi Strauss for financial support. Strauss agreed since Davis was a regular customer. Together, Levi Strauss and Jacob Davis got a patent for the reinforced pants in 1873.

Although legend has it that Levi Strauss sold his first jeans to miners during the California Gold Rush, this is actually a myth. The first pair of Levi's wasn't created until the 1890s—about 31 years after the Gold Rush had ended. The rumor came about due to a false advertising campaign.

The first people to purchase blue jeans were factory workers. Over time, the trend caught on and the rest is history!

Popsicles

Did you know the Popsicle almost never came to be? It was invented in California by accident!

Back in 1905, an 11-year-old boy by the name of Frank Epperson accidentally left a fruit drink out overnight on the back porch of his home in Oakland. The temperature dropped to below freezing overnight. The following morning, Epperson found the frozen drink on the "stick," which inspired him to invent the fruit-flavored ice pop.

The idea stuck with Epperson over the years. He didn't go public with his invention until he was in his late 20s. In 1923, he sold the frozen treat, which came in seven flavors, at Neptune Beach amusement park. In 1924, he got a patent for his invention, which he originally named the "Epsicle Ice Pop". His children later convinced him to change its name to the Popsicle.

Martinis

Have you ever wondered where the martini came from? The famous cocktail got its start in California!

There has been some argument as to where, exactly, in California the now famous cocktail came from. Some argue that the cocktail came from Martinez, which is the city the cocktail is believed to have been named after. Others say the cocktail originated from San Francisco. In the early 1860s, the Occidental Hotel in San Francisco served a drink called the "Martinez Cocktail." In both versions of the story, a California Gold Rush miner requested a drink and the bartender came up with the idea of the martini.

No matter where it got its start, the martini is one of the most well-known cocktails today. The original martini is made with gin and vermouth and garnished with either an olive or a lemon twist.

Since its invention, the martini has been offered in numerous flavor varieties, ranging from appletinis to chocolate martinis. There are even martini bars, which serve different types of martinis.

California Rolls

There has been some controversy over who actually invented the California roll.

It's been said that California rolls were invented by a Los Angeles sushi chef named Ichiro Mashita in the early 1970s. When he was working at the Tokyo Kaikan in LA, Mashita began to substitute avocado for toro (fatty tuna) and constructed the roll inside-out.

However, a chef named Ken Sousa at the Kin Jo sushi restaurant near Hollywood was the first to be formally credited with the California roll's invention. It was reported by the *Associated Press* in 1979 until it was later contested.

Regardless of who actually invented them, California rolls were an instant hit in southern California. The trend began to spread like wildfire throughout the rest of the country. By the 1980s, it was one of the most popular sushi dishes in America. California rolls have inspired sushi restaurants to serve many other different types of rolls.

Apple Inc.

Did you know the iPhone started out in Cupertino, California? Apple Inc. was founded by Steve Jobs, Steve Wozniak, and Ronald Wayne in 1976.

The company made computers for both businesses and consumers. The very first computer released by the company was the Macintosh. It was the iMac, however, that really gained Apple attention. The iMac, which was first introduced in 1998, gained a lot of fans for being easy to use and design-oriented.

Apple later went on to take over the music player industry with its iPod and the phone industry with the iPhone in 2007. Today, the iPhone has more than 100 million users in the United States alone and more than 700 million users throughout the world. It's crazy to think it all started in California!

McDonald's

Today it's the largest chain restaurant in the entire world, but did you know the first McDonald's opened in San Bernardino, California in 1940?

The restaurant was opened by siblings Maurice and Richard McDonald. It wasn't the same as the McDonald's of today.

By 1948, McDonald's had a "Speedee Service System." It wasn't the first of its kind, however. It was a more advanced version of the fast food service that White Castle, which had opened 20 years earlier, had in place.

You might be surprised to learn that the original McDonald's mascot was *not* Ronald McDonald. The restaurant's first mascot was "Speedee," a chef hat on top of a hamburger. In the early 1960s, Speedee was replaced by the now-famous Golden Arches. In 1965,

Ronald McDonald was introduced in advertisements to help target children.

In 1954, McDonald's was changed forever when Ray Kroc joined the chain. He ultimately turned it into a global franchise and, ultimately, the most successful fast food chain.

You can still visit the first McDonald's location, but you won't find an actual McDonald's restaurant there. The chain sold the site to the Juan Pollo fast food chain in 1976. You'll also find a McDonald's and Route 66 museum.

Slot Machines

Today, slot machines can be found in casinos throughout the entire world. But did you know they pretty much originated from California?

While he didn't invent the first slot machine, a San Franciscan car mechanic named Charles Fey did a lot of fine touching. His redesigned concept is what brought the slot machine, which was originally called the "Liberty Bell" machine, to what it is today.

Fortune Cookies

While you might think fortune cookies came from China, you'd be wrong. Fortune cookies actually originated from California. While there are several theories on who actually came up with the idea, the most popular theory is that they were invented by a Japanese immigrant named Makoto Hagiwara. Hagiwara was a gardener, who was best-known for designing the Japanese Tea Garden in Golden Gate Park.

As the story goes, the Mayor of San Francisco fired Makoto Hagiwara from his gardening job. When the new Mayor hired him back, Hagiwara made him cookies with "thank you" notes inside. The concept of a cookie with a note inside became popular.

The Golden Gate Park is the first place to have ever served fortune cookies.

In 1973, the fortune cookie folding machine was invented in Oakland, California. This made it possible for Chinese fortune cookies to be mass produced for the first time.

Orange Julius

A trip to the mall in the 1990s or early 2000s wouldn't have been the same without Orange Julius. Did you know Orange Julius started out in California?

In 1929, Orange Julius was founded in Los Angeles. Julius Freed, an orange juice stand owner, was inspired by his friend who suffered from stomach problems. His friend couldn't drink orange juice because of the acidity. Freed wanted to make a drink everyone could enjoy.

To make orange juice stomach-friendly, Julius Freed mixed the juice with milk, sugar, egg, vanilla, and ice to create the Orange Julius.

The frothy drink was an instant hit with the customers. Almost overnight, Julius Freed's daily sales went from $20 a day to $100 a day.

Taylor Guitars

If you're a musician, then you've probably heard of Taylor Guitars. Did you know Taylor Guitars is headquartered in El Cajon, California?

In 1972, an 18-year-old named Bob Taylor got a job at American Dream, a guitar-making shop. When the owner decided to sell the guitar shop, Bob Taylor and his two co-workers—Kurt Lustig and Steve Schemmer—bought it.

They knew they needed to rename the shop and opted for Bob's last name, Taylor because it sounded most American. Bob Taylor also did most of the guitar-making, while Kurt Lustig handled the business aspects.

Taylor Guitars is known for producing some of the best-sounding guitars in the industry. The company also helped make the acoustic guitar what it is today.

Some of the most famous musicians who have played Taylor Guitars include Taylor Swift, Jewel, Prince, Dave Matthews, Jason Mraz, and Steven Curtis Chapman.

You can take a free, guided tour of the Taylor Guitars Factory in El Cajon at 1 p.m. Monday through Friday.

The Gap

The Gap, Inc. currently operates the Gap, Old Navy, Banana Republic, Weddington Way, Athleta, and Intermix. But did you know the very first Gap store started out in the Golden State?

Don Fisher was inspired by the success of The Tower of Shoes, which advertised that it had whatever brand, style or size of shoes a woman could want. Using the same business model, Don Fisher opened the store on Ocean Avenue in San Francisco in 1969. Doris Fisher, his wife, and co-founder of the Gap, gave the store its name.

Originally, the Gap only sold Levi's clothing. Don Fisher grouped the clothing by sizes. The store also guaranteed that it wouldn't go out of stock, as it replenished sold items from Levi's overnight warehouse. The store also offered LP records to attract a teenage audience.

Today, the Gap, Inc. is the largest specialty retailer in the United States and the 3rd largest international retailer. There are more than 2,000 locations of its stores in the USA and over 3,000 throughout the entire world.

The Hot Fudge Sundae

Although the origins of the hot fudge sundae have been contested, it's believed that the hot and cold treat got its start in Los Angeles.

Clarence Clifton Brown allegedly created the first hot fudge sundae in 1906 at C.C. Brown's, the ice cream shop he owned. Brown is said to have experimented with a few hot fudge recipes before getting it right.

He put it on the menu at C.C. Brown's when it was at its first location at 7th and Flower Downtown. The hot fudge sundae was an instant hit! In fact, the success of the hot fudge sundae brought in so many customers that Brown was able to move his ice cream parlor to Hollywood Boulevard. C.C. Brown's became a hotspot for both tourists and celebrities. The hot fudge sundae's popularity caught on and quickly became an American classic.

RANDOM FACTS

1. The Egg McMuffin was invented by Herb Peterson, who co-owned a McDonald's franchise in Santa Barbara, California. He first introduced the egg, cheese, and Canadian bacon sandwich, which is served on an English muffin, to his menu in 1972.

2. The jukebox got its start in California in 1889. The coin-operated phonograph, the invention that would later lead to the modern-day jukebox, started out at San Francisco's Palais Royale Saloon. Customers were charged a nickel a pop. In its first six months of use, the machine earned more than $1,000, which is estimated to be more than $25,000 in modern times.

3. The origins of the Shirley Temple drink have been disputed. One Hawaii resort takes credit for the virgin cocktail. However, most historians believe the drink, which was named after the child actress, was invented in California. Rumor has it that a bartender at Chasen's in Beverly Hills created the drink to serve the young actress a non-alcoholic beverage. The Shirley Temple drink is made of ginger ale, grenadine, and a maraschino cherry garnish.

4. **The Cobb Salad got its start at the Hollywood Brown Derby restaurant in the 1930s. The owner of the restaurant, Robert Howard Cobb, was working late one night when he decided to make himself a snack. He opted for a salad and leftover bacon, which he mixed together with some French dressing. He added the salad to the restaurant's menu not long after. The salad is made up of bacon, chicken, eggs, and avocados. Cobb Salad is still traditionally served with French dressing.**

5. **While sourdough bread wasn't actually invented in California, it did get its start in America in the Golden State. During the California Gold Rush, French bakers brought**

sourdough bread to Northern California. Boudin's has made sourdough bread since those times. Sourdough bread has been scientifically proven to taste better from San Francisco due to its tastier bacteria, which is used to achieve the sour flavor.

6. Pet rocks were created as a joke by Gary Dahl after listening to his friends complain about how much work their pets required. He told his friends rocks would be the perfect pets because they didn't require any care. Dahl created a humorous instructional manual for the pet rock, which was included when people purchased the product. In 1975, more than one million people bought Pet Rocks during the holiday season. Within one year, Gary Dahl became a millionaire on his invention.

7. The first working laser was invented by Theodore Harold Maiman in 1960. It was designed using a ruby crystal in his Malibu laboratory.

8. The first cable car in the world made its debut down Clay Street in August of 1873. Since then, they have been commonplace in San Francisco (though they were removed temporarily in the late 1940s, they were later brought back). While they're not the best method of transportation, they're still a pretty cool sight to see.

9. The modern hula hoop became popular after the plastic ring was sold by Wham-O Toy Company, which is based in Carson, California. The toy was inspired by Native American Hoop Dance. Four months after the toy was released in 1958, 25 million hula hoops were sold. Within two years, 100 million had been sold. The craze eventually died out in the United States in the 1980s, though it remained popular internationally.

10. The Mai Tai is made of rum, curacao, lime, and orgeat. The cocktail was created by Victor Bergeron, who owned Trader Vic's restaurant in Emeryville, California. Bergeron came up with the idea when his friends were visiting from Tahiti in 1944.

Wondering how the drink got its name? As the story goes, Bergeron made the cocktail for them and one of his friends said, *"Maita'i roa ae!"*, which means "out of this world!"

11. The waterbed got its start in California. Charles Hall created the waterbed for his Master's Thesis project at San Francisco State University in 1968. Waterbeds were trendy in the 1970s when they were considered sexy.

12. The first wetsuit was invented in California back in 1952. It was designed by Hugh Bradner, a physicist at the University of California Berkeley. Sadly, his invention didn't take on right away. A lot of other brands began to develop wetsuits of their own. It wasn't until the 1990s that Brander actually got credit for being the wetsuit's original inventor.

13. The first videotape recorder was invented by a California native. Charles Ginsburg was working as an engineer at the AM-radio station KQW (today's KCBS). When he joined Ampex in 1951, he was behind the development of the world's first video tape recorder.

14. WD-40, which helps prevent and reduce rust, was invented in San Diego. It was created by Norm Larsen, who founded the Rocket Chemical Company. He also invented WE-40 as well.

15. The Gay Pride Flag, which is also often referred to as the Rainbow Flag or the LGBT Flag, was created in San Francisco by an artist named Gilbert Baker. Designed in 1978, the flag represents support and unity for the LGBTQ community and is used during Pride month celebrations.

16. **Fantasy football originated in California. It all happened back in 1962 when two Oakland Raiders employees, a sports reporter, and an *Oakland Tribune* sports editor took a three-week trip to the East Coast together with the Raiders. After they returned from the trip, they started the Greater Oakland Professional Pigskin Prognosticators League, which met**

weekly at King's X bar (today's Kona Club). This paved the way for fantasy football.

17. Skateboarding was invented back in the 1950s as an alternative to surfing. It was considered to be an ideal alternative when the waves in Southern California weren't good for surfing. Skateboarding has come a long way since it was first invented. The very first skateboard was a simple wooden board attached to disassembled roller blades. By the 1970s, the boards became more elaborate and an entire culture had been formed around skateboarding. In fact, skateboarding is going to be added as an Olympic sport in 2020.

18. The Nicotine Patch was invented by Murray Jarvik, a professor at UCLA, and one of his colleagues. Their research on the effects of nicotine absorption into the skin led them to develop the now-famous nicotine patch, which helps people quit smoking. The nicotine patch was released in 1992.

19. The California burrito got its start at an unknown San Diego restaurant in the 1980s and has been a popular part of San Diego's culture ever since. The California burrito is generally made from chunks of carne asada meat and contains a surprising ingredient: French fries. It also generally includes pico de gallo, cilantro, sour cream, onion, and/or guacamole. With the combination of American and Mexican ingredients, the California burrito is considered a border fusion food.

20. The Jack in the Box fast-food chain got its start in San Diego when Robert O. Peterson opened it in 1951. It was the first fast food restaurant to make the drive-thru its primary focus, as well as the first to use a two-way intercom system for its drive-thru. Today, the chain has over 2,000 locations, which are located primarily on the West Coast and in select urban areas on the East Coast.

Test Yourself – Questions and Answers

1. Who was the Barbie doll named after?

    a. The inventor of the Barbie Doll
    b. The inventor's daughter
    c. A doll from Europe

2. Which cold treat was *not* invented in California?

    a. The hot fudge sundae
    b. The frozen margarita
    c. Popsicles

3. Who brought sourdough bread to the Golden State?

    a. French bakers
    b. Native Americans
    c. Latvian bakers

4. Fortune cookies were first served where?

    a. SeaWorld
    b. Universal Studios
    c. Golden Gate Park

5. Which popular snack food was first served at Disneyland?

    a. Marshmallow Peeps
    b. Doritos
    c. Fritos

Answers

1. b.

2. c.

3. a.

4. c.

5. b.

CHAPTER FIVE

CALIFORNIA'S UNSOLVED MYSTERIES, SUPERNATURAL, AND OTHER WEIRD FACTS

Do you know which unsolved mysteries have taken place in California? Due to Hollywood, it's no surprise that many of these unsolved mysteries involve celebrities. Have you heard about the creepy folklore and urban legends that haunt the Golden State? Some of the facts you read in this chapter may give you goosebumps. Others may surprise you. Some of them are just plain weird. To find out about some of the creepiest and most bizarre things that have happened in California, read on!

The Black Dahlia Murder Mystery

You've probably heard of the Black Dahlia by now. The case is one of the most famous unsolved murder cases in the history of the United States, as well as one of the oldest unsolved murder cases in Los Angeles County. But how much do you really know about it?

Twenty-two-year-old Elizabeth Short's body was found in Leimert Park in Los Angeles on January 15th, 1947. Her body, which was severely mutilated, was found severed in two pieces. The killer had also drained Short of all her blood before cleaning her body with gasoline to remove any fingerprints. Police were able to identify the victim based on her fingerprints, which matched fingerprints on a previous arrest record.

As the case began to unravel, the LAPD found that Short had last been seen six days before her murder. This led investigators to believe the victim had been kidnapped prior to being killed.

Elizabeth Short's boyfriend had dropped her off at a bar where she was supposed to meet her sister from Boston. One of the last people to have seen Elizabeth Short was a wealthy man named Mark Hansen, a movie theater and nightclub owner.

Newspapers often gave nicknames to murder victims during that time. There have been several theories about how Short came to be known as the Black Dahlia. There was a murder mystery film called *The Blue Dahlia*. Short also wore dahlias in her hair. It's been said that Short had already been given the nickname at the drug store she worked at prior to her murder.

Within the week following Short's murder, a person who claimed to be the killer called the editor of the *Los Angeles Examiner*, James Richardson. The alleged killer told Richardson he planned to turn himself in, but he wanted the police to pursue him further. The killer also told Richardson to expect some of Short's "souvenirs" in the mail.

Three days after the call was made, a manila envelope was discovered which contained newspaper clippings and Elizabeth Short's birth certificate, photographs, business cards, and an address book with the name Mark Hansen embossed in gold on the front. Like Short's body, the envelope had been cleaned with gasoline. While some fingerprints were still able to be lifted from the envelope, they were compromised on their way to the FBI and could not be used.

Due to the address book, Mark Hansen became a suspect in the investigation. Hansen knew Elizabeth Short and was able to confirm that a purse and shoe belonged to her. Ann Toth, who was Short's roommate, told investigators that Hansen had made sexual advances which Short had reject prior to her murder.

Mark Hansen was cleared as a suspect. However, author Piu Eatwell argues in her book about the case, *Black Dahlia, Red Rose*, that Hansen played a role in Short's death. She believes that the murder was committed by Hansen and a man named Leslie Duane Dillon, a mortician's assistant and bellhop. At one point, Dillon was a lead suspect in the investigation. Piu suggests that both suspects were let off the hook because LAPD Sergeant Finis Brown, who was one of the two cops who led the investigation, was a corrupt cop with ties to Hansen.

More than 150 suspects were interviewed, but no one has ever been arrested for the murder.

Over 500 people have confessed to the murder. Some people who have confessed to killing Short were not even born at the time of her death.

Conspiracy Theories Surround Marilyn Monroe's Death

Marilyn Monroe was found dead at her home on August 4th, 1962. The actress, who was found naked, had an empty bottle of pills nearby.

While Marilyn Monroe's death was believed to be a suicide, a lot of people aren't so sure. A lot of conspiracy theories came about after the actress's death. Nearly all of these theories revolve around Monroe's alleged involvement with the Kennedy family.

It was rumored that Marilyn Monroe was sleeping with John F. Kennedy. The rumor drew even further attention when Monroe famously sang "Happy Birthday" to the then President a few months before she was found dead. There was another rumor, too—that Marilyn Monroe was also having an affair with JFK's brother, then-Attorney General Robert "Bobby" Kennedy.

One popular theory is that Bobby Kennedy had Monroe murdered to cover up their affair. Another theory was that she had a diary with incriminating information about the family, which Bobby had her murdered for.

Other conspiracy theories were that the Mafia or the CIA had Monroe killed in order to hurt the Kennedys.

In a documentary called *Unacknowledged*, Dr. Steven Greer suggests another theory. He says that the United States government has been covering up extraterrestrial existence. Greer reveals a wiretap, which states that Marilyn Monroe knew about the government's cover-up and threatened to hold a press conference in which she would reveal all.

Is it possible that Marilyn Monroe was murdered due to her knowledge of aliens? Could this have been the same incriminating information she had about the Kennedy family?

In 2014, the diary of a late Hollywood detective named Fred Otash was found. Otash claimed that he heard Marilyn Monroe die. He claimed that Monroe argued with Kennedy before they had sex with her, causing her to scream. He said Bobby Kennedy used a pillow to muffle her cries so the neighbors wouldn't overhear. Bobby allegedly left immediately after that and Monroe's body was later found.

To date, many people still consider Marilyn Monroe's death to be a mystery.

Natalie Wood's (Not So) Accidental Drowning

Natalie Wood was an actress who was known for her roles in the movies *Miracle of 34th Street*, *West Side Story*, and *Rebel Without a Cause*. She also dated famous celebrities, including Elvis Presley.

On November 28th,1981, while she was filming the movie *Brainstorm*, Natalie Wood and her husband Robert Wagner took a weekend boat trip to Catalina Island. They were on board a boat called the *Splendour* with Wood's *Brainstorm* co-star Christopher Walker and Dennis Davern, the captain of the boat.

The following morning, Natalie Wood's body was found dead one mile away from the boat. A dinghy was found on the beach.

Robert Wagner claimed that Wood wasn't in bed when he retired to his cabin.

Alcohol was found in Wood's bloodstream. Thomas Noguchi, the Los Angeles County coroner, believed she was drunk and slipped when trying to re-board the dinghy. Noguchi ruled her death an accidental drowning and hypothermia.

In 2011, Dennis Davern publicly stated that he lied during the investigation. Davern claimed that Wood was having an affair with Walker and Wagner, who was jealous and angry, had killed her.

Police have officially cleared Walker as a suspect, but Robert Wagner was named a person of interest in February 2018.

Californians Report Lots of Bigfoot Sightings

Did you know California is the 2nd state with the most reported Bigfoot sightings in the United States?

In fact, Bigfoot sightings are so commonplace in California that there's even a museum in Willow Creek, which is known as the Bigfoot Capital of the World. The Bigfoot Museum has the largest collection of sasquatch artifacts in the entire world. Most of the collection is from Bigfoot researcher Bob Titmus. Some of the artifacts you'll find include newspaper clippings, Bigfoot hair, and casts of Bigfoot footprints.

According to urban legends, Yosemite National Park was home to the world's very first Bigfoot. During one sighting at Yosemite, a camper was woken up by a strange sound. He ran out of his tent screaming, hoping to scare off whatever had woken him up in the first place. Instead, the camper found himself face-to-face with Bigfoot, who let out an even scarier scream before running off into the woods.

Redwood National and State Park is another place which is believed to possibly be where the first Bigfoot originated from. The very first widely publicized reported sighting of Bigfoot came from the park back in 1958.

The Patterson-Gimlin Film is the first recorded footage of what might be Bigfoot. The short film was shot alongside Bluff Creek near Orleans, California. The film was made by Roger Patterson and Bob Gimlin. Patterson maintained that the creature in the film was real up until his death in 1972. In 1999, however, Gimlin said that he believed it may have been a hoax set up by Patterson—one that Gimlin fell for himself.

A number of Bigfoot sightings have been reported at Mount Shasta. In 1962, one woman allegedly saw Bigfoot have a baby at Mount Shasta.

In 1993, a group of hikers reported seeing sasquatch across from Aloha Lake in Northern California. Since then, a number of Bigfoot sightings have been reported in the area.

The most recent famed Bigfoot sighting happened in 2017 when a woman named Claudia Ackley, who had been researching the urban legend for 20 years, took her two daughters hiking near Lake Arrowhead in the San Bernardino mountains. A few yards away and 30-feet up in a tree, Ackley spotted what she believed to be an 800-pound creature that looked like a hairy Neanderthal. When Ackley called authorities to report the Bigfoot sighting, they told her she had seen a bear and refused to offer assistance. What drew attention to Claudia Ackley's sighting was the lawsuit she filed a year after her report was made. The lawsuit is against the California Department of Fish and Wildlife for "dereliction of duty to protect Bigfoot" and infringing on her own constitutional rights.

The Death of Elisa Lam at the Cecil Hotel in Los Angeles

The story behind Elisa Lam's death at the Cecil Hotel in Los Angeles is so eerie that many believe it to be an urban legend, but it's not. It's all real—and it's all completely terrifying.

But before we talk about Elisa Lam's death, let's start at the beginning. The Cecil Hotel has a long history of murders and suicides. In fact, so many suicides took place at the hotel that it was once referred to as "The Suicide" instead of "The Cecil."

Attention was first drawn to the hotel when the Black Dahlia was said to have been spotted at the Cecil's Bar just days prior to her death.

In the early 1960s, one of the hotel's residents, "Pigeon Goldie" Osgood, was found dead in her room, which had been ransacked. Osgood had been raped, stabbed, and beaten. While a man named Jacques B. Ehlinger was charged with her murder, he was later cleared. Her death is still a mystery.

In the 1980s, the Cecil Hotel was said to have been where a serial killer named Richard Ramirez, who was nicknamed the "Night Stalker," had been staying for a few weeks. It's believed that Ramirez may have done some of his murders while he was staying at the Cecil.

Richard Ramirez isn't the only serial killer who stayed at the Cecil. In 1991, Austrian serial killer Jack Unterweger is believed to have stayed there to pay homage to Ramirez. During his stay at the Cecil, Unterweger strangled and killed at least three prostitutes. He was later convicted of the murders in Austria.

In 2013, the creepiest death took place at the Cecil Hotel, which had been renamed Stay on Main. After hotel guests began to complain that their water was a darker color, hotel maintenance discovered a young woman's nude body inside the water tank, located on the roof of the hotel. Her body had been decomposing in the tank for at least two weeks.

The body was identified as Elisa Lam, a young Canadian student who was traveling at the time. Lam had originally been sharing a hotel room before her roommates complained of her "odd behavior," and she got her own hotel room.

When police went through the hotel's security cameras on the day Lam is believed to have died, what they found was... well, bizarre and disturbing. In the video footage, Lam pressed the elevator buttons erratically and then looked out the elevator door when it opened as if someone had been following her. Once she exited the elevator, the doors opened and a closed a second time, but the person was never seen—leading some people to believe that Lam was being followed.

Although the Los Angeles County Coroner ruled Lam's death an accidental drowning, many have questioned how her body ended up in the water tank at all. There was no way to access the hotel roof, aside from the fire escape. Others have questioned if it was possible for her to have gotten into the water tank herself, which has led to speculation that someone may have murdered her and placed her body inside the tank. Could she have been trying to flee from the murderer when she was in the elevator?

Some believe that paranormal involvement may have played a role in Lam's death and that it could explain her erratic behavior in the hotel. Others have questioned if Lam, who suffered from bipolar disorder, may have been having a relapse at the time of her death. And still, others wondered if she may have been on ecstasy or another drug at the time of the video footage.

People have also pointed out that certain points of the viral video were slowed down. This has led to speculation that the video may have been tampered with before it was put on the internet.

One unusual theory is that Elisa Lam may have been suffering from tuberculosis. Part of the logic behind this theory is the fact that the TB test is called LAM-ELISA.

People have compared the circumstances surrounding the death to the 2005 horror movie, *Dark Water*.

Things got even creepier when posts on Elisa Lam's blog continued to publish even after she had died. While it's most likely that Lam had pre-scheduled the blog posts, some believe it's her ghost. Lam's phone was never found, which also made people wonder if a possible murderer may have continued to post from the blog.

The mystery of Elisa Lam's death remains unsolved.

Alcatraz is One of the Most Haunted Spots in America

Did you know that Alcatraz Island is considered to be one of the most haunted places in the United States?

The theory of the island being haunted dates back to when the Native Americans visited Alcatraz Island before it was ever used for a prison. The Native Americans believed the island was home to "evil spirits." And they weren't the only ones who found the island to be... well, *eerie*. Author Mark Twain visited Alcatraz at one point and described it as "cold as winter, even in the summer months."

It's also been said that there are ghosts of prisoners and prison guards who died at Alcatraz who haunt the former prison. One of the most scary places in the prison that's believed to be haunted is "the hole," which was once used for solitary confinement.

Rumor has it that a man was put in "the hole" in the 1940s. During the night, the man allegedly told the guards he was being tormented by a demon-like creature with glowing eyes who he believed was trying to kill him. The guards ignored the man's screams because they thought he was just trying to get out of the cell, but the following morning the man was found strangled to death. No one knows for sure how the man died, but people claim to hear the man's screams to this day.

The Zodiac Killer Once Killed in Northern California

You've probably heard of the Zodiac Killer, one of the most famous serial killers in American history. But you might not know that he killed his victims in northern California.

The killer's murder spree began in December 1968. Betty Lou Jansen and David Faraday were murdered in Benicia, California. They were both shot dead while sitting in their parked car. Without any witnesses or evidence, there wasn't much of an investigation.

In July 1969, Darlene Ferrin and Michael Mageau were attacked in Vallejo, California. While Ferrin's gunshot wounds killed him, Mageau managed to survive the attack.

In August, three newspapers in San Francisco received letters from the killer. With the letter, the killer sent a cryptogram that he said would reveal his identity if it was solved. It was eventually solved, but it didn't reveal his identity.

On August 7th, 1969, the killer sent a letter in which he wrote his famous phrase— "This is The Zodiac speaking"—and it drew national attention and gave the killer his name.

In September of the same year, Cecilia Shepard was shot dead on the shore of Lake Berryessa, while her boyfriend Bryan Hartnell survived his wounds.

In October, Paul Lee Stine was shot to death in a taxi in San Francisco. It's believed that Stine was the final victim, though some investigators believed that the Zodiac Killer may have been responsible for up to 37 murders in total.

Following Stine's death, the Zodiac Killer sent a piece of Paul Stine's shirt with his letters to the newspapers. The killer also sent another cryptogram, which no one could solve, and a seven-page letter.

Throughout 1970, the newspapers received six more letters and greeting cards. The letters contained details about some of the things the Zodiac Killer had done in the past, as well as what he had planned for the future. Unfortunately, the letters didn't help police enough for them to come up with any potential leads or suspects.

The Zodiac Killer didn't give up, however. He continued to send letters for eight more years.

There was evidence that made investigators believe the Zodiac Killer may have also murdered victims in Lake Tahoe, Riverside, and Santa Barbara.

While the police have come up with several suspects over the years, there was never enough evidence for them to make an arrest.

In his book, *The Black Dahlia Avenger*, a retired police detective named Steve Hodel suggests that his own deceased father, a physician named George Hill Hodel, Jr., was the Zodiac Killer. Steve Hodel also believes his father was responsible for the Black Dahlia's murder.

The Zodiac Killer's letters stopped coming in 1978. While the case was marked inactive in 2004, it was re-opened at some point prior to 2007.

Dark Watchers May Haunt the Santa Lucia Mountains

The Dark Watchers are one of the most popular California urban legends. If you've never heard the story, it's a little creepy, to say the least.

The legend originates from the Chumash Indians, who lived in the region. The cave walls in the Santa Lucia Mountains were painted to show dark phantom-like shapes on the mountains looking down, as though they were watching.

In his story *Flight*, author John Steinbeck described the same figures as "dark forms against the sky."

A Monterey high school principal claimed to see the Dark Watchers.

Since then, there have been mixed reports about what the Dark Watchers look like. Some describe them as ghostly figures that wear dark capes and hats, while others report phantom-like figures like those described by the Chumash Indians. In every account, however, these figures are said to stay still as they watch from the mountaintop before vanishing into thin air.

The legend of the Dark Watchers has been around for centuries, so it seems safe to say that it will be around for years to come.

The Hollywood Sign is Believed to be Haunted

Did you know the Hollywood Sign is said to be haunted? According to urban legend, death is supposed to follow anyone who visits it alone.

So, what fueled this urban legend? A second urban legend. Almost every state has a legend about a Lady in White, and California is no exception. A Lady in White, with a skeletal face and eyes, is said to haunt the Hollywood Sign at night. It's believed that the Lady in White is late actress Peg Entwistle, who was allegedly driven to commit suicide from the top of the H after a bad review in 1932.

Entwistle isn't the only one who has died at the Hollywood Sign, however. The sign has been a popular suicide location. A man's decapitated head and body parts were also discovered near the sign.

If you're planning to try to get past the Hollywood Sign's security system, just make sure you don't go alone.

A Former Navy Pilot's Story About UFOs in California is Eerie

There have been numerous sightings of UFOs in California. In fact, based on information from the National UFO Reporting Center and the Mutual UFO Network, California is the state with the most UFO sightings in America. But one former Navy pilot's story is a little creepy, to say the least.

In 2017, former Navy commander David Fravor recounted his story of seeing UFOs off the coast of California in 2004. During his 15th year as a Navy pilot, Fravor was on a routine training mission when the squadron he was in charge of was ordered to go check out some strange unidentified flying objects that were being tracked for weeks.

The objects were making a descent at 80,000 and 20,000 feet before disappearing.

According to the *Washington Post*, Fravor said what he found was a "white Tic-Tac, about the same size as a Hornet, 40-feet long with no wings" hanging above the water. Fravor said the UFO didn't create visible air turbulence the way helicopters do. He said the UFO mirrored pilots as they got closer before accelerating into thin air, moving faster than anything he had ever seen in his life.

When Fravor checked out the water, he didn't find anything besides blue water.

Fravor told *ABC News* that what he saw was "not from this world."

The Monster That Once Haunted Elizabeth Lake

Surely, you've heard of the Lochness Monster, but have you heard of the Elizabeth Lake Monster? In fact, there are several urban legends surrounding Elizabeth Lake, which is located near Lancaster in Los Angeles.

For starters, it's been said that Elizabeth Lake is a secret passage to Hell. The legend says that to get to the underworld, one must swim deep enough into the lake.

It has also been said that the lake was created by the devil himself as a home for one of his pets. In 1780, Spanish missionary Father Junipero Serra named the lake "La Laguna de Diablo," or Devil's Lake because people who lived nearby believed it contained the devil's pet. The lake was later renamed after a girl named Elizabeth Wingfield slipped and fell into the water. While the girl was okay, people began to call it Elizabeth's Lake as a joke and it caught on.

One of the first records of the monster came about in the 1830s, when a guy named Don Pedro Carrillo's ranch mysteriously burnt down. In 1855, people tried to settle in the area, but they were driven away by unnatural nighttime noises and other odd occurrences.

Not too long after, Don Chico Lopez, Chico Vasquez, and Don Guillermo Mentiroso gave the first description of the monster. They compared it to the size of a whale with huge bat-like wings. They claimed the monster roared and splashed water with either flippers or legs. Lopez also claimed that his livestock had been disappearing. Not convinced this wasn't a hoax? Lopez abandoned his ranch along the lake.

A rancher named Don Felipe Rivera reported seeing the lake monster in 1886. Not long after, another rancher named Miguel Leonis reported the loss of his livestock. He claimed to shoot the monster, only for the bullets to bounce off of it. The monster allegedly went back to the lake after Rivera's attack.

The good news is that this is the last report of the Elizabeth Lake Monster. In fact, it's believed that Don Felipe Rivera's attack on the monster drove it away from the lake.

Not long after it was believed to leave the area, there were reports of a similar lake monster in Tombstone, Arizona. There, the monster was seen flying in the area. A group of ranchers claimed to trap and kill the monster in the Huachuca Mountains. There is a photo from the 1890s of the ranchers holding what looks like a pterodactyl, which is what many believe the Elizabeth Lake Monster to have been.

The Most Haunted Ship in the USA is Docked in California

Did you know the most haunted ship in the United States is docked in the Golden State? The Queen Mary, which is larger in size than the Titanic, was used from 1936 to 1967. Since then, she has been docked in Long Beach, California.

So, why is the Queen Mary so haunted? It's been said that someone was murder inside one of the ship's engine rooms. Staff members have claimed to see apparitions in the room. Other allegedly haunted areas of the ship include the nursery and a few passenger cabins. Both staff and guests have reported hearing children laughing when no children were aboard the ship. People have also claimed to smell cigars, even though no one was smoking a cigar.

If you want to find out if the Queen Mary is haunted for yourself, you're in luck. The ship is a haunted attraction that's open to tourists. There are even haunted overnight stays aboard the ship, but beware: most of the guests end up having sleepless nights!

Writer Adam Mock wrote about his overnight experience for the site Crixeo. According to him, the entire ship is haunted, but most guests have more paranormal experiences on the B deck. Room B340 has even been closed to overnight visitors because so many guests were scared by poltergeist-like activity.

The Winchester Mystery House Might be Home to Spirits

Have you ever heard of the Winchester Mystery House? The house is the former residence of Sarah Winchester, widow of William Wirt Winchester, who founded the Winchester Repeating Arms Company. It's believed to be one of the most haunted houses in California.

After Sarah's infant daughter died and her husband died of tuberculosis, she was told by a medium in Boston that she needed to build a home in the West for herself and the spirits of people who had been killed by Winchester Rifles. In 1884, Sarah purchased a home in San Jose, California.

Sarah had builders work on the house day and night until it became a seven-story mansion. Since she didn't hire an architect, the house has a lot of strange architectural features, such as doors and staircases that lead nowhere. The mansion also contains secret passageways. Winchester was believed to have felt haunted by the spirits who had been killed by Winchester rifles and continued to have more work added to the house until she died.

Since 2017, people have been able to tour the Winchester Mystery House. You'll get a chance to see rooms that had never previously been open to the public, as well as rooms that hadn't been finished before Sarah Winchester's death in 1922. You can also participate in a séance in the house or spend the night if you're brave enough.

The Mystery of California's Gravity Hills

There are a number of "gravity hills" in California where a car will roll uphill when it's in neutral.

California's gravity hills can be found at the following locations:

- 1054 E. Loma Alta Drive in Altadena.
- Rohnert Park in Sonoma County. The gravity hill starts at the "Gracias San Antonio" sign.
- 465 Mystery Spot Road in Santa Cruz.
- Rose Hills Memorial on Workman Mill Road in Whittier

Although scientists have come up with a number of possible theories for this crazy phenomenon, gravity hills have been the subject of urban legends.

The legend behind the gravity hill in Whittier is perhaps the creepiest. The gravity hill located at the cemetery used to be a sacred burial ground. It has been said that the spirits were awoken from their slumber by Satanic cult rituals and construction. To get revenge, they forcefully push vehicles down the hill. Some people have even claimed to hear strange knocking sounds on their cars when driving on the hill, which has said to be the spirits' hands.

The Skinwalkers of Joshua Tree National Park

In Native American culture, there's a legend known as "skinwalkers." Skinwalkers are said to be harmful witches or medicine men who have the ability to possess or turn themselves into an animal. It's believed that most skinwalkers take the form of a coyote or wolf. Skinwalkers are believed to exist in Joshua Tree National Park.

It has been said that skinwalkers terrorize and even *kill* campers at the park. The eerie part about it all is that people are often found dead at Joshua Tree National Park, while others have gone missing, never to be heard from again. Is it possible that skinwalkers could be possible for some of these deaths or disappearances?

RANDOM FACTS

1. Known for his role as Superman in the TV show *Adventures of Superman* in the 1950s, George Reeves died from a gunshot wound in 1959. While his death was ruled a suicide, it has been a controversial subject. His friends didn't believe he had committed suicide. Reeves was allegedly having an affair with MGM vice president Eddie Mannix's wife, Toni Mannix. It has been suggested that Eddie Mannix, who had mafia ties, might have had Reeves killed.

2. It's believed that Marilyn Monroe's ghost has been spotted throughout Hollywood. It's been said that her spirit appears near her tomb in the Westside Memorial Cemetery. There have also been sightings of Marilyn Monroe in full-length mirrors at the Roosevelt Hotel, one of the late actress's old favorite hangout spots.

3. **People have claimed to see lost ships in California's Colorado Desert. While the Lost Ship of the Desert may sound like nothing more than a ridiculous urban legend to some since ships can't travel on land, it *may* be possible. There's a theory that former river ways may have led the ship to sink in the Salton Sea.**

4. **One of the most intense haunted houses in America is located in San Diego. In fact, the Haunted Hotel has been ranked as the 2nd top haunted house in America. The haunted house gets about 24,000 visitors a year, and hardly any of them actually make it through the entire thing. You can expect to be pushed, grabbed, and exposed to numerous graphic displays. Do you dare to enter?**

5. **While California is best-known for Bigfoot, there's a scarier legendary monster who's believed to reside in Ventura County. The legend, which originates back to World War II,**

says the Billiwhack Dairy was home to some horrifying experiments. An OSS officer named August Rubel allegedly conducted the experiments in an attempt to make a "super-soldier" that would help win the war. Instead, Rubel created a half-goat/half-man monster, which he left behind while he went overseas to fight. The Billiwhack Monster is believed to haunt students who attend Santa Paula High School.

6. Turnbull Canyon was once known as "Hutukngna," a name it had been given by the Gabrielino Indian tribe meaning "the place of the Devil." The legend involves the region being haunted by spirits of Native Americans who were murdered for not converting to Catholicism. During the Great Depression, a Satanic cult was said to hold their satanic rituals in Turnbull Canyon. They were known to sacrifice babies they bought and children from the local orphanages. One night, the cult mysteriously vanished. Hikers and locals began to report sightings of the children sacrificed, the spirits of the cult members in the form of hooded figures, and other paranormal occurrences. Since the reports began, other deaths have taken place in the area. A teenager was exploring the ruins of an old asylum in the canyon and ended up getting electrocuted. In 1978, 29 people died when a plane crashed in the canyon.

7. Highway 299 is said to be the most haunted highway in the United States. While the highway is believed to be haunted in more than one location, the stretch of highway near Old Shasta City is said to be the most haunted. Once a booming gold-mining town, Old Shasta City is now in ruins. Spirits are said to haunt the town's old courthouse and jail.

8. In 1922, silent film director William Desmond Taylor was found dead in his home. While he had been shot in the back, a supposed doctor had claimed he'd died of natural causes. While Taylor's butlers were considered suspects, the primary suspect in the case was then-young actress Mary Miles Minter's mother. Mary Miles Minter claimed in her unpublished autobiography

that her mother, who didn't approve of Mary's relationship with Taylor, was behind his death.

9. Bodie was once one of California's gold-mining towns. Today, it's a ghost town that's frequented by tourists. It's been said that the residents of Bodie were possessive about their town. But today, there's said to be a curse that goes like this: if you take anything from Bodie when you visit—even a rock—the spirits of the town residents will haunt you, *even if* you return whatever you've taken. There's an album at the park with letters from people who are suffering from the curse.

10. The disappearance of Anna Waters isn't only tragic. It's mysterious, too. Waters, who was just five years old at the time, disappeared from her family's backyard in San Mateo County. No one ever saw or heard from the girl, who went missing in 1973, again. Authorities believe she may have been kidnapped by a non-family member, but no one knows for sure.

11. The legendary "Dogman" is believed to be a type of werewolf. It's said to stand upright like a human, but it's generally covered in fur and has the head of a dog. There have been reports of the Dogman in Southern California. One sighting was reported in the foothills of the San Bernardino National Forest.

12. Rudolph Valentino was an actor who passed away at the ripe age of 31 due to complications from an ulcer. The late actor, who was a character in *American Horror Story: Hotel*, is said to haunt Studio Five at Paramount Studios.

13. The Battery Point Lighthouse, which is one of the oldest lighthouses in California, has been said to be haunted for more than 100 years. Paranormal researchers believe the lighthouse to be haunted by the ghosts of a child and two adults. Museum visitors have been said to feel their shoulders being touched or

sense a presence, see a rocking chair move back and forth when no one is sitting on it, and hear the sound of footsteps climbing the lighthouse stairway when no one is there.

14. The cemetery that lays adjacent to Mission San Jose, Fremont has been said to be haunted. People have reported the sound of cries and cold spots. There have also been reported sightings of what are believed to be Native American spirits. People have claimed to see Native Americans cross the street and then disappear once they enter the courtyard of the Mission.

15. Located in Grass Valley, the Holbrook Hotel opened in 1852 during the California Gold Rush. Today, it's said to be haunted by multiple ghosts, including the Suicide Gambler. Rumor has it that he was found in a pool of blood after slitting his own throat.

16. The mystery of James Gilmore Jr.'s death is an unsettling one. Known as a high school bully and a member of a motorcycle gang, 14-year-old James Gilmore Jr. disappeared after leaving his family's home in Baldwin Park in 1962. His remains were found 20 years later in a shallow grave underneath the family's house. The circumstances surrounding his death remain a mystery.

17. The Colorado Street Bridge Curse is one of Pasadena's eeriest urban legends. As the story goes, a construction worker fell off the bridge back when it was being built. His body was allegedly encased in concrete and his remains were never found. It's been said that the man's spirit haunts the bridge, which is what has driven many people to commit suicide or attempt to commit suicide by jumping off the bridge.

18. Stow Lake in San Francisco is believed to be home to a ghost known as the "Ghost of Stow Lake." As the story goes, two women were sitting on a park bench when one of the women didn't notice that her baby's stroller had rolled away. The woman allegedly looked everywhere in the park for the baby, asking park goers, "Have you seen my baby?" The woman

searched the lake for her baby and she never resurfaced. Today, there's a statue at the park in her honor. Her spirit is believed to haunt Stow Lake at night. She's been said to ask people if they've seen her baby. Depending on how you answer her, she might haunt or kill you.

19. Thelma Todd was an actress in the late 1920s/early 1930s who was known as "Hot Toddy." Her dead body was found inside a garage, but the circumstances surrounding her death didn't exactly line up. Her nose was broken and her blood alcohol level was so high that people didn't think she would have been able to climb the stairs to the garage. Rumor has it that Ronald West, Todd's boyfriend at the time of her death, confessed on his deathbed to accidentally locking the actress in the garage. However, others have questioned if Thelma Todd may have been killed by her ex-husband or gang leader Charles "Lucky" Luciano, who she'd allegedly gotten into confrontations with not long before she died.

20. Since people began hiking Mount Shasta, there have been reports of "little people." They have been said to live in caves, which leads many to believe they could be fairies. These people come out and are said to act like gremlins who try to sabotage people hiking the mountain. To try to keep them happy, some hikers leave out peace offerings in the form of food.

Test Yourself – Questions and Answers

1. Which of the following is recognized as one of the most haunted places in America?

   a. Catalina Island
   b. Alcatraz
   c. San Francisco

2. Skinwalkers are said to exist at which of California's national parks?

   a. Yosemite National Park
   b. Sequoia National Park
   c. Joshua Tree National Park

3. The most haunted highway in California is:

   a. Route 66
   b. Highway 299
   c. State Route 1

4. What is the name of America's most haunted ship, which is docked in Long Beach?

   a. The Titanic
   b. The Mary Celeste
   c. The Queen Mary

5. The Black Dahlia's real name was:

   a. Elizabeth Short
   b. Marilyn Monroe
   c. Dahlia Black

Answers

1. b.

2. c.

3. b.

4. c.

5. a.

CHAPTER SIX

CALIFORNIA'S SPORTS

Whether or not you're a sports fanatic, California has a rich sports history. For example, do you know which international sporting event has been held in the Golden State? Do you know which famous athletes got their start in California? To find out the answers to these questions and other cool facts about California's sports, read on!

California is the Only State That's Hosted Both the Summer *and* the Winter Olympics

Not only does California hold the record of being the only state to host both the Summer and Winter Olympics, but it's also hosted the Olympics *three times*!

The Summer Olympics were held in Los Angeles in both 1932 and 1984, while Squaw Valley hosted the Winter Olympics in 1960. Here are some of the American highlights from each of these three games.

1932 Summer Olympics:

- The Victory Podium made its debut.

- Babe Didrikson won two gold medals in javelin and hurdles.

- Helene Madison won three swimming gold medals.

- Los Angeles' Tenth Street's name was changed to Olympic Boulevard in honor of the Olympics' 10th anniversary.

1984 Summer Olympics:

- The Olympic rings were formed by the United States Army for the opening ceremony.

- The U.S.A. set the record for the highest number of gold medals won in a single Summer Olympics. A total of 83 gold medals were won that year.

- Track and field athlete Carl Lewis won four gold medals.

- Edwin Moses won a gold medal for the first time in 8 years.

1960 Winter Olympics:

- *CBS* bought exclusive rights to broadcast the Olympics.

- Walt Disney produced the opening and closing ceremonies.

- The United States won an unexpected gold medal in ice hockey.

- David Jenkins won the Olympic gold medal in men's figure skating, while Carol Heiss took home the gold in women's figure skating.

- Women competed in speed skating for the first time.

Today, the Olympic Museum in Squaw Valley honors the legacy of the 1960 Winter Olympics games. At the museum, you can expect to find athlete memorabilia, authentic American Olympics uniforms, a hockey stick and puck from the 1960 games, and other artifacts.

There are More Professional Sports Teams in California Than Any Other State

Did you know the Golden State is home to more professional sports teams than any other state in the country?

California professional sports teams include:

Major League Baseball:

1. Los Angeles Angels
2. Los Angeles Dodgers
3. San Diego Padres
4. Oakland Athletics
5. San Francisco Giants

National Football League:

1. San Francisco 49ers
2. Los Angeles Chargers
3. Los Angeles Rams
4. Oakland Raiders

National Basketball Association:

1. Los Angeles Clippers
2. Los Angeles Lakers
3. Golden State Warriors
4. Sacramento Kings

National Hockey League:

1. Anaheim Ducks
2. Los Angeles Kings
3. San Jose Sharks

Major League Soccer:

1. LA Galaxy
2. Los Angeles FC
3. San Jose Earthquakes

Women's National Basketball Association:

1. Los Angeles Sparks

The Oldest College Bowl Game Takes Place in California Every Year

The country's oldest college football bowl game is held in Pasadena, California. Every January, the game is held at the Rose Bowl—the oldest stadium and one of only four stadiums that's recognized as a National Historic Landmark in the United States!

The first Rose Bowl game was played in 1902. Early on, the game was held at Tournament Park. At that point, the game was called the Tournament East-West Football Game.

It wasn't until 1922 that the Rose Bowl stadium was built. The following year, the game was held there for the very first time. The game has been held at the stadium ever since, except for in 1942 when the game was moved to Duke University following the attack on Pearl Harbor.

Today, the Rose Bowl is a highly anticipated televised event among college football fans. The game was televised for the very first time in 1952.

A number of well-known professional football players have won the MVP award for the Rose Bowl. Some of these include O.J. Simpson, Ernie Nevers, Charley Trippi, Jim Plunkett, Sam Cunningham, Mark Sanchez, Jack Del Rio, and Andy Dalton.

Tiger Woods's Career Started at a Navy Golf Course in California

Did you know that the golf legend Tiger Woods is from California?

Tiger, whose real name is Eldrick Tont Woods, was born in Cypress, California. The name Tiger came about to honor his father's friend, who was also nicknamed Tiger.

Tiger Woods grew up in Orange County where he began to play golf at the age of two. Tiger's father, Earl Woods, is the one who introduced him to golf. Earl was in the military and was given privileges to play golf at the Navy golf course in Los Alamitos. Tiger also played golf at several courses throughout Long Beach.

Tiger Woods began to receive recognition at a very young age. Most people considered him a child golf prodigy. When Woods was just three years old, he putted against Bob Hope on *The Mike Douglas Show*. The same year, Woods shot a 48 over nine holes. At five years old, he made it into an issue of *Golf Digest* and was also featured on ABC's *That's Incredible!*

Tiger Woods won the Junior World Golf Championships a total of six times, which included four consecutive wins. The first time he won, he was only eight years old and competed in the 9-10 boys event.

While Tiger Woods was attending Western High School in Anaheim, he became the youngest U.S. Junior Amateur Champion. He held this record until 2010 when it was broken by Jim Liu. Woods played on his high school's golf team and was recruited to Stanford University thanks to his achievements in the sport.

By the age of 20, Tiger Woods became a professional golfer and signed a deal with Nike, Inc.

Major Surfing Competitions are Held in California

When you think of surfing competitions, Hawaii might be the first state that comes to mind. But did you know that some major surfing competitions are held in California?

The biggest surfing competition that's held in the state is the U.S. Open of Surfing, which is held every year in Huntington Beach. The week-long event is the largest surfing competition in the entire world. The first U.S. Open in Surfing was held in 1959. Today, it adds $21.5 million to Orange County's economy and is attended by nearly half a million people every year. During the event, people are also added to the Surfers' Walk of Fame and the Surfers' Hall of Fame, which are both located across from the Huntington Beach Pier.

245

Titans of the Mavericks is another major surfing competition that's held in the Golden State. Held in Mavericks, California, it's a big wave surfing competition. Thirty of the best international surfers compete each year. Waves can reach up to 60 feet in height. The first competition was held in 1999.

California is Home to the Salinas Rodeo

The California Rodeo Salinas is the largest rodeo in the Golden State. It's considered to be one of the top 20 rodeo events in the United States, as well as one of the 10 rodeos that are aired on ESPN, FOX Sports, and other television networks every year.

The Salinas Rodeo got its start back in 1910. At that time, it was a Wild West Show and took place on the old race track ground. Today, it's held at the Salinas Sports Complex—a 17,000-seat stadium.

The rodeo, which takes place every year, is a four-day event. The top cowboys and cowgirls from the Professional Rodeo Cowboys Association compete at the event for both money and the gold and silver belt buckles that are given out as prizes each year. Some of the events that are held at the rodeo each year include bull riding, steer wrestling, team roping, and more.

The California Rodeo Salinas also gives back approximately $400,000 each year to local non-profits.

One California NFL Team Was Named After the Gold Rush

Did you know the San Francisco 49ers got their name because of the California Gold Rush?

During the California Gold Rush, gold miners were called "49ers." The reason for this was because they migrated to California in search of gold in 1849.

The team's franchise is actually legally registered as the "San Francisco Forty Niners."

The team's name relating to California doesn't end there. The mascot for the San Francisco 49ers is also named thanks to the city. The mascot is a gold miner named Sourdough Sam. Sourdough, of course, came from San Francisco's reputation and history of being the best place to get sourdough bread.

A New York Yankees Legend is From California

Famous New York Yankees player Joe DiMaggio's baseball career got started in California! DiMaggio, who was born in Martinez, California, got his start as an athlete thanks to his older brother, Vince DiMaggio.

Vince was playing as a shortstop for the San Francisco Seals of the Pacific Coast League, a former minor league baseball team when he asked his manager to let Joe fill in for him in 1932.

Joe DiMaggio, who was named the Pacific Coast League's MVP, had his contract purchased by the New York Yankees for $55,000.

DiMaggio is considered one of the Yankees most legendary players. He played in nine World Series championships, in which the Yankees won.

Joe DiMaggio was given his nickname "The Yankees Clipper" in 1939 by Arch McDonald, the New York Yankees stadium announcer. McDonald compared DiMaggio's speed and range to the Pan American outline, which was a novel invention at the time.

DiMaggio was also well-known for his widely publicized marriage to Marilyn Monroe.

And So is a Boston Red Sox Legend!

Did you know that the late Red Sox legend Ted Williams was born in San Diego, California?

When Ted Williams was growing up in the North Park neighborhood of San Diego, his uncle Saul Venzor taught him how to throw a baseball. Throughout his career as a semi-professional baseball player, Venzor had pitched against Babe Ruth, Joe Gordon, and Lou Gehrig.

Williams attended Herbert Hoover High School in San Diego. He was the star of the school's baseball team, for which he was the pitcher.

Ted Williams was offered to join the New York Yankees and the St. Louis Cardinals while he was still in high school! His mom thought he was too young, however, so Williams played for the San Diego Padres with the local minor league instead.

He later went on to join the Boston Red Sox, who traded Ben Chapman to the Cleveland Indians just so they could make room for Ted Williams.

To this day, Ted Williams is still considered to have been the best hitter of all time.

These Famous Tennis Sisters are From California

Famous tennis-playing sisters Serena and Venus Williams are from California! Both sisters were born in Lynwood, California. They were raised in Compton, California.

Serena Williams began playing tennis in Compton when she was just three years old! By the time Venus was seven and Serena was eight, their talents on the tennis court began to gain recognition.

When the girls were 10 and 11, their parents moved the family from Compton to West Palm Beach, Florida so they could receive better tennis training.

Today, Venus Williams is a four-time Olympic gold medalist and one-time silver Olympic medalist. She ties with Kathleen McKane Godfree for the most tennis medals to ever be won by a tennis player.

Serena Williams has won four Olympic gold medals.

O.J. Simpson Had a Troubled Youth While Growing Up in California

Today, he's most well-known for the controversial murder of his wife. But did you know that former football player O.J. had a troubled youth growing up in California?

Orenthal James "O.J." Simpson was born in San Francisco. He was raised in the housing projects of the Potrero Hill neighborhood of San Francisco.

O.J. Simpson attended Galileo High School in San Francisco. During his teens, he got involved in a street gang called the Persian Warriors. He spent some time in a juvenile detention center called the San Francisco Youth Guidance Center.

After he was arrested for the third time, O.J. Simpson met former MLB player Willie Mays. Mays encouraged Simpson to reform his life and stay out of trouble. This encouraged O.J. Simpson to play for the high school football team, the Galileo Lions.

Simpson later went on to play college football, even winning the Heisman Trophy. He later went on to play for the Buffalo Bills and then the San Francisco 49ers. While his wife's murder remains a highly controversial topic, especially after O. J. Simpson's book *If I Did It*, many still consider him to have been one of the most successful football players of all time.

The First African-American to Play Major League Baseball Grew Up in California

Jackie Robinson was the first African-American to play for the MLB. Did you know he grew up in California?

Although Jackie Robinson was born in Cairo, Georgia, his mother moved the family to California after his father abandoned them when Jackie was just one year old. Robinson lived with his family at 121 Pepper Street in Pasadena.

Robinson grew up poor in an otherwise wealthy community, which led him to join a neighborhood gang. However, his friend encouraged him to leave.

Robinson attended Washington Junior High School and John Muir High School (Muir Tech) in Pasadena. When he attended Muir Tech, Robinson played varsity baseball where he played in the catcher and shortstop positions. He also played football, track, basketball, and tennis.

In 1936, Jackie Robinson earned a spot on the Pomona baseball tournament all-star team. The team also included Ted Williams and Bob Lemon. Robinson, Williams, and Lemon were all later inducted into the Baseball Hall of Fame.

After he graduated from Muir Tech, Robinson went to Pasadena Junior College where he continued to play in baseball, basketball, track, and tennis. He was the shortstop and leadoff hitter for the team.

He continued in all four sports when he later attended UCLA, becoming the first athlete from the school to win varsity letters in baseball, basketball, football, and track.

After Robinson was drafted and returned from the military, he began a career in professional baseball. He started out playing in the Negro leagues before playing in minor leagues.

History was made when Jackie Robinson signed a contract with the Brooklyn Dodgers, which marked the end of segregation in professional baseball. Robinson had a major influence on the Civil Rights Movement.

The First Owner of the Los Angeles Angels May Surprise You

Did you know that the Los Angeles Angels' first owner was a celebrity? It was none other than the legendary Gene Autry!

The Los Angeles Angels weren't the first team Gene Autry owned, either. Autry, who had once turned down playing in the minor leagues himself, owned the minor league team, the Hollywood Stars in the 1950s.

When the MLB announced that it wanted to start a team in Los Angeles, Gene Autry wanted the broadcast rights to the games. Major League Baseball executives found the plan so impressive that they convinced Autry to become the team's franchise owner.

The Los Angeles Angels, which got their start in 1961, were named after a minor league of the same name of the former Pacific Coast League. Gene Autry paid $350,000 for the right to name the team the Angels! The Dodgers were actually going to be called the Los Angeles Angels first, but Autry bought the rights from Walter O'Malley, the former owner of the Dodgers.

The Los Angeles Angels' team name has changed quite a few times. When the team moved to Anaheim in 1966, they were renamed the California Angels. In 1997 through 2005, they were the Anaheim Angels. Then they became the Los Angeles Angels of Anaheim. They became the Los Angeles Angels again in 2016, which is what they are currently known as. Time will tell if the team changes their name again in the future!

Bethany Hamilton is Honored at the California Surf Museum

Famous professional surfer Bethany Hamilton rose to fame after she survived a shark attack. Hamilton lost her arm during the attack but with hard work and determination, she was able to return to professional surfing. The movie *Soul Surfer*, which is based on Hamilton's book of the same name, made her a household name.

Did you know you can see artifacts from Hamilton's attack at the California Surf Museum in Oceanside, California? At the museum, you will find Hamilton's shark-bitten surfboard and the bathing suit she wore during the attack.

Fun fact: Bethany Hamilton came in 5th place at the U.S. Open of Surfing in 2008!

A Famous Figure Skater is From the Golden State

Michelle Kwan may be one of the most recognizable names when it comes to female figure skaters. Did you know the former figure skater is from California?

Kwan was born in Torrance, California. Her parents had immigrated to the state from Hong Kong.

When Michelle Kwan was just five years old, she began to develop an interest in ice skating, a sport in which both of her older siblings participated in. Her brother, Ron, was an ice hockey player, while her sister, Karen, was also a figure skater. When Michelle was eight years old, both she and Karen began to receive serious coaching in figure skating. They trained for 3-4 hours daily, before and after school.

The cost of training took a financial toll on the Kwan family, however, and they were unable to afford a coach when Michelle reached 10. Fortunately, a fellow member of the Los Angeles Figure Skating Club offered the family financial assistance. The girls trained at the Ice Castle International Training Center, which is located in Lake Arrowhead, California.

Michelle Kwan attended Soleado Elementary School in Palos Verdes, California prior to her homeschooling, which began when she was in the 8th grade. Kwan attended UCLA for one year before transferring to the University of Denver.

By 2003, Kwan won two Olympic gold medals and was a five-time World champion in figure skating. Kwan and Carol Heiss (who has also won five World Championship titles) both hold the American record for the highest number of World titles. She also holds nine world medals, which is the highest number of any American figure skater. And to think her success all started out in California!

RANDOM FACTS

1. NASCAR legend Jeff Gordon was born in Vallejo, California. The first racetrack Gordon ever raced on is the Roy Hayer Memorial Race Track in Rio Lindo, California when he was five years old.

2. The San Francisco 49ers were the city's first professional sports team. The team entered the NFL in 1950.

3. Downhill ski racing got its start in California! The oldest downhill ski racing on record took place in Plumas County in 1860. The Plumas-Eureka Ski Bowl is a yearly competition held in the region.

4. New England Patriots quarterback Tom Brady is from San Mateo, California. Brady went to Junipero Serra High School in San Mateo where he was first a backup quarterback on the junior varsity team. As a kid, Tom Brady regularly went to San Francisco 49ers games and was a big fan of Joe Montana, who Brady has said was his role model.

5. The Los Angeles Chargers used to be known as the San Diego Chargers. The team started out playing in Los Angeles, but they relocated to San Diego in 1961. They later relocated back to Los Angeles. The name was changed back to the Los Angeles Chargers in 2017. "Chargers" came from a contest that was held by Barron Hilton, the team's first owner. His father, Conrad Hilton, liked "Chargers" because of its association with yelling "charge."

6. Nick Gabaldon was the first surfer of African-American and Latino descent, according to California records. Gabaldon was born in Los Angeles. While he was a recreational surfer, he is often recognized as a huge influencer of African-Americans in the surfing world of California.

7. Mark Spitz was considered the Michael Phelps of his time. Born in Modesto, California, Spitz once won seven gold medals in swimming during one Olympics—a record he held until 2008 when Phelps beat him!

8. Magic Johnson is part owner of the Los Angeles Dodgers. In 2012, Johnson and the team's co-owners paid $2 billion for the team, which is the highest amount of money anyone has ever paid for a professional sports team. As of 2014, Johnson also became co-owner of the Los Angeles Sparks.

9. Former professional boxer Oscar De La Hoya is a Mexican-American who was born in East Los Angeles. He graduated from Garfield High School in East Los Angeles and won an Olympic gold medal in the lightweight division not long after.

10. Former quarterback Warren Moon is a Los Angeles native! He attended Alexandra Hamilton High School. Moon began his professional football career in the Canadian Football League (CFL), where he played for the Edmonton Eskimos. He later went on to play for four NFL teams: the Houston Oilers, Minnesota Vikings, Seattle Seahawks, and Kansas City Chiefs. Moon was inducted into the Pro Football Hall of Fame, making him the first African-American quarterback to ever accomplish that.

11. Former Baltimore Orioles player and Hall of Famer Eddie Murray was born in Los Angeles. Murray went to Locke High School in LA where he played on the baseball team. He batted .500 during his senior year. He was classmates with former St. Louis Cardinals player Ozzie Smith.

12. The Los Angeles Lakers have more Facebook fans than any other sports team in the United States! They're also the NBA team with the highest number of Twitter followers.

13. Cayla Barnes, who plays ice hockey for both Boston College and the American national team, is from California! Barnes was

born in Eastvale, California. She played in the 2015, 2016, and 2017 Women's World Championships.

14. In 2012, professional athletes in California paid a combined $216.8 million in income taxes!

15. The Los Angeles Dodgers weren't originally a California-based baseball team. They were the Brooklyn Dodgers first. The team moved to Los Angeles in 1958 and were renamed the Los Angeles Dodgers.

16. Leigh Steinberg is an American sports agent whose client list has included Troy Aikman, Warren Moon, Ricky Williams, and Oscar De La Hoya. Steinberg, a California native, is said to be the inspiration of the sports agent in the movie *Jerry Maguire*.

17. The San Diego Padres named their team in honor of the former Pacific Coast League minor league team. The minor league Padres was led by Ted Williams. The name, which means "fathers" in Spanish, honors the Spanish founders of San Diego.

18. Sean McVay, head coach of the Los Angeles Rams, set a historical record in 2017 when he became the youngest head coach in the history of the modern NFL. McVay became head coach at just 30 years old.

19. Former NFL player Larry Allen was born in Los Angeles and grew up in Compton. Allen went to four different high schools, spending only one school year at each. These included Centennial High School for his freshman year, Tokay High School in Lodi for his sophomore year, Edison High School in Stockton, and Vintage High School in Napa. Allen didn't graduate from high school, but he went to Butte College in Oroville where he played on the football team. He later attended Sonoma State University before eventually going on to play for the Dallas Cowboys and the San Francisco 49ers. Throughout the course of his career, Allen played in more Pro

Bowls than any other Dallas Cowboy in history. Allen was also inducted into the Pro Football Hall of Fame.

20. The Oakland Raiders are one of only three teams in the NFL that is known not to retire players' jerseys. It's said that the reason is that they believe reusing players' jerseys helps keep their memory alive. The only exception to this rule is 00, a number which was banned by the NFL.

Test Yourself – Questions and Answers

1. Which major surfing competition is held in California every year?

    a. The World Open in Surfing
    b. The U.S. Open in Surfing
    c. The California Open in Surfing

2. Which former NFL player is *not* from California?

    a. Peyton Manning
    b. O.J. Simpson
    c. Larry Allen

3. Which New York Yankees legend is from California?

    a. Babe Ruth
    b. Joe DiMaggio
    c. Lou Gehrig

4. Gene Autry was the first owner of which of California's MLB teams?

    a. Los Angeles Angels
    b. San Diego Padres
    c. Los Angeles Dodgers

5. Which of California's professional sports teams has the most Facebook followers of any sports team in the United States?

    a. Los Angeles Angels
    b. Los Angeles Dodgers
    c. Los Angeles Lakers

Answers

1. b.

2. a.

3. b.

4. a.

5. c.

DON'T FORGET YOUR FREE BOOKS

OTHER BOOKS IN THIS SERIES

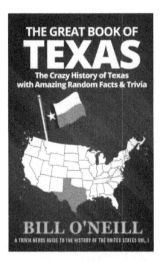

Are you looking to learn more about Texas? Sure, you've heard about the Alamo and JFK's assassination in history class, but there's so much about the Lone Star State that even natives don't know about. In this trivia book, you'll journey through Texas's history, pop culture, sports, folklore, and so much more!

In The Great Book of Texas, some of the things you will learn include:

- Which Texas hero isn't even from Texas?
- Why is Texas called the Lone Star State?
- Which hotel in Austin is one of the most haunted hotels in the United States?
- Where was Bonnie and Clyde's hideout located?
- Which Tejano musician is buried in Corpus Christi?
- What unsolved mysteries happened in the state?
- Which Texas-born celebrity was voted "Most Handsome" in high school?

- Which popular TV show star just opened a brewery in Austin?

You'll find out the answers to these questions and many other facts. Some of them will be fun, some of them will creepy, and some of them will be sad, but all of them will be fascinating! This book is jampacked with everything you could have ever wondered about Texas.

Whether you consider yourself a Texas pro or you know absolutely nothing about the state, you'll learn something new as you discover more about the state's past, present, and future. Find out about things that weren't mentioned in your history book. In fact, you might even be able to impress your history teacher with your newfound knowledge once you've finished reading! So, what are you waiting for? Dive in now to learn all there is to know about the Lone Star State!

GET IT HERE

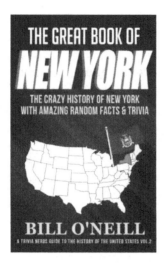

Want to learn more about New York? Sure, you've heard about the Statue of Liberty, but how much do you really know about the Empire State? Do you know why it's even called the Empire State? There's so much about New York that even state natives don't know. In this trivia book, you'll learn more about New York's history, pop culture, folklore, sports, and so much more!

In The Great Book of New York, you'll learn the answers to the following questions:

- Why is New York City called the Big Apple?
- What genre of music started out in New York City?
- Which late actress's life is celebrated at a festival held in her hometown every year?
- Which monster might be living in a lake in New York?
- Was there really a Staten Island bogeyman?
- Which movie is loosely based on New York in the 1800s?
- Which cult favorite cake recipe got its start in New York?
- Why do the New York Yankees have pinstripe uniforms?

These are just a few of the many facts you'll find in this book. Some of them will be fun, some of them will be sad, and some of them will be so chilling they'll give you goosebumps, but all of them will be fascinating! This book is full of everything you've ever wondered about New York.

It doesn't matter if you consider yourself a New York state expert or if you know nothing about the Empire State. You're bound to learn something new as you journey through each chapter. You'll be able to impress your friends on your next trivia night!

So, what are you waiting for? Dive in now so you can learn all there is to know about New York!

GET IT HERE

MORE BOOKS BY BILL O'NEILL

I hope you enjoyed this book and learned something new. Please feel free to check out some of my previous books on Amazon.

THE GREAT BOOK OF NEW YORK

The Crazy History of New Your with
Amazing Random Facts & Trivia

**A Trivia Nerds Guide
to the History of the
United States Vol.2**

BILL O'NEILL

DON'T FORGET YOUR
FREE BOOKS

<u>GET THEM FOR FREE ON WWW.TRIVIABILL.COM</u>

CONTENTS

INTRODUCTION

How much do you know about the state of New York?

Sure, you know New York City is a tourist hotspot. You know it's home to the New York Yankees, the New York Giants, and Broadway. But what else do you *really* know about the city?

You know the Statue of Liberty was a gift from France, but do you know which popular New York City attraction sees more annual visitors than the Statue of Liberty?

Have you ever wondered how New York came to be known as the Empire State? Do you know why people call New York City the "

'Big Apple'? Have you ever wondered if it actually has anything to do with apples?

Do you know which war New York state played a key role in or which President was sworn into office in New York?

If you have ever wondered the answers to any of these questions, then you've come to the right place. This book is filled with stories and facts about the state of New York.

This isn't just any book about New York. It will highlight some of the key facts that have helped shape New York into the state it is today. You'll learn facts about the state that you've probably never even wondered about. Once you've finished reading, you'll know all there is to know about New York.

New York is a state that's rich in both history and culture. We'll go back in time before New York City was what it is today. We'll jump around and look at some of the coolest (and most shocking) elements of the state's history and explore some of the more recent happenings of the state.

Although, we'll mostly stick to a timeline of historical events, we'll also jump around some as we talk about some of New York's past and some of the most famous people who live in the state.

This book is broken up into easy to follow chapters that will help you learn more about the Empire State. Once you've finished each chapter, you can test your knowledge with trivia questions.

Some of the facts you'll read about are sad. Some of them will give you goosebumps. Some of them are shocking. But the one thing they all have in common is that all of them are fascinating! Once you've finished reading this book, you're guaranteed to walk away with a wealth of facts you didn't know before.

This book will answer the following questions:

Why is New York City called 'The Big Apple'?

How did the state of New York come to be known as the Empire State?

Which iconic late comedian is honored by a festival that's held in her hometown every year in New York?

Which BBQ restaurant in the Big Apple is owned by a former '90s boy band member?

What famous lake monster is believed to live in one of New York's lakes?

Which famous athletes were born in New York?

And so much more!

CHAPTER ONE

NEW YORK'S HISTORY AND RANDOM FACTS

New York City Got Its Name from the Duke of York

It's hard to imagine New York City being called anything else today, but did you know NYC was once called something else? The city's former name was New Amsterdam.

An early Dutch settler named Peter Minuit purchased what is now the present-day island of Manhattan from the Native Americans in the early 1620s. The reason he bought it was to legitimize Dutch claims to the territory. Minuit is said to have paid the Lenape tribe in $24 worth of trinkets or jewelry. It's been estimated that he paid the equivalent of about $1,000. Minuit named the island New Amsterdam, of which he became the first governor of.

In 1664, the territory of New Amsterdam was seized from the Dutch settlers by the British. During that time, King Charles II changed the territory's name. He named it after his brother the Duke of York, who was responsible for organizing the mission.

New York Was a Key Battlefield During the Revolutionary War

Did you know New York played a critical role in the Revolutionary War? Due to its central location in the American colonies, the state was at the forefront of the war, especially early on.

Opposition from New York residents also played a big role in the war. The people of the state were opposed to the Stamp Act in 1765, which required everyone to pay a tax on paper products such as newspapers, licenses, and playing cards. Many became resistant to the act.

A secret society called the Sons of Liberty was formed to protest the Stamp Act. While it was formed in Boston, there was a large New York branch.

Some of the most significant battles of the Revolutionary War took place in New York. In fact, one of the first battles of the war took place in 1775 when Ethan Allen and Colonel Benedict Arnold captured Fort Ticonderoga. The cannons that were captured at Fort Ticonderoga were dragged to Boston and used to help stop the British attack that was happening there at the time.

On August 27th, 1776, the Battle of Long Island occurred. The battle was the largest of the entire Revolutionary War. The British won the battle against George Washington and his troops, leading the British to gain control over Manhattan.

At that time, Washington withdrew from the battles. Many of his supporters viewed his withdrawal as a smart tactic because it caught the British army off guard.

After Washington had left Manhattan in British hands, many New Yorkers fled. As they fled, however, many American prisoners were also brought to the city. In fact, at one time, Manhattan was housing 30,000 American prisoners, many of which were being kept there under horrible conditions. Many of the Continental soldiers were also held as prisoners on British ships in the New York Harbor, where they were also treated under awful conditions.

The Battle of Saratoga was another one of the most important battles of the Revolutionary War. Led by Horatio Gates and Benedict Arnold, the battle is considered the turning point of the war. It's the battle that convinced France to enter the war as America's ally. The battle also gave Americans renewed hope for winning the war.

After the Revolutionary War was won, the last British troops left Manhattan on November 25th, 1783, which would later come to be known as Evacuation Day. The day was celebrated throughout the country into the 1800s.

New York City Was the First Capital of the United States

Today, it's hard to imagine the nation's capital being located anywhere other than Washington D.C.. You probably know that Philadelphia was the country's capital at one point, but did you know that New York City was actually the very first capital of the United States?

New York City became the first capital in the United States in January of 1785. The old City Hall on Wall Street is where the Congress of Confederation convened at that time. The old City Hall building was later remodeled so that it could become the United States' capitol building. At that time, Congress met and held their meetings at Fraunces Tavern.

At one point, lower Manhattan was going to become a federal district. The presidential mansion was to be built on Governor's Island. However, keeping NYC as the nation's capital was very controversial. Some feared that the city was too aristocratic and leaned towards England's styles of clothing too much.

Needless to say, New York City's time spent as the country's capital was short-lived. It only lasted for five years, between 1785 and 1789. The last time Congress convened in New York City's Federal Hall was on August 12th, 1789.

George Washington was sworn into office as the first President of the United States at Federal Hall on April 30th, 1789. This is why a statue of Washington can be located outside of a reconstruction of Federal Hall can be found today!

New York Was Probably Nicknamed the "Empire State" by a United States President

New York is known as the 'Empire State', but no one actually knows for sure how the state got its nickname. That being said, there are a number of theories.

A lot of people very wrongly assume the state was nicknamed after the Empire State Building. In reality, the state's nickname came first.

It has been theorized that the state was nicknamed the 'Empire State' because of its variety of resources, such as its fertile soil, rich timberland, and its abundance of water. This may be at least part of the reason New York got its nickname. Even in early history, the state's growth and prosperity likely had to do with the reason it got its nickname.

It's believed that George Washington may have been responsible with nicknaming New York the Empire State. The first time the state was referred to by its nickname in documents was in 1784. During that time, George Washington said his vision for the state was as "the seat of the empire." He believed New York's central location and its abundance of resources would make it a significant unifying state for the rest of America.

No matter how New York got its name, it's quite fitting. The state is somewhat of an empire with both national and global significance.

The nickname was used on New York license plates from 1951 until the mid-1960s and again from 2001 until now.

The Fight for Women's Rights Started In New York

Did you know that the fight for women's rights kicked off in the state of New York? In July of 1848, the first *ever* convention for women's rights in America took place in Seneca Falls, New York. It was held at the Wesleyan Chapel.

Nearly 200 women attended the convention, which was started by two abolitionists named Lucretia Mott and Elizabeth Cady Stanton.

The convention was attended by famous African-American abolitionist Frederick Douglass.

Two weeks after the convention, there was an even larger one held in Rochester, New York. After that, women's rights conventions were held every year.

In 1917, women won the right to vote in New York. By 1920, the 19th Amendment had been adopted, which gave all American women the constitutional right to vote.

The Five Boroughs of New York City Used to Be Cities of Their Own

Modern-day New York City is known for its famous five boroughs: Manhattan, Queens, Brooklyn, the Bronx, and Staten Island. But did you know that there once was a time when the five boroughs were cities entirely of their own?

In fact, it wasn't until 1895 that people in Queens, Brooklyn, the Bronx, and Staten Island voted to consolidate with Manhattan in order to form 'Greater New York.'

Brooklyn almost didn't become part of New York City. There was an anti-consolidation movement in the city. It voted in favor of consolidating with Manhattan but only by 278 votes.

The consolidation had a huge effect on the size of New York City. In December of 1897, New York City's size was 60 square miles and its population was just over 2 million. When the five boroughs officially consolidated on January 1st, 1898, NYC's size grew to 360 square miles – or six times its previous size – and its population increased to more than 3.35 million people.

Why is New York City Called the 'Big Apple'?

Have you ever wondered how New York City came to be known as the 'Big Apple'? For a long time, no one really knew where the nickname came from. People speculated and came up with many theories.

Some people figure the city got its nickname because New York State is the second top state in the country for apple production and has a lot of apple orchards. This isn't the reason, however.

Another popular theory was that there was a brothel-operator named Eve in New York City and that the name originated from Adam, Eve, and the forbidden apple. This theory was eventually to put to rest as nothing more than a rumor.

So, what's the real reason New York City came to be known as the Big Apple? The nickname actually stems from horse racing.

The big horse racing tracks throughout New York City were referred to as 'apples.' It's believed that the nickname was given to the tracks because horses liked apples.

A reporter named John J. Fitz Gerald was the first one to mention the "Big Apple" when he described it in *The New York Morning Telegraph* around 1920 as going to the "big time." Fitz Gerald allegedly heard African-American stable workers in New Orleans say they were going to "the Big Apple," since NYC was known for its big-time horse racing venues.

Fitz Gerald continued to call New York City the Big Apple in his newspaper columns. The nickname caught on in the 1930s when jazz singers began to use the term regarding NYC's big-time music clubs. In 1950, Frank Sinatra used the name when describing the city in an NBC radio program. The rest is history!

Ellis Island Was Used for Pirate Hangings in the 1700s

Ellis Island was one of the main immigration stations in the United States. More than 12 million immigrants passed through the station. It has been estimated that four out of 10 Americans can trace at least one of their ancestors to Ellis Island. But before it became a federal immigration station in 1892 and for sixty years after, Ellis Island had a past that might surprise you.

Ellis Island was once used as a hanging site for convicted pirates. Mutinous sailors and other criminals were also executed there.

During the 1760s, the island became known as 'Gibbet Island' due to the gibbet—or wooden post—where the dead bodies were displayed after they were hung.

The last hanging took place on Ellis Island in 1839. After that, the island's name was reverted back to 'Ellis Island,' which it had been given after Samuel Ellis, who owned the island.

The island, which was leased from Ellis by the State of New York in 1794, later went on to become a military post. It served as a military post for almost 80 years before it was eventually chosen to be a federal immigration station.

The first immigrants who passed through Ellis Island in 1892 were unaccompanied minors. They were 17-year-old Annie Moore and her two younger brothers, who had immigrated from Ireland to meet their family in New York. Annie Moore was given a $10 reward for being the first immigrant to pass through the station. Today, a statue of the siblings can be found at the Ellis Island Immigration Station.

In1954, Ellis Island saw its last immigrant come through the station, a Norwegian merchant named Arne Peterssen.

The island, which opened to the public in 1976 and then again in 1990, now gets about 3 million visitors a year!

There Was a Holocaust Refugee Shelter in Oswego, NY

A little-known fact of American history is that President Franklin D. Roosevelt saved the lives of 982 war refugees during WWII. They were brought to Safe Haven, a refugee shelter located in Oswego, New York.

In 1944, President Franklin D. Roosevelt sent his Special Assistant to Italy to carefully select which refugees to bring back to the United States. The first priority was given to refugees who had managed to escape from concentration camps, but people who had skills that would benefit the camp were also chosen.

The refugees technically had no legal right to be in the United States. President Roosevelt promised Congress that the refugees would later return home to their original countries once the war was over.

The refugees traveled aboard the USS Henry Gibbons. The trip is said to have been an awful one, with the refugees suffering from seasickness, cramped quarters, and overheating during the two-week journey. When they arrived at the New York Harbor, they were excited to be greeted by the Statue of Liberty.

When the refugees got to Safe Haven, however, they didn't feel entirely free. Despite being provided with food, healthcare, and shelter, they still felt imprisoned by the barbed wire fences that surrounded the camp and by the military personnel who guarded them.

There were some silver linings of being at the shelter. Children went to school. One pair of refugees got married. The people of Oswego were friendly and helped sneak food into the camp.

Despite Roosevelt's promise to Congress, many of the refugees never went home and instead were provided with clearance to remain in the United States.

The Safe Haven Holocaust Refugee Shelter Museum serves as a memorial to the war refugees who lived there. It preserves the history of the only war refugee shelter in the United States.

New York's Hospitals Helped Shape the Healthcare Industry of Today

Today, New York is known for some of the best hospitals in the country. According to a 2013 *US News & World* report, New York-Presbyterian Hospital of Columbia and Cornell ranked as the seventh best hospital in the United States.

But did you know that over the years, New York's hospitals helped shape the healthcare industry today? The state is home to a number of historically significant medical achievements.

The first public hospital in the United States opened in New York in 1902. The Ellis Island Immigrant Hospital was used to house wannabe immigrants who were found to be too unfit to enter the United States. The hospital ran until 1930. It was later abandoned in 1954. The main building became a museum in 1990 and in 2014, the entire hospital could be viewed in hard hat tours. Even today, the hospital is viewed as an extraordinary part of the history of the public health field.

New York is also home to the oldest hospital in America to still be in operation today. Bellevue Hospital in Manhattan was founded in 1736. When the hospital was first founded, it was an almshouse for the poor. In 1787, it became a place of instruction for Columbia University's College of Physicians. In 1861, it was turned into Bellevue Hospital Medical College. It was the first medical college that had connections to a hospital in New York.

Since then, Bellevue Hospital Medical College has made some historical programs and achievements that have helped shape the healthcare industry of today. Some of these include:

- 1869 – The hospital opened the first ambulance service ever. The ambulances were horse-drawn carriages and used a gong to make it through crowded streets.

- 1873 – The first nursing program in the country that incorporated Florence Nightingale's principles opened at the hospital.

- 1874 – The first children's clinic in the United States was opened.

- 1875 – The first emergency room in the form of an emergency pavilion was founded.

- 1879 – The first mental ward was opened at the hospital in the form of a 'pavilion for the insane.'

- 1883 – A residency training program was started at the hospital. The concepts from that program are still used as a model for surgical training today.

- 1884 – Carnegie Laboratory, the first laboratory to study pathology and bacteriology in the country was opened at the hospital.
- 1888 – The first men's nursing school in the country opened at Bellevue.

Bellevue Hospital was home to New York City's first morgue, which opened in 1866.

The hospital also treated more AIDS patients than any hospital in the country. More AIDS patients also died at the hospital than they did at any other hospital in the United States.

America's First and Oldest State Park is in New York

Niagara Falls State Park is a popular tourist attraction today, but did you know that it was the first state park to be developed in the United States?

It took a lot of fighting for the state park to become what it is today. During the 1800s, early environmentalists were worried about the reduction in the Niagara River's flow. This led to the Free Niagara Movement, in which people believed the land surrounding the Niagara River should be free to the public and should also be preserved from commercialization and exploitation. The most noteworthy person who was a part of this movement was Frederick Law Olmsted, the landscape architect who was responsible for designing Central Park.

It took 15 years of fighting from the Free Niagara crusaders for the state to sign the Niagara Appropriations Bill into law in 1885. This led to the development of the Niagara Reservation. Niagara Falls State Park was designed by Frederick Law Olmsted.

Today, Niagara Falls State Park sees more than 8 million visitors a year. It's home to three waterfalls, which were formed over 12,000 years ago during the last glacial period.

One of the oldest American flags can also be found in the state park. Located at Old Fort Niagara, the flag was captured from the British by the Americans during the War of 1812.

Uncle Sam May Have Originated From New York

Uncle Sam is a popular cartoon that is used to represent the American government. Did you know that the cartoon may have originated from New York?

It has been said that the cartoon was actually a caricature of a man named Samuel Wilson. Wilson, a Troy resident, worked a meat packer. In 1812, Wilson supplied rations for American soldiers during the war. He labeled his meat packages with "U.S.", which stood for the United States. When asked what the 'U.S.' stood for, one of Samuel Wilson's workers jokingly said, "Uncle Sam."

However, there are some historians who doubt the credibility of the story. The earliest reference to 'Uncle Sam' was in 1810. Wilson's meatpacking contract with the government didn't take place until two years later.

NYC Has Some Surprising Former Burial Grounds

Perhaps one of New York City's most chilling secrets is that there are a number of parks, squares, and other locations throughout the city that were once used as burial grounds.

Washington Square Park rests above one of the city's biggest burial grounds. Between the years of 1797 and 1825, the area was used as a potter's field. Most of the people buried there died due to an outbreak of yellow fever. It has been estimated that more than 20,000 people were buried at the site the park was built on top of. Excavators often dig up bodies. During the 19th century, people claimed to see a blue mist that hung over the park at night due to the remains beneath it.

Madison Square Park was built over an estimated 1,300 corpses. Like Washington Square Park, it was used as a potter's field. Many of the people buried there came from local poorhouses or the nearby Bellevue Hospital. In 1806, the area was turned into an Army arsenal and then later was turned into a parade ground.

Central Park may be one of the city's most bustling places today, but it was built upon a cemetery belonging to All Angels Church. It seems that the bodies were never moved. Over the years, the coffins and graves of people buried in the 1800s have been dug up.

Another spot in the city that was a popular burial ground lays just south of Collect Pond. In the 1690s, African-American slaves and even freedmen were forced to bury their loved ones just outside of the city limits. In 1788, bodies were illegally removed from the burial ground for medical experimentation. Businesses were later built on the burial ground. It wasn't until the 1990s when bodies were dug up by excavators that the area became marked. A memorial was built in 2007.

Today, New York City buries its unclaimed bodies on Hart Island. The island, which is off the coast of the Bronx, is a burial ground to nearly one million bodies that have been buried there since the late 1860s. Hart Island is not open to the public.

These are just some of the many places throughout the city where bodies were once buried.

New York City is Rich in Titanic History

Whether you're a Titanic history buff or you loved the depiction of the tragedy in the film *Titanic* starring Leonardo DiCaprio and Kate Winslet, you might not know that there are a number of historical landmarks throughout New York City honoring the tragedy.

For starters, you might start by checking out what remains of Pier 54. This is where the Carpathia arrived, carrying the survivors of the Titanic. Although the pier is gone now, the gate can still be seen today.

Down the street, you'll find the Jane Hotel, the hotel where surviving crew members were housed after the tragedy. There is a fountain and memorial for the Titanic in the front lobby of the hotel, which was restored in 2008.

Titanic Memorial Park is located at the entrance of South Street Seaport in Manhattan. There's a lighthouse monument with a plaque that honors those who were lost in the tragedy.

There's a monument located at Broadway and 106th Street, which honors Isidor and Ida Strauss. Isidor Strauss, who helped Macy's become the world's largest department store, is regarded by many as one of the biggest icons who died on the Titanic. His wife Ida was given the option to leave on one of the lifeboats, but she chose to die with her husband instead.

In Central Park, you'll find a memorial dedicated to William T. Stead. Regarded as one of the ship's heroes, Stead was a British journalist who allegedly helped others get off the ship before dying about it himself.

If you pay a visit to Battery Park, you'll find the Wireless Operators Memorial. One of the names you'll find written on it is Jack Phillips, a wireless operator who stayed in the wireless room seeking out help until he died.

These are just some of the historical sites in New York City that mark the history of the Titanic.

New York City Really is America's Melting Pot

New York City has been called America's melting pot, and for good reason. Estimates have found that one out of every three people who live in New York City was born outside of the United States.

The city is home to some of the highest populations of people from various ethnicities and cultures. As a result, a number of different cultures have influenced the businesses and culture of New York City.

New York City is home to a huge Hispanic population. As of 2010, it was estimated that more than 8 million Hispanics live in the city. Of those, 33% are Puerto Rican, 25% are Dominican, and 13% are Mexican. The Bronx is the borough with the largest Hispanic population, with estimates showing that more than half of its residents have Hispanic roots.

Manhattan's Chinatown boasts the largest Chinese community that can be found outside of Asia. In 2015, it was estimated that there were more than 800,000 Chinese-Americans living in New York City. In Chinatown, you can find everything from Chinese food to Chinese clothing styles. A visit to Chinatown isn't complete without making a stop at the Original Chinatown Ice Cream Factory, which serves Chinese-influenced ice cream flavors, such as almond cookie and peanut butter with toasted sesame seeds. Chinese New Year is also a huge celebration in Chinatown each year.

As of 2011, it was estimated that there were more than 100,000 Koreans living in New York City, making it the second largest population outside of Korea. Two out of three of those live in Queens. There's also a Koreatown in Manhattan, which is well-known for its Korean restaurants and karaoke clubs. Don's Bogam is a popular Korean BBQ restaurant.

In Astoria, Queens, you'll find the highest number of Greek people outside of Greece. This population has grown since 2010 after the country of Greece experienced a financial crisis. Taverna Kyclades is known as one of the top authentic Greek restaurants.

Brighton Beach in Brooklyn is home to a large Russian community. In 'Little Odessa,' you will find plenty of Russian specialties, including pierogi, borscht, and vodka.

More Jewish people can be found in New York City than anywhere in the world besides Israel. It's been estimated that 1.1 million Jews are living in NYC. This is a huge number when you consider that America's overall Jewish population is around 6.5 million. Borough Park is home to a very large community of Orthodox Jews.

Aside from Warsaw, New York City has the largest Polish population.

New York City is also the city with the largest Irish population. Due to the potato famine and politics, more people from Ireland lived in NYC in 1850 than they did in Dublin. Things haven't changed much. New York still has more people with Irish ancestry than Dublin.

One area in which you might notice the influence of other cultures in the city? When having a conversation with someone! More languages are spoken in New York City than any other city in the world. The most languages are spoken in Queens, lending it the nickname of 'most linguistically diverse capital of the world.' It has been estimated that about 800 languages are spoken in the Big Apple.

Wondering how so many languages could be spoken in New York City? Dozens of Native American languages, languages from the Mariana Islands, native Mexican languages, Pennsylvania Dutch, and Yiddish are just a few of the *hundreds* of languages that are spoken in the city. It is also believed that at least half of all people living in NYC speak a language other than English at home.

RANDOM FACTS

1. New York City has a huge population. It has the third highest population in America, with only California and Texas having more residents. It has been estimated that one in every 37 people who live in the United States are residents of NYC. There are more than 8 million people who live in the city. More popular live in New York City alone than they do in both Switzerland and Australia combined.

2. Contrary to what you might think, New York City is *not* the capital of the state of New York. The capital of New York is Albany. Founded by Dutch settlers, Albany was originally named Fort Orange.

3. Manhattan's current name came from the Native Americans. Its meaning may surprise you: 'island of many hills.' Although Manhattan did have a lot of hills at the time, most of them have since been flattened in order to make room for urban development.

4. No Walmart can be found in the Big Apple. Since it's the largest corporation in the world, this may come as a surprise to some. It all comes down to unions. New York is a highly unionized city and Walmart does not allow unions to be formed among its employees. Walmart's attempts to open stores in Brooklyn, Queens and Staten Island have all been unsuccessful.

5. Early Dutch settlers found that there were huge oyster beds in Manhattan. This is why Ellis Island and Liberty Island were originally called Little Oyster Island and Big Oyster Island.

6. Five United States presidents were born in the state of New York. These include Martin Van Buren, Theodore Roosevelt, Franklin Delano Roosevelt, Millard Fillmore, and Donald Trump.

7. Just like every other state, New York has a number of strange laws. It's illegal to wear slippers after 10 p.m., you can be fined $25 for flirting, and farting in an NYC church can get you a misdemeanor. It's also illegal to honk your car horn in New York City (aside from emergency situations), but everyone still does it.

8. A plane crash happened at one point in Park Slope in Brooklyn. In 1960, two commercial planes collided with one another in midair. One of the planes crashed on Staten Island, while the other crashed at the intersection of Sterling Place and Seventh Avenue. Despite the fact that 128 passengers and six people on the ground died in the accident, there is no memorial. However, the color of the bricks at the top 126 Sterling Place are different in color from the rest of the building due to the crash.

9. The Catskill Mountain House in Palenville, New York was the first grand resort hotel to open in the United States in 1824.

10. New Yorkers love their coffee. It's been estimated that they consume seven times more coffee than other people living in the United States. This should probably come as no surprise, considering NYC is home to more than 1,600 coffee shops.

11. A lot of rich people call New York their home. It has been estimated that one out of every 21 people residing in New York are millionaires.

12. Albert Einstein's eyes can be found in NYC. A doctor who removed Einstein's brain to study it also removed his eyes. The eyes were given to Einstein's eye doctor, who kept them in a safe deposit box in New York City. They still remain there to this day.

13. The Bronx is the only NYC borough which is located on the mainland. The other four boroughs are located on islands. Queens and Brooklyn are both located on Long Island, while Manhattan and Staten Island are both islands of their own.

14. Former first lady and presidential candidate Hillary Clinton's career started out in New York. She served as the first female senator from New York after she was elected in 2000 and was re-elected to office in 2006.

15. The American Museum of Natural History is home to President Theodore Roosevelt's memorial.

16. The oldest cattle ranch in America was not started in the West. It's Deep Hollow Ranch, which is located in Montauk on Long Island. Founded in 1747, the ranch is still open today.

17. The "I love New York" (often represented by a heart symbol in place of "love") was created as a tourism campaign during a countrywide recession to draw more interest in the state. It has been around for more than 30 years and has become a popular slogan both nationally and globally.

18. After the stock market crashed during the Great Depression, a number of New Yorkers committed suicide. It's even been said that one hotel clerk started asking guests if they needed to get a hotel room to jump from the balcony. Some New Yorkers handled the financial crisis differently and began selling apples. In fact, an estimated 6,000 people were selling apples in NYC.

19. In 1992, it became legal for women to go topless in New York City.

20. Apples are the official state fruit of New York. European settlers first brought apple seeds to New York in the 1600s.

Test Yourself – Questions and Answers

1. Which United States President may have nicknamed New York the Empire State?

    a. George Washington
    b. Abraham Lincoln
    c. Bill Clinton

2. Who was the first female senator of the state of New York?

    a. Elizabeth Warren
    b. Condoleezza Rice
    c. Hillary Clinton

3. New York City was the nation's first capital for how many years?

    a. Two years
    b. Five years
    c. One year

4. Which of the five boroughs almost didn't become a part of New York City?

    a. Brooklyn
    b. Queens
    c. The Bronx

5. The Native American meaning of Manhattan is "island of many..."

    a. hills
    b. roads
    c. birds

Answers

1. a.

2. c.

3. b.

4. a.

5. a.

CHAPTER TWO

NEW YORK'S POP CULTURE

Since New York City is one of the biggest tourist attractions in the entire world, it should come as no surprise that the Empire State is rich with pop culture. Do you know which movies and films have been filmed in New York? Do you know which hit TV show that's set in New York City was based on a book? Do you know which movie was based on a true story that happened in New York? Read on to find out the answers to these and other fascinating pop culture facts about the state.

Lucille Ball's Life is Celebrated Every Year in Jamestown, New York

If you're a fan of *I Love Lucy*, then you may already know that Lucille Ball was born in Jamestown, New York. Though her family lived in Michigan, Montana, and New Jersey, Lucille Ball's mom later moved the family back to Celeron, NY, near Jamestown.

Lucille Ball later attended the John Murray Anderson School for the Dramatic Arts in NYC. Her instructors didn't think she would make it in show business, but Lucy was determined to prove them wrong.

Lucy and her real-life husband Desi Arnaz met when they were both cast in the New York production of *Too Many Girls*. The couple later went on to self-produce *I Love Lucy*, which is set in a New York City apartment building.

Today, Lucy's life is celebrated every year in Jamestown. The Lucille Ball Comedy Festival, which is held each August, draws in almost 20,000 people every year from nearly every state!

Each year, there are stand-up comedy performances. Some of the past performers at the event have included Jerry Seinfeld, Ellen DeGeneres, Jay Leno, and more. There are exhibits showcasing Lucille Ball's career. Some of these exhibits have included *Lucy I'm Home* and *The Desi Arnaz Exhibition*. There are Lucy tribute shows with impersonators, a block party, and so many other things for Lucille Ball fans to enjoy!

If you're unable to make it to the festival, that's okay! Jamestown is also home to the Lucille Ball Desi Arnaz Museum, which is open year-round. The museum, which opened in 1996, preserves both the personal life and productions of Lucille Ball and Desi Arnaz. Some of the things you'll be able to find at the museum include the set that was used for Lucy and Ricky's living room on *I Love Lucy* (which you can see in color for the first time), a set from the *I Love Lucy* Vitameatavegamin episode and a number of other exhibits and artifacts from the late comedian's life and career.

Woodstock Was Held at a Dairy Farm in New York, and You Can Visit the Site Today!

By now, you probably know that Woodstock took place in New York. But did you know that it did *not* take place in the town of Woodstock?

Although the festival planners originally wanted to hold the event in Woodstock, they couldn't find a venue. The festival was later set to take place at an industrial site near Middletown, New York, but that fell through when their permits were revoked.

The festival was saved by a dairy farmer named Max Yasgur, who owned a 600-acre farm in Bethel, New York. Yasgur agreed to allow the festival to be held on his property. The festival didn't take place on his dairy farm, however. It took place on one of his hay fields.

Woodstock is considered the most significant music event of all time. *Rolling Stones* named it as one of the "50 Moments That Changed the History of Rock and Roll." Some of the musicians and bands who performed include: Janis Joplin, Jimi Hendrix, The Who, Creedence Clearwater Revival, Johnny Winter, Santana, and Joe Cocker.

The festival took place over the course of three days, beginning on August 15th and ending on August 18th, 1969. Though only 200,000 people were expected to attend the festival, there were nearly half a million attendees.

In 2006, the Bethel Woods Center for the Arts opened on the site where Woodstock was held. The Bethel Woods Pavilion hosts outdoor concerts during the months of summer. There's also a museum with exhibits that honor Woodstock, rock and roll, peace and love, and so much more! The Museum at Bethel Woods is open from April to December.

Hip Hop Originated from the Big Apple

Hip hop music is frequently played on the radio today, but have you ever given any thought as to where it all got started?

Hip hop, both as a music genre and a culture, originated from New York City. It all began in the 1970s when young people in the Bronx threw house and block parties in predominantly African-American ghetto neighborhoods. At these parties, DJs would play percussive breaks of songs using a DJ mixer and two turntables. They used techniques such as scratching, beatmatching, and Jamaican toasting, in which they would chant over the beats. It was during this time that rapping was also born.

Early on, the only recorded hip hop was of live shows and mixtapes recorded by DJs. In 1977, DJ Disco Wiz is said to have recorded the first mixed dub recording.

It wasn't until 1979, however, that hip hop was recorded for radio. This was mostly due to lack of acceptance of hip hop out of ghetto neighborhoods. It was also due to a lack of financial resources.

"Rapper's Delight" by the Sugarhill Gang is widely recognized as the first hip hop record, though some consider "King Tim III (Personality Jockey)" by the Fatback Band to be the first. That being said, "Rapper's Delight" was the first to gain mainstream attention and experience commercial success.

Wizard of OZ is Honored in a Town in Upstate New York

Are you a fan of *The Wizard of Oz*? If so, you might want to take a trip to Chittenango in upstate New York. The town is the birthplace of Lyman Frank Baum "L. Frank Baum", author of the book series *The Wonderful Wizard of Oz*.

To honor Baum and his works, the sidewalks are painted like the yellow brick road. Throughout the town, you'll also spot signs of the characters from *Wizard of Oz*.

A number of businesses in the town of Chittenango are *Wizard of Oz* themed. Some of these include Emerald City Lanes Bowling, Tinman Hardware Store, End of the Rainbow Gift Shop, and Auntie Em's Pantry, which is best known for its Oz Cream Cones. There's also an *Oz*-themed casino called the Yellow Brick Road Casino, which is operated by the Oneida Indian tribe.

In downtown Chittenango, you'll also find the All Things Oz Museum. The museum is home to many *Wizard of Oz* themed collectibles, Judy Garland's autograph, props and costumes from the movie, and so much more!

Every year, the town also holds an annual *Wizard of Oz* themed festival called Oz-Stravaganza. The festival generally takes place the first week of June. It features a parade, live shows, and community groups. Special guests often attend the festival. In 2017, one of the special guests was Jane Lahr, daughter of Bert Lahr, the actor who played the "Cowardly Lion". You can even buy one of the bricks from the town's "yellow brick road" to help Chittenango raise money.

Lots of Celebrities Own Restaurants in New York City

Do you want to eat at a restaurant that's owned by one of your favorite celebs? If so, then you've come to the right place. A number of celebrities own restaurants in the Big Apple. Here are some of the most well-known celeb-owned restaurants in NYC:

- Southern Hospitality BBQ: Justin Timberlake pays homage to his Memphis roots at his restaurant in Midtown Manhattan. The casual restaurant has been known to serve up some awesome traditional Southern BBQ. Some celebrities who have appeared at the restaurant include: Channing Tatum and wife Jenna Dewan-Tatum (who re-enacted the iconic dance scene from *Dirty Dancing* at the restaurant), as well as former couple Minka Kelly and Derek Jeter.

- Joanne Trattoria: Lady Gaga and her parents co-own this traditional Italian restaurant in the Upper West Side. The restaurant is named after Lady Gaga's aunt Joanne, who died at seventeen years old from lupus complications.

- The Spotted Pig: Co-owned by Jay-Z, this restaurant serves both British and Italian cuisine. The West Village restaurant is best known for its burgers and sheep's milk ricotta gnudi. Celebrities who frequent the restaurant include: Luke Wilson, David Schwimmer, Jade Law, and Mario Batali.

- Tribeca Grill: This restaurant, which is owned by Robert De Niro, serves up American cuisine and steakhouse food. Other restaurants De Niro co-owns include Nobu and Locanda Verde (where you might spot Mary-Kate Olsen, Gwyneth Paltrow or Bradley Cooper!)

- Mermaid Oyster Bar: Co-owned by *Scrubs* actor Zach Braff, this upscale restaurant in Greenwich Village is known for its East coast oysters and lobster roll.

- Laughing Man Coffee and Tea: Hugh Jackman owns this café, which is all based on the concept of self-sustainability. Its coffee beans are self-sustainability grown in countries such as Peru, Guatemala, Ethiopia, and Papua New Guinea. Located in Tribeca, all profits go to charity.

- Jack's Wife Freda: Co-owned by Piper Perabo of *Coyote Ugly* fame, Jack's Wife Freda is a popular brunch spot. In fact, it's been said to be one of the most common brunch spots people post about on Instagram. With locations in both Soho and the West Village, the bistro is also known for its Israeli-inspired foods.

- SPiN New York: Actress Susan Sarandon co-owns this establishment in Midtown Manhattan. There are 17 ping-pong tables, a bar, and a restaurant, which is known for its sliders and shared plates. Not only has Kim Kardashian been spotted at SPiN, but Jake Gyllenhaal, David Schwimmer, and other celebs have competed in ping-pong charity events.

The Most Popular Radio Talk Show in the Country Airs From New York City

Did you know the most popular radio talk show in the country airs from New York City?

Elvis Duran and the Morning Show airs live in New York City on the Z100 radio station. The show is now aired on more than 80 other stations, reaching listeners in Philadelphia, Miami, Cleveland, Atlantic City, Fort Myers, New Haven, Richmond, Syracuse, and more.

The radio show, which is hosted by Elvis Duran and his colleagues, reaches 10 million listeners. As of 2018, it is the most-listened-to Top 40 morning program in the entire country.

The show's format has been so successful that other stations have used it as a model. *Elvis Duran and the Morning Show* consists of a celebrity gossip "Entertainment Report", a prank phone call segment called "Phone Taps", song parodies, contests, the occasional celebrity interview, and more.

Friends Fans Can Visit Some of the Show's Landmarks in NYC

If you're a fan of the show *Friends*, then you know landmarks throughout New York City regularly appeared in the show. There are a number of places you can go throughout the city to pay homage to the show, which first aired in 1994.

For starters, you might choose to visit the Pulitzer Fountain, which is featured in the opening credits of *Friends*. The fountain can be found in the Grand Army Plaza. Something you might not know is that the actual fountain was *not* used in the opening credits. What you really see is an exact replica of the fountain.

Although the interior of the characters' apartment building was filmed on-set in Los Angeles, the exterior of the apartment building was shot on the corner of Bedford and Grove in Greenwich Village. Fun fact: it has been estimated that an apartment in the building would cost someone $3.5 million.

Many *Friends* fans want to visit Central Perk, the iconic coffee shop from the show. Unfortunately, the only way to visit a pop-up version of Central Perk (and see that classic orange couch from the show) is to take the Warner Bros. Studio Tour.

NYC Was Once the East Coast's Hollywood

Before the film industry emerged in Hollywood in the early 1930s, New York City was considered to be American film industry central. Many of the major film studios were based in NYC. Paramount Pictures, which is the 2nd oldest film studio in the country and the 5th oldest in the world, was headquartered in the city.

The Return of Sherlock Holmes, *Goodfellas*, and *Carlito's Way* were a few of the many movies that were filmed at Paramount's Kaufman

303

Astoria Studios in Queens. Later on, TV shows like *The Cosby Show*, were shot at the film studio.

Kaufman Astoria Studios is located near the Museum of the Moving Image, the only museum that honors the moving image. It has a collection of over 130,000 artifacts from the TV and film industry. The museum is home to the Jim Henson Exhibit, which is dedicated to the director known for *The Muppet Show, Fraggle Rock, Sesame Street*, and other classics. The exhibit also contains some of his puppets. If you've ever wanted to see the original puppets used for Kermit the Frog, Miss Piggy, Elmo or Big Bird, then this exhibit is for you.

Kaufman Astoria Studios isn't the only place where filming has taken place in New York City. In fact, Central Park has long been a hotspot for films. It has been featured in more movies than any other location in the entire world!

Romeo and Juliet was the first movie to be filmed in Central Park in 1908. Since then, more than 300 movies had been filmed in the park. Some of the most popular movies to be filmed there include: *When Harry Met Sally, Breakfast at Tiffany's, Home Alone 2: Lost in New York, Ghostbusters, The Avengers, Elf, Maid in Manhattan, Serendipity, Enchanted, 13 Going on 30, Big Daddy, Night at the Museum,* and *Friends with Benefits*.

Gangs of New York is Loosely Based on a True Story

You've probably heard of the movie *Gangs of New York*, but did you know that it's based on a true story?

The movie, starring Leonardo DiCaprio and Daniel Day-Lewis, takes place in the Five Points district of Lower Manhattan in 1863.

It's based on a 1928 nonfiction book called *The Gangs of New York: An Informal History of the Underworld* by Herbert Asbury. The book focuses on several gangs that were prominent in New York City during the 1800s. These included: the Bowery Boys, Plug Uglies, Dead Rabbits, Shirt Tails, and True Blue Americans.

Director Martin Scorsese read the book in 1970 and believed it would make a good movie. He spent more than twenty years trying to make it happen.

While the book the movie is based on is nonfiction, there has been a lot of controversy over its accuracy. According to a modern historian named Tyler Anbinder, elements of the book were exaggerated. For example, Asbury claimed there was a murder every day in the neighborhood, while Anbinder claims that there was only a murder a month in all of New York City at that time.

A gang fight in the movie that's portrayed as taking place in 1846 is fictional. Meanwhile, the movie leaves out a major fight between the gangs that took place in Five Points in 1857.

The movie depicts Chinese-Americans as a large enough population to have their own community within the neighborhood. While there were Chinese-Americans residing in New York City at the time, it wasn't until 1869 that Chinese immigration to America really increased. The Chinese Theater shown in the movie wasn't built at the time, while the Old Brewery portrayed in the movie had already been demolished during some of the years it had been shown.

While *Gangs of New York* is inspired by actual events, it's important to remember that it's categorized as historical fiction and not 100% accurate.

Many Famous Authors Got Their Start in New York City

Over the years, many authors have moved to New York. Some of them moved in hopes of making connections to get their works published, while others just happened to have success while working other jobs.

Here are some of the most famous American authors of all-time whose careers got started after they moved to the Big Apple:

- Walt Whitman: Known for his collection of poems, Whitman worked in the newspaper industry. He worked as a devil's printer, a typesetter, and even created *The Long Islander* newspaper.

- Harper Lee: The author of *To Kill a Mockingbird* dropped out of college and moved to New York City, where she worked as an airline ticket agent and wrote in her free time. *To Kill a Mockingbird* was written after one of Lee's Broadway composer friends gave her enough money to quit her job and work on a novel for a year.

- Herman Melville: *Moby Dick* author Melville moved to Manhattan for work. Melville worked as a cabin boy on the St. Lawrence merchant ship. The time he spent there inspired his first work, *Redburn: His First Voyage*, along with his other nautical-themed works, including *Moby Dick*.

- Scott Fitzgerald: Best known for *The Great Gatsby* and "The Curious Case of Benjamin Button," Fitzgerald moved to New York City in pursuit of work. He began his career as a journalist before being told to give it up and later became a typist instead.

These are just a few of many authors who got their start in New York City!

The Legend of "Rip Van Winkle" Took Place in the Catskill Mountains of New York

Have you ever heard of the story of "Rip Van Winkle"? In the story, Rip Van Winkle is a Dutch villager who lives in a village at the foothill of the Catskill Mountains. The story begins before the American Revolution takes place.

Rip Van Winkle enjoys the great outdoors, spending time with his friends, and telling stories and repairing toys for the children in town. He doesn't like working, however, which causes his wife to nag him.

To get away from his wife, Rip Van Winkle heads into the woods with his dog one day. He comes across some men who he's never met before and drinks their Dutch gin. Shortly after, he falls asleep.

When Rip Van Winkle wakes up, his dog is gone and he has a foot-long beard. He goes to the local village where people ask him who he voted for. Not knowing the Revolutionary War took place, Rip says he's a supporter of King George III. He almost gets in trouble until an old woman in the town recognizes him as the "long lost" Rip Van Winkle. Rip learns that most of his friends died in the war and also comes across another man named Rip Van Winkle—his son, who is now grown up.

Rip Van Winkle learns that the strange men who he came across in the woods were actually the ghosts of Henry Hudson and his crew. Rip Van Winkle also learns that he was sleeping for at least 20 years.

Although some people believe that the legend of Rip Van Winkle is true, it's not. Author Washington Irving admitted that he had never been to the Catskill Mountains before writing the story.

That being said, an author named Joe Gioia said the story of Rip Van Winkle closely resembles a legend from Seneca Falls, New York. The legend says a squirrel hunter met the elusive "Little People," who he spent one night with. When he returned to his village, he found that all of the people were gone and the village was overgrown by forest. The night he'd spent with the "Little People" had turned into a year.

Sex and the City is Based on a New York City Newspaper Column

Sex and the City is one of the most well-known TV shows set in New York City. The series has even been credited for jumpstarting HBO. Did you know the show is actually based on a newspaper column?

In 1994, Candace Bushnell began writing a column called "Sex and the City" for the *New York Observer*. The humorous column, which ran for two years, was based on both her and her friends' dating experiences.

The first article Candace Bushnell wrote for the column was called "Swingin' Sex? I Don't Think So...." It was about a "couples-only sex club," which Bushnell and her male partner attended and were severely let down. The column featured several lines that went on to be famous quotes from the show.

In 1997, Bushnell's entire column was published in an anthology, which was also called *Sex and the City*. The show would later go on to be based on the book.

Though she initially used her own name, Candace Bushnell later used the name 'Carrie Bradshaw' in her columns for privacy reasons. Bushnell's alter-ego shares her own initials. In the show, Carrie Bradshaw, played by Sarah Jessica Parker, is a writer, too!

A Number of Reality Shows Have Been Filmed in New York

There's no doubt that Americans love their reality TV shows. Did you know that many of your favorite reality shows have been filmed in New York?

Some of the many reality shows that have been filmed in the Empire State include:

- *Judge Judy*
- *America's Next Top Model*
- *Basketball Wives*
- *Project Runway*
- *Newlyweds: The First Year*
- *Mob Wives*
- *The Real Housewives of New York City*
- *Love & Hip Hop*
- *Long Island Medium*

- *Growing Up Gotti*
- *Kourtney & Khloe Take the Hamptons and Kourtney & Kim Take New York*
- *The Apprentice and All-Star Celebrity Apprentice*
- *What Not to Wear*
- *The Real World: New York*
- *The Millionaire Matchmaker*
- *Queer Eye for the Straight Guy*

New York City is Talk Show Central!

If you've always wanted to see a talk show as it's being recorded, then you might want to visit the Big Apple! There are a number of talk shows that are recorded in New York City.

As of 2018, you can be an audience member at one of the following talk shows:

- *The View*
- *The Rachael Ray Show*
- *Dr. Oz*
- *Good Morning America*
- *The Chew*
- *The Daily Show with Trevor Noah*
- *The Tonight Show with Jimmy Fallon*
- *The Late Night Show with Steven Colbert*

The Big Apple is Known as the "Jazz Capital of the World"

If you love jazz music, then you partially have New York City to thank! The Big Apple has long been known as the "jazz capital of the world." A number of jazz music milestones have occurred in NYC.

309

One of the first successful jazz bands got their start in New York City. That band was the Original Dixieland Jazz Band, and they played in the Big Apple back in 1917.

Cabaret also originated in New York City. It got its start in the 1920s during the prohibition era. It was during this time that bars and nightclubs began to allow musicians to perform. The Cotton Club in Harlem was one of the most famous venues for jazz musicians during that time.

Duke Ellington was a famous bandleader of a jazz orchestra. His orchestra gained national attention after playing at the Cotton Club in Harlem in the mid-1920s.

In 1939, Billie Holiday played her song "Strange Fruit" at Café Society in Greenwich Village. It was the first integrated nightclub at the time.

Stride, which was the first piano style to ever be incorporated into jazz music, originated in NYC.

Jazz music is celebrated every year in New York City at the Winter Jazzfest. Voted as the "#1 Jazz Festival in North America," the festival pays homage to jazz music icons of the past and celebrates the jazz music being made today.

RANDOM FACTS

1. Fran Drescher grew up in Flushing, Queens. The actress went on to star in the hit '90s show *The Nanny* where she played Fran Fine, a nanny from Flushing, Queens who moves to New York's upper East side and falls in love with her wealthy boss.

2. Actress Michelle Trachtenberg was born and raised in Sheepshead Bay in Brooklyn. She later went on to play Georgina in the CW show *Gossip Girl*, which focuses on elite teens who live in the Upper East Side and teens from Brooklyn who struggle to fit in.

3. After dropping out of college, Madonna moved to NYC in 1978 in order to pursue a career in modern dance. When she moved to the city, she worked at Dunkin' Donuts. She was fired after she squirted jelly on a customer.

4. Actress Julia Stiles is a Manhattan native. At eleven years old, she started her acting career with New York's La MaMa Theater Company. Her son, Strummer, was born in 2017 at Mount Sinai hospital in NYC!

5. Lady Gaga, who was born and raised in Manhattan, honored her home state by doing a remake of Frank Sinatra's song "New York, New York."

6. Lenny Kravitz was born in Manhattan and raised in both Manhattan and Brooklyn. The musician recorded a song about his hometown called "New York City."

7. Barbara Streisand was born and raised in Brooklyn. She went to Erasmus High with fellow musician Neil Diamond! They were in the school choir together and hung out and smoked cigarettes in front of the school.

8. Actor Heath Ledger, who is best-known for his role in his final film *The Dark Knight*, was found dead in an apartment in Manhattan in 2008.

9. Vanessa Williams, who was born and raised in the Bronx, won Miss New York in 1983. She was recognized as the first African-American woman to ever win Miss America, but she was later pressured to give up the title after *Penthouse* published unauthorized nude photos of her. Williams has since gone on to have success in singing and acting.

10. *Sesame Street*, which is the longest-running television series for kids, is filmed in Astoria, Queens. The set is designed to capture the feel of different neighborhoods throughout NYC.

11. Mariah Carey was born in Huntington, New York. She is currently a resident of New York City. Her grandfather immigrated from New York to Venezuela and adopted the last name, Carey.

12. The show *Will & Grace* featured several famous buildings throughout New York City. The roommates lived at 155 Riverside Drive, while the location of Grace's design studio was in the Puck Building.

13. Taylor Swift paid $18 million for a townhouse located in the Tribeca neighborhood of Lower Manhattan. It's located next to her penthouse.

14. Christina Aguilera was born in Staten Island. Though her family was forced to move to New Jersey, Texas, Japan, and other locations because her father was in the military, the musician can always be found in NYC at Madame Tussauds wax museum.

15. Musicians Alicia Keys and Jay-Z, who are both NYC natives, paid homage to their home state in their song "Empire State of Mind."

16. Sean Combs, who has been known as Puff Daddy, P. Diddy, and many other nicknames, was born in Harlem. He was

raised in Mount Vernon, NY. Combs began his career as an intern at Uptown Records in New York. Combs later went on to become a talent director at the record company. During that time, he played a role in developing Jodeci and Mary J. Blige.

17. A number of songs have been written about New York City. Some of these include: "Living for the City" by Stevie Wonder, "No Sleep Till Brooklyn" by the Beastie Boys, "Guaranteed Raw" by the Notorious B.I.G., "Visions of Johanna" by Bob Dylan, "Black Jesus + Amen Fashion" by Lady Gaga, "Spanish Harlem" by Ben E. King, "I Am… I Said" by Neil Diamond, "Mona Lisas and Mad Hatters" by Elton John, and "14th Street" by Rufus Wainwright.

18. Actress/musician Jennifer Lopez was born and raised in the Bronx. She announced this to the world in her song "Jenny from the Block." Lopez has said that growing up in the Bronx has influenced everything about her.

19. Cyndi Lauper was born and raised in Queens, New York. In the early '70s, the musician performed with a number of cover bands. One of the bands she was in, Flyer, was popular throughout the New York metro area.

20. All four members of the Beatles have performed at Madison Square Gardens, but the band never performed there together. In 1974, John Lennon gave his second to last performance at MSG.

Test Yourself – Questions and Answers

1. Which hit '90s TV show was *not* set in New York?

    a. Friends
    b. The Nanny
    c. Boy Meets World

2. Which genre of music got its start in New York City?

    a. Hip hop
    b. Country
    c. Blues

3. Which city in New York celebrates Lucille Ball's life every year?

    a. Huntington
    b. Jamestown
    c. Manhattan

4. Who is the DJ behind the New York-based radio talk show that's one of the most popular in the country?

    a. Ryan Seacrest
    b. Mark Larson
    c. Elvis Duran

5. Which female musician is *not* from New York?

    a. Alicia Keys
    b. Mariah Carey
    c. Beyoncé

Answers

1. c.

2. a.

3. b.

4. c.

5. c.

CHAPTER THREE

FACTS ABOUT NEW YORK CITY'S ATTRACTIONS

Whether you're thinking about visiting New York City or you already have, you may have never considered the history of some of its most popular tourist attractions. For example, do you know which architect designed the Statue of Liberty? Do you know who started the annual New Year's Eve bash in Times Square? Did you know there's a place in the city where couples can feel "sparks fly" when they kiss?

The Statue of Liberty Has a Full Name

Even though most of us only know her as the Statue of Liberty, the statue actually has a full name! It's "Liberty Enlightening the World."

How did the statue get its name? It came from the statue's torch, which is a symbol of enlightenment. According to the National Park Service, the torch "lights the way to freedom showing us the path to liberty."

Unfortunately, the statue's torch isn't the same torch it was originally built with. The original torch was damaged in the Black Tom explosion on July 30th, 1916. The explosion, which was a German act of sabotage to destroy American-made ammunition that was going to be supplied to the USA's allies during World War I, left the Statue of Liberty with $100,000 worth of damage. Due to structural damages caused by the explosion, the torch hasn't been open to the public ever since.

In 1986, a newly constructed replacement torch was added to the statue. Its flame, which is made of copper, is covered in 24k gold. During the daytime, the gold reflects the sun's rays. At nighttime, the torch glows due to its lights.

The original torch can be found in the lobby of the Statue of Liberty.

Central Park is Designed to Represent the State of New York

With 42 million visitors a year, Central Park is one of the most bustling places in all of New York City. The park, which was the first public park to ever be landscaped in America, spans across 843 acres of land and 3.5 square miles. Whether you've been to Central Park or not, here's a fact that you probably don't know about it: the park was designed to resemble New York state.

The park, which was designed by Frank Olmstead, is meant to be a mini-scale representation of New York. The south side of Central Park was designed to give off a more elite, less woodsy feel. This area of the park is meant to represent New York City.

As you enter the northern part of the park, you'll notice more hills and woods. This rustic area also contains more benches and gazebos. This area of the park is supposed to remind you of the Catskills and the Adirondack Mountains.

Broadway's Longest-Running Show Isn't Its Highest Earning

Whether you've always dreamt of going to a Broadway show or if you already frequent them, you may be wondering which show has been around the longest and which has earned the most money. You might be surprised to learn that they are *not* one in the same!

The longest-running Broadway show is *The Phantom of the Opera*. The show first made its Broadway premiere back in 1988. Since then, it has run more than 11,000 times. The show is still running today. *Chicago* is the second-longest running Broadway show. Since it opened in 1996, *Chicago* has run more than 7,000 times and continues to run to date. Neither of these shows has been the highest-earning Broadway show, however.

The highest-earning Broadway show is *Lion King*, which has grossed a whopping $1.09 billion. *The Phantom of the Opera* is the second highest earner, hitting $850 million. The third highest earner is *Wicked*, with earnings of $477 million.

The Empire State Building May be More Romantic Than You Thought

The Empire State Building was built at a time when builders were in a race to build the world's highest skyscraper. Unveiled in 1931, the Empire State Building was the world's tallest landscaper. It maintained that title until 1970 when the first World Trade Center tower was built.

Since the Empire State Building was built, more than 30 people have committed suicide by jumping from the building.

When it comes to romance, the Empire State Building might not be the first place that comes to mind. However, it might be one of the most romantic spots in the city. In fact, couples see "sparks fly" here—*literally*.

Some couples have noticed sparks fly—and the feeling of being jolted—when they kiss at the top of the Empire State Building. This is due to static electricity at the top of the building.

You can even get married at the Empire State Building. If you want to have your wedding here, you'll have to do it on Valentine's Day, though, as this is the only day of the year when weddings are allowed on the building. Weddings are held in the form of a contest, however. In 2017, 13 lucky couples were chosen to hold their weddings or vow renewal on the 86th Floor Observatory.

There's also an Empire State Building Wedding Club for people who have their wedding at the Empire State Building. This grants them free entry into the observatory on Valentine's Day every year.

The Rockefeller Center Christmas Tree Topper is Massive!

Sure, you know the Rockefeller Center Christmas Tree is huge. But have you ever given any thought to how big the tree topper is?

The Swarovski star that tops the tree is a whopping 550 pounds. It's 9.5 feet in diameter and is made up of 25,000 crystals. There are also 1,024 programmable channels to ensure that the star keeps twinkling.

You might be wondering how that 550-pound star stays on top of the tree. The tree weighs enough to support the weight of the topper.

To put things into perspective, the 2017 Rockefeller Center Christmas Tree was 75 feet tall and weighed 24,000 pounds. This wasn't even the largest Christmas Tree that's been displayed at Rockefeller Center. In 1999, the tree, which came from a farm in Killingworth, Connecticut, stood 100 feet tall (though that tree only weighed 14,000 pounds).

So, how much is the Rockefeller Center Christmas Tree topper worth? Although the Swarovski star's value has been kept a secret, it's estimated to be worth more than $1.5 million.

One World Trade Center is 1,776 Feet Tall for a Reason

One World Trade Center is the rebuilt World Trade Center. It was named after the North Tower, one of the two towers on the World Trade Center that were destroyed during the terrorist attacks on September 11th, 2001.

Here's something you might not know about One World Trade Center. The reason it was built to stand 1,776 feet tall is an intentional reference to the year the Declaration of Independence was signed. The United States has been known to hide references to the Declaration of Independence in other places, such as the dollar bill.

With its height, One World Trade Center is often considered to be the tallest building in the United States, but some beg to differ. The Willis Tower in Chicago, which stands 1,451 feet high, still holds the national record as the world's tallest building. How can this be? Well, a spire was added to One World Trade Center to ensure it hit 1,776 feet tall. Without the spire, One World Trade Center stands at only 1,368 feet tall—making it technically shorter than the Willis Tower.

Regardless of whether or not it's the tallest building in America, One World Trade Center was built with careful planning to memorialize the lives lost in 9/11. The building is also located just north of the National September 11 Memorial & Museum, which was built where the original World Trade Center once stood.

The First New Year's Eve Bash in Times Square Was Thrown by a New York City Newspaper Company

Today, nearly a million people ring in the New Year in Times Square. Even when not in attendance, many people throughout the country watch the ball drop live from Times Square on *Dick Clark's New Year's Rockin' Eve* with Ryan Seacrest. In 2018, the TV program drew 15.7 million viewers. Have you ever given any thought to how the tradition of celebrating New Year's in Times Square got started?

The first New Year's Eve celebration in Times Square was held by the *New York Times*. The newspaper company hosted the event to celebrate its opening in 1903. Fireworks were shot off to ring in the New Year. About 200,000 people were in attendance the first year. By 1904, the popularity of the event grew.

The ball was introduced in 1907. Replacing the fireworks show that had been held in previous years, the electrically-lit ball was lowered on a flagpole when the clock struck midnight to ring in the year of 1908.

The Times Square Ball has dropped every year since 1908, with the exception of 1942 and 1943. The celebration was not held during those years due to wartime blackouts.

Since the introduction of the Times Squares Ball, it's come a long way! Back in 1907, the ball contained 100 light bulbs and was lowered on a 141-foot pole. The ball that's dropped down a 475-foot pole today in Times Square has a computerized LED multi-colored lighting system and reflective crystal panels.

Dick Clark began to host *Dick Clark's New Year's Rockin' Eve* in 1972. He created the program with a younger audience in mind. At the time, there was another program run by Guy Lombardo. Clark was well-known as the host of *American Bandstand. Dick Clark's New Year's Rockin' Eve* grew in popularity, especially once Guy Lombardo died.

Dick Clark's New Year's Rockin' Eve is under contract to air on ABC until at least 2024.

Coney Island Was Probably Named After Rabbits

Have you ever wondered where Coney Island got its name? No one knows for sure, but there are a few theories.

The Lenape tribes are said to have called the island "the island without shadows." When the Dutch settled on the island, they renamed it *"Konijnen Eiland,"* the Dutch term for "Rabbit Island," due to the large population of rabbits on the sandy island.

Some theorists believe the island may be named after "Conyn," which may have been one of the surnames among early Dutch settlers. Others believe it may be named after John Coleman, one of Henry Hudson's crew members who was killed by Native Americans. Overall, however, the rabbit island theory is the most widely believed.

Madison Square Garden Has Hosted Some of the Biggest Benefit Concerts of All-Time

Benefit concerts have become a popular way to raise money for tragedies and natural disasters. Did you know that Madison Square

Garden has hosted some of the highest-earning benefit concerts of all-time?

In fact, the MSG arena was the first to host a benefit concert when it held "The Concert for Bangladesh." The event took place in 1971 and raised money for Bangladeshi refugees after the Bangladesh Liberation War-related genocide. Forty thousand people came out to see former Beatle member Ringo Starr, Eric Clapton, Bob Dylan, Leon Russell, Billy Preston, and Badfinger perform, raising nearly $250,000 for Bangladesh relief. Albums from the event were also sold, which raised an additional $12 million.

"The Concert for New York City" also took place at Madison Square Garden. In addition to raising money, the concert was also used as a way to honor the first responders and lives lost in the terror attacks. The concert, which was aired live on VH1, raised over $35 million. More than 60 performers participated in the event, including: Bon Jovi, Elton John, Jay-Z, Destiny's Child, the Backstreet Boys, and Adam Sandler. Performers also autographed memorabilia, which earned an extra $275,000.

"From the Big Apple to the Big Easy" was a benefit concert that was held at Madison Square Garden, in collaboration with nearby Radio City Music Hall. The benefit was held for Hurricane Katrina relief efforts. The concerts from: Elton John, Bette Midler, Jimmy Buffett, Elvis Costello, and other performers helped raise approximately $9 million for the cause.

The largest benefit concert to ever be held (both at MSG and of all-time) was "12-12-12: The Concert for Sandy Relief." The event raised $60 million for the victims of the hurricane, with $30 million of that being raised from ticket sales alone. The concert was aired live on 39 TV stations, streamed on more than 25 websites, and broadcasted on more than 50 radio stations. Performances were given by: Paul McCartney, Kanye West, Alicia Keys, Bon Jovi, The Who, Bruce Springsteen, Billy Joel, Eric Clapton, and the Rolling Stones.

Central Park Zoo Animals Were Featured in the First Ever Macy's Day Parade

Watching the Macy's Thanksgiving Day Parade has become a pastime for many Americans. You might be surprised to learn the very first Macy's parade was much different from the one that takes place in the streets of Manhattan today.

The parade was originally called the "Macy's Christmas Parade" when it first made its debut on Thanksgiving Day in 1924. The parade was held to celebrate the expansion of the Macy's store in Manhattan. As you can probably guess, the parade was Christmas-themed. What you might not guess is that there were no balloons in the first Macy's Day Parade. Live animals were used instead!

The animals included goats, camels, donkeys, and elephants. These animals came from the Central Park Zoo. Horses were also used to pull the floats.

Live animals were used in 1925 and 1926, as well. Lions, tigers, and bears were included in the parade those years. However, the animals scared the children who were watching the parade. As a result, the parade stopped using animals.

In 1927, Macy's introduced its giant helium balloons in place of animals. The very first balloons that year included Felix the Cat, Toy Soldier, The Dragon, and The Elephant. It was also renamed "Macy's Thanksgiving Day Parade" the same year.

Grand Central Terminal Was Saved by a Former First Lady

Grand Central Terminal is one of New York City's most famous landmarks. It's been featured in everything from the movie *Avengers* to the first episode of the show *Gossip Girl*. But did you know the terminal would have been destroyed if it weren't for a former First Lady?

In 1975, there were plans to destroy Grand Central Terminal to make room for the railroad. When Jackie Kennedy Onassis read about these plans in the *New York Times*, she was outraged. The terminal meant a lot to the former First Lady. She saw it as symbolic of Manhattan, a city her grandfather had helped build.

After Onassis read about the city's plans to destroy Grand Central, she fought against it with the Municipal Art Society. The Municipal Art Society was a well-respected group that had previously been involved with the creation of the city's first zoning code, planned the subway lines, and the development of the Landmarks Preservation Law in 1965.

Jackie Kennedy Onassis played a key role in saving Grand Central. She was the highlight speaker at a press conference about the plans. Onassis also wrote a letter to New York Mayor Abraham Beame asking him to preserve the city's beauty and history by stopping the plans from going through. Mayor Beame announced that he would appeal the plans a week after receiving her letter.

Staten Island Ferries Were Once Used for More Than Transporting People

Between 2014 and 2015, 22 million people rode on the Staten Island Ferry! But did you know that Staten Island's ferries weren't always used just for transportation?

During the Civil War, the Union army used ferry boats from all over the country. The ferries they purchased from Staten Island — the Clifton and Westfield — were used as gunships, fully equipped with cannons. They were considered to be some of the best used in the war. While they were not used on a long-term basis, they were very useful.

In 1863, the Westfield was destroyed in a surprise attack from the Confederates. The ship was blown in half and the crew was killed. Remains of the ship could be seen off the coast of Galveston for years, serving as a reminder of the Confederate defeat.

In 1987, ferries from Staten Island served another purpose. Due to prison overcrowding on Rikers Island, Mayor Ed Koch came up with a plan to turn two former ferries into prison barges. The ferries held more than 300 prisoners off the coast of the Bronx. The ships were used by the Department of Corrections until 1997.

Many Sculptures Can be Found in Central Park

Central Park is home to a number of sculptures. Most of these sculptures were donated to the park by organizations or people. Here's a list of some of the most popular sculptures you'll find there:

- *Alice in Wonderland* is, by far, the most popular statue that can be found in Central Park. The sculpture features: Alice, the White Rabbit, the Mad Hatter, the Cheshire Cat, and the dormouse. Created by Jose de Creeft and added to the park in 1959, the sculpture attracts many children.

- *Ludwig van Beethoven* is a sculpture that was created in honor of the late composer by German-American sculptor Henry Baerer. The statue was added to Central Park in 1884.

- *Hans Christian Anderson* features the famous fairy-tale writer sitting and reading to a duck, in honor of his most famous story "The Ugly Duckling." The sculpture was created by Georg J. Lober in 1956.

- *Still Hunt* is a sculpture that was created by Edward Kemeys. Added to Central Park in 1863, the sculpture features a cougar on a rock ledge about to pounce. The sculpture has scared many joggers.

- *The Angel of the Waters*, otherwise known as the Bethesda Fountain, is located at the center of the lower terrace. Sculpted by Emma Stebbins, the sculpture was unveiled when Central Park was completed in 1873. It's the only sculpture in the park that was commissioned by the city of New York.

- *Group of Bears* is a bronze and granite sculpture of three bears. Created by Paul Howard Manship, the statue was unveiled to the park in 1990.

- *William Shakespeare* is a bronze statue of the late poet on a stone pedestal. Sculpted by John Quincy Adams Ward, the statue was added to the park in 1872.

- *Dancing Goat* and *Honey Bear* are two statues created by Frederick George Richard Roth. Both are fountains in the Central Park Zoo and were installed in 1937.

- *Seventh Regiment Memorial* honors the lives lost from that regiment during the Civil War. The park became home to the statue is 1874.

- *Christopher Columbus* is a replica of a sculpture created by Jeronimo Suñol in Madrid. The replica was added to the park in 1892.

- *Eagles and Prey* is the oldest sculpture of any New York City park. Created by Christophe Fatin in 1853, the statue was added to the park in 1863. The sculpture depicts a goat that's about to be devoured by two eagles.

- *Untermyer Fountain* is a bronze cast of Walter Schott's sculpture, *Three Dancing Maidens*. It was donated to the park by the Untermyer family in 1940.

- *Alexander Hamilton* is a granite sculpture that honors the American founding father. Commissioned by Hamilton's son, the statue was sculpted by Carl Conrads and donated to the park in 1880.

- *Balto* is a statue that honors the sled dog who led his team through a snowstorm in 1925 to deliver medication that stopped a diphtheria outbreak. Sculpted by Frederick George Richard Roth, the statue was added to the park the same year of the storm.

- The *Burnett Memorial Fountain* was created by Bessie Potter Vonnoh between the years of 1926 and 1936. The sculpture, which was placed in the Conservatory Garden, was designed as a storytelling memorial in memory of author Frances Hodgson Burnett. It's believed the boy and girl in the sculpture are Mary and Dicken, from Burnett's famous book *The Secret Garden*.

- *Indian Hunter* depicts a Native American hunting with a wolf. Sculpted by John Quincy Adams Ward, the sculpture was added to the park in 1866.

- The *107th Infantry Memorial* is a monument that pays homage to the men who served in the infantry regiment of the same name during World War I. It was created by Karl Illava, who served as a sergeant in the Infantry Regiment. The memorial was added to the park in 1927.

- *Simón Bolívar* can be seen riding a horse in a sculpture overlooking Central Park West. The sculpture sits where the Bolivar Hotel once stood.

- The *King Jagiello Monument* depicts the King Wladyslaw II Jagiello of Poland and Grand Duke of Lithuania on a horse. The statue, which sits on a tall pedestal, is considered to be one of the most impressive statues in all of Central Park. It was added to the park in 1945.

A total of 22 statues depicting historical figures can be found throughout the park. All of these statues are of men.

The Bronx Zoo is the Largest Metropolitan Zoo

Did you know the Bronx Zoo is the largest metropolitan zoo in the United States? The zoo is set on 265 acres of land!

When it opened on November 8th, 1899, the zoo was home to 843 animals and exhibits. Today, you can see more than 6,000 animals from more than 600 species.

Since it first opened to the public, the Bronx Zoo has accomplished some of the "firsts" in the zoo world.

In 1901, the Wildlife Conservation's first veterinary department was formed at the Bronx Zoo. In 1916, the zoo also opened the first fully equipped animal hospital.

An exhibit called "Lion Island" was opened in 1940. It was the first exhibit in the country that allowed animals in the African Plains habitat to wander without a cage.

The Bronx Zoo opened the African Plains Exhibit in 1941. It was the first exhibit that allowed visitors to view predator and prey in a naturalistic setting.

The zoo opened the world's first nocturnal animals exhibit. The exhibit, which was called "The World of Darkness," ran until 2009.

The New York Public Library is Home to a Number of Odd Artifacts

The New York Public Library is the second largest library in the United States, second only to the Library of Congress. It's the fourth largest library in the entire world. It's home to a lot of books—53 million, to be exact—but did you know a number of other surprising artifacts can be found at the New York Public Library?

For starters, you can find locks of hair from a number of famous people throughout history. Some of these include: Wild Bill Hickok, Charlotte Bronte, and Walt Whitman. The locks of hair are signed and dated.

Charles Dickens' favorite letter-opener can be found in one of the library collections. The shaft is made of ivory, but the handle is the embalmed paw of Dickens' cat, Bob.

The original stuffed animals the Winnie-the-Pooh stories were written about can also be found at the New York Public Library. Winnie-the-Pooh, Piglet, Eeyore, Tigger, and Kanga have called the library home since 1987.

These are just a few of the many odd artifacts you'll find at the New York Public Library!

Random Facts

1. The Statue of Liberty used to be dark brown in color, but its copper exterior has since turned green. While this is caused by deterioration, the green coating also protects the statue from seeing any further damage—meaning, the statue's green color is here to stay!

2. Although the Empire State Building falls within the boundaries of Manhattan's zip code, the building has its own zip code! In 1980, it got the zip code of 10118.

3. The Bronx Zoo is the largest metropolitan zoo in the entire United States. It houses more than 4,000 animals and 500 species.

4. Times Square wasn't called that at first. It was named after the *New York Times* when the world-famous newspaper moved there in 1904. Prior to that, Times Square was known as Longacre Square.

5. Despite the fact that the American Museum of Natural History is home to one of the best dinosaur collections in the entire world, most of its fossils remain in storage.

6. The Macy's Thanksgiving Day Parade was put on hiatus during World War II due to a shortage of rubber and helium. It stopped in 1942 and resumed in 1945. The following year, its route was cut in half.

7. The Statue of Liberty was sculpted by Frédéric Auguste Bartholdi. It has been said that the statue's face was modeled after Bartholdi's mother. Gustave Eiffel, who was the architect behind the Eiffel Tower in Paris, built the Statue of Liberty. The Statue of Liberty gets fewer visitors than the Eiffel Tower does. In 2016, the Statue of Liberty had 4.5 million visitors, while the Eiffel Tower had 7 million.

8. St. Patrick's Cathedral, which is a National Historic Landmark, is the largest Gothic Roman Catholic Cathedral in all of

America. The cathedral sees 5 million visitors each year—more than the Statue of Liberty!

9. Radio City Music Hall is connected to Rockefeller Center through a secret underground tunnel. It was previously used by commuters and then as a general admission seating entrance for schools and large groups. Today, it's used by the performers as a private entrance to the music hall. Almost all performers use the tunnel to avoid the Paparazzi.

10. Brooklyn Botanic Garden opened one of the first children's gardening programs in 1914. There are still garden programs offered for kids today!

11. One of the most famous trees in all of New York City can be found in Prospect Park. The elm tree, which has been named Camperdown Elm, was transplanted from Scotland to Prospect Park. The tree has gained so much popularity due to how its branches grow parallel to the ground. While the tree almost died in the 1960s, it was able to be preserved. It can be found today behind the Prospect Park Boathouse.

12. The movie *Night at the Museum* is based on a fictional book that takes place at the American Museum of Natural History. Though the interior scenes in the movie were shot in Vancouver, the exterior scenes were shot at the actual museum. This isn't the only time the American Museum of Natural History has been featured in film, either! Ross Geller in *Friends* worked at the museum at one point during the show. The AMNH also appears in *The Devil Wears Prada* and *K-Pax*.

13. Mickey Mouse didn't debut in the Macy's Thanksgiving Day Parade until 1934! Macy's designers worked personally with Walt Disney to create the balloon, which was held down by 25 people. Surprisingly, Mickey isn't the character who's appeared in the parade most often! That would be Snoopy, who first premiered in the parade in 1968 and has had a total of 39 appearances. However, Snoopy was replaced by Charlie Brown in 2016.

14. The Brooklyn Bridge is said to be the inspiration for more art than any other manmade structure in America. The bridge has been painted by Georgia O'Keeffe, Andy Warhol, and other famous artists. It's also been the focus of photographers, poets, musicians, filmmakers, and more.

15. Sea-Lion Park, the first enclosed amusement park in the United States, was opened on Coney Island in 1895 by Captain Paul Boyton. Boyton, who was famous for being an aquatic daredevil, did one thing differently when he opened Sea-Lion Park. He enclosed it with a fence. He also charged a single admission fee, which was something that had never been done before. Some of the attractions included a water chute and an aquatics shower. Sea-Lion Park was later replaced by Luna Park in 1903.

16. Times Square has a free visitor center and museum, which is located in the Embassy Theater. The Embassy Theater, which is the world's first newsreel theater, was the only theater in the United States that was once managed and run by women only. At the museum, you'll see some of the costumes used in Broadway productions, learn about the history of Times Square, and write a wish on confetti that will be released when the ball drops on New Year's Eve.

17. If you're not that into art, you won't want to skip out on a visit to the Metropolitan Museum of Art. The oldest surviving piano can be found at the museum—along with approximately 5,000 other instruments that can be found at the MET. The museum also has an Arms and Armor department, where you'll find Henry VIII's armor and other historical battle gear. More than 35,000 historically significant pieces of clothing and accessories can be found at the MET's Costume Institute. You'll also find an Egyptian temple, Chinese Garden Court, a 16th-century Spanish patio, and so much more.

18. Bryant Park sits above some literary masterpieces. In 1989, the New York Public Library built a space beneath the park for

additional storage. Currently, 40 miles of bookshelves can be found beneath Bryant Park. It's been estimated that there's enough space underneath the park to store 3.2 million books and 50,000 reels of film.

19. Everyone from the Beatles and Judy Garland to Billie Holiday has performed at Carnegie Hall, but the first composer to ever perform at the music hall was Tchaikovsky. Tchaikovsky performed on April 5th, 1891, which was opening night. Maestro Walter Damrosch knew they needed a big-name performer to make the music hall succeed. Tchaikovsky traveled to America from Russia and conducted five of his pieces at the hall.

20. There's an area in the city known as "Little Britain." Situated in the West Village, there's a corner that's unofficially known as "Little Britain Boulevard." One of the most popular businesses in Little Britain is Tea & Sympathy, a restaurant serving traditional British tea and cuisine ranging from scones to Shepherd's pie. A Salt & Battery is a popular fish and chips restaurant in the area. A little shop called Carry On sells traditional British loose and bagged tea.

Test Yourself – Questions and Answers

1. What is the Statue of Liberty's full name?

    a. Liberty Enlightening the World
    b. Liberty of the World
    c. Liberty Freedom of the World

2. What is the longest-running Broadway show?

    a. Lion King
    b. Wicked
    c. The Phantom of the Opera

3. Which New York City attraction has the highest number of visitors a year?

    a. St. Patrick's Cathedral
    b. Central Park
    c. The Statue of Liberty

4. Which former First Lady saved Grand Central Terminal from destruction?

    a. Jackie Kennedy Onassis
    b. Michelle Obama
    c. Hillary Clinton

5. The first Times Square New Year's Eve bash was thrown by who?

    a. The New York Observer
    b. The New York Times
    c. The New York Post

Answers

1. a.
2. c.
3. b
4. a.
5. b.

CHAPTER FOUR

NEW YORK INVENTIONS, IDEAS, AND MORE!

Have you ever wondered what inventions have come out of New York? New York has been the origin of a number of foods, products, and other inventions that you use on a day to day basis! Read on to learn more about some of the things that started in New York!

Pizza

It's often said that you haven't tasted pizza until you've tried pizza in New York, and for good reason! Pizza got its start in NYC.

While pizza originated from Italy, Americans can thank New York City for the pizza they eat today. Lombardi's, which is located in the Little Italy section of Manhattan, was the first pizzeria to open in the United States. The pizzeria opened in 1905.

Lombardi's first served pizza that was cooked with wood fires. However, in 1905, the owner of Lombardi's served the first coal-fired pizza. Although it's illegal to cook a pizza that way, Lombardi's and other pizzerias throughout the city still use coal ovens during their pizza-cooking process.

Since then, pizza has come a long way! Now, pizzerias across the country serve a variety of different types of pizza, ranging from New York-style and deep-dish pizza to stuffed crust pizza and pizza bagels.

So, what exactly sets a New York-style pizza apart from other pizzas? Well, several things. For starters, NY-style pies are wide, hand-tossed, and have thin crust. It's meant to be folded into a V. New York-style pizza is always made from fresh mozzarella, and there's never an overabundance of tomato sauce.

Toilet Paper

Today, many of us take toilet paper for granted. Have you ever wondered who you should thank for its invention?

Joseph Gayetty began selling toilet paper in 1857 in New York City. He marketed it as "medicated paper for the water-closet." At the time, his toilet paper was made of Manilla hemp paper, which contained aloe for lubrication. It was intended to help prevent hemorrhoids. His toilet paper was sold throughout the 1920s.

Despite the fact that Gayetty has been credited with inventing American toilet paper, the first patent for toilet paper and toilet paper dispensers was issued to Seth Wheeler of Albany, New York.

It took a long time for toilet paper to be perfect. In the 1930s, people were still getting splinters from their toilet paper!

Hot Dogs and Hamburgers

Ever wonder where hot dogs and hamburgers came from? It's what Americans eat to celebrate their independence on the Fourth of July, but where did these foods come from? Both of these all-American foods originated in New York City!

While hot dogs weren't invented in the United States, American hot dogs got their start on Coney Island. This isn't surprising, considering a trip to Coney Island is incomplete without stopping at Nathan's Famous hot dogs. But did you know that Nathan's wasn't the first Coney Island hot dog stand?

A German immigrant named Charles Feltman has been credited with inventing hot dogs on a bun (though his original "hot dogs" were actually pork sausages on a bun). Feltman originally started out his business in 1867 in the form of a push-cart stand. His hot dogs came to be known as Coney Island's red hots and sold for ten cents. Feltman later opened a restaurant, along with an entire empire that took up a street of the seaside town.

In 1916, one of Feltman's former employees changed everything. Nathan Handwerker, a Polish-American, was encouraged by his friends Eddie Cantor and Jimmy Durante to open a competing business. Handwerker saved up $300 and opened his own hot dog stand called Nathan's Famous. He used his wife Ida's hot dog recipe and sold the hot dogs for five cents each. Before long, his hot dogs were the most popular on Coney Island and began to gain popularity through the rest of the United States.

The story of how hamburgers came to be is a little less clear. It has been said that in the 1820s, restaurants throughout New York City began to serve Hamburg-style steak in a bowl with breadcrumbs and onions. The idea was to draw German immigrants, who journeyed to America from Hamburg. Eventually, restaurants began to serve Hamburg-style steak on bread and named it the "hamburger."

The Bloody Mary

Have you ever wondered who invented the Bloody Mary cocktail?

The origin of the Bloody Mary isn't entirely known. Here's what we *do* know: in the United States, the cocktail got its start in New York City. What we don't know for sure is who actually invented the drink.

A bartender named Henry Zbikiewicz at New York's 21 Club claimed that he invented the cocktail in the 1930s.

However, Fernand Petiot claimed that he invented the Bloody Mary in the early 1920s. At the time, he was working at the New York Bar in Paris, France, which was frequented by Ernest Hemingway. The bar, which was later renamed Harry's New York Bar, claimed the drink was created at the spur of the moment. He then said he began to make the drink New York's St. Regis Hotel's King Cole Role. In 1964, he told *The New Yorker* his secret recipe. He also said the hotel was serving 100-150 Blood Mary's every day.

So, who invented the Bloody Mary in the USA? Who knows. All we know is that it did come from New York City.

General Tso's Chicken

It's a popular item on Chinese food menus across the United States, but do you know how General Tso's chicken started out?

Although there are several claims circulating out there involving the creation of General Tso's chicken, Peng's Restaurant on East 44th Street in New York claims that it was the first to serve the menu item.

It all started with a Taiwanese chef named Peng Chang-Kuei. Peng was forced to flee Taiwan during the Chinese Civil War.

In the 1990s, Peng opened a restaurant in Hunan, a province in China. He included General Tso's as a menu item. However, the local people found the recipe too sweet. Peng later closed the restaurant.

Peng later moved to New York where he opened Peng's in 1973. After he added sugar to his original General Tso's recipe, the menu item became a hit! A 1977 review of Peng's General Tso chicken called it "a stir-fried masterpiece."

It has long been rumored that General Tso's chicken was a favorite of General Tso of the Qing Dynasty. However, there is nothing to prove whether or not that this is actually true.

Air Conditioning

Willis Carrier created the "Apparatus for Treating Air" in 1902. However, his system wasn't created for people! The "Apparatus for Treating Air" was originally designed to prevent the humidity from causing the paper to warp at a printing company in Bushwick, Brooklyn. It was an added bonus that the workers were kept comfortable in the summer heat.

Prior to Carrier's invention, people used to wrap buildings in cloth soaked in melted ice water with a fan that blew hot air. While this cooling method was effective, it wasn't practical as it required more than 250,000 pounds of ice each month.

ATMs

The first money-dispensing device was introduced in New York in 1939 by Luther George Simjian. The contraption was called the Bankograph. Simjian convinced the City Bank of New York—which is today's Citibank—to test his invention for six months.

Surprisingly, the first ATM didn't go over too well. Unlike today's ATMs, the Bankograph didn't dispense cash. It only accepted coins, cash, and checks. Due to lack of customer acceptance, the Bank of New York didn't use the Bankograph past the trial period. The bank claimed the only ones using the device were prostitutes and gamblers.

While Simjian is credited with developing the ATM, the first ATM with cash features would later go on to be developed in the United Kingdom.

Credit Cards

Most of us can't live without credit cards. Wondering who to thank for those late fees or all that credit card debt? You can blame it all on John Biggins, a banker and credit promoter at the Flatbush National Bank in Brooklyn.

In 1946, Biggins created the "Charg-It" program, which allowed local retailers to offer credit to bank customers. The bank would pay the retailers and then collect the debt owed from the cardholders. The program, which was the first of its kind, would later be accepted throughout the country.

Potato Chips

Have you ever given any thought to who invented potato chips? The inventor of one of America's favorite junk foods goes to George Crum, the head chef at a restaurant in Saratoga Springs, New York called Moon's Lake House.

Potato chips were born in 1853 when one of the people dining at the restaurant was unsatisfied with how thick Crum's french fries were. The customer also claimed the fries were too moist and didn't have enough salt.

In an attempt at insulting the customer, Crum sliced up some really thin potatoes, fried them to a crisp, and drenched them in salt. The customer ended up loving the invention, leading to "Saratoga Chips."

George Crum later went on to meet Herman Lay—the same Herman Lay who would go on to become co-founder of the Frito-Lay company. The rest is history!

Christmas

Did you know that Christmas the way it's celebrated in the United States today came from New York? Obviously, Christmas itself didn't originate from New York. However, the idea of a commercialized Christmas involving giving gifts did.

A little-known fact is that Christmas was once banned in the United States by the Puritans in 1659. People were actually forced to (gasp) work during the Christmas holiday. People who were caught celebrating or feasting were even fined five shillings.

In the early 1800s, early settlers of New York City (which at the time was New Amsterdam) decided to bring back the Dutch tradition of Sinterklaas, including gift-giving. Clement Clarke Moore wrote a poem in 1823 called "A Visit from St. Nicholas," which most of us know today as "Twas the Night Before Christmas." Moore's poem brought about the idea of Santa riding a sleigh that was pulled by reindeer and entering people's homes through the chimney to deliver gifts. A cartoonist named Thomas Nast later developed an image of Santa Claus, which over time led to the man with the white beard and red suit that we all recognize today.

New York City store owners quickly caught on to the fact that Christmas could be commercially beneficial. They all began to promote the holiday. Even back in 1830, the week before Christmas became the busiest shopping season of the year.

State Fairs and Ferris Wheels

The New York State Fair was the first state fair to ever take place. Today, it's the longest-running state fair in the United States.

The first Ferris wheel in the United States appeared at the state fair back in 1849. The Ferris wheel, which was made from iron and oak, was 50 feet high and had wooden buckets that were large enough for four adults or six children. It used ropes and was operated by hand power. It was developed by the operator of the State Fair, along with a carpenter from Scotland who had seen a similar Ferris wheel design in Edinburgh.

Soon, New York City will also be home to the second tallest Ferris wheel in the world! The New York Wheel, which is expected to be completed by 2018, will be 630-feet tall. With its location on Staten Island, the New York Wheel is expected to be one of the city's greatest landmarks. It will be one of the best places in the city to view the New York skyline, New York Harbor, and the Statue of Liberty.

Spaghetti and Meatballs

Spaghetti and meatballs are a staple in most American households. Today, people enjoy everything from zoodles (zucchini noodles) and meatballs to gluten-free spaghetti. But have you ever wondered where the original spaghetti and meatballs recipe came from? We'll give you one hint: it's not Italy.

In fact, people from Italy have been known to mock spaghetti and meatballs, recognizing the recipe as *non*-Italian! In Italy, meatballs are never served with spaghetti. The only time restaurants serve them is for American tourists.

Italy does have meatballs, but they're usually smaller than American meatballs. They're also made from different types of meats, such as turkey or fish, versus the American version of ground beef meatballs. Only certain regions of Italy, including Sicily, serve meatballs with pasta. In those instances, they're usually served with egg-based pasta or rigatoni.

So, where did spaghetti and meatballs come from? Italians who immigrated to Little Italy in New York City in the 1880s through the 1920s created the recipe. In America, food was much cheaper and the meat was more plentiful, which allowed them to eat meatballs over pasta. Spaghetti was one of the only Italian ingredients that were available in the United States at the time. They made marina sauce because canned tomatoes were easily found at local grocers.

The first recipe for spaghetti and meatballs was published in the 1920s by the National Macaroni Manufacturers Association (now known as the National Pasta Association).

Thomas' English Muffins

Thomas' is known for its English muffins, bagels, and other bread products. Did you know the company got its start in New York City?

It all started back in 1880 when an English immigrant named Samuel Thomas opened a bakery in New York City. He created the Original "Nooks & Crannies" English muffin that so many Americans have come to enjoy today.

The secret to his English muffins was all in the cooking process. Thomas used a griddle to create an English muffin that was soft on the inside and crunchy on the outside. Although Thomas is credited for the first English muffin, his cooking method had been used in the past by other people.

It has been said that Thomas was actually trying to create a crumpet but accidentally invented the English muffin instead. Due to their name, many people believe that English muffins were popular in England before making their way to America but this isn't true.

When Samuel Thomas died in 1919, Thomas' was left to his daughter and nephews. George Weston Bakeries later went on to buy the company.

Today, Thomas' English muffins are the #1 best-selling English muffins in the United States. The company also now owns Sara Lee, Entenmann's, Stroehmann, and Arnold bread.

Red Velvet Cake

Red velvet cake, which usually consists of layers and white cream cheese frosting, has a cult-like following. Do you know how the recipe got to be so popular?

Red velvet cake got its start in 1959 at the Waldorf Astoria in New York City. It was called the "Waldorf Astoria Cake" on the hotel's menu. One guest at the hotel liked the cake so much that she asked for the recipe. Although the hotel gave it to her, she later discovered she'd been charged $100 for it. The woman was infuriated.

To get revenge on the hotel, the woman chain-mailed the recipe to hundreds of people. This helped the recipe gain popularity and sparked America's love for red velvet!

Bagels

It's often said that there's no bagel like a New York bagel.

The bagel has a long history in the Big Apple, dating back to the late 1800s when they were brought to New York by Eastern European Jewish immigrants.

Bagels were first produced in private bakeries owned by Jewish immigrants. By 1900, there were 70 bakeries in the Lower East Side alone. The International Beigel Bakers' Union was founded in 1907 to monopolize bagel production in New York City.

Zabar's and Russ & Daughters were both opened in the early 1900s. They are two of the most iconic bagel shops that were started by Jewish immigrants.

Over time, bagel shops were no longer owned only by Jewish immigrants.

New York bagels have come a long way since they first became popular in America. For starters, the New York Bagel, as we know it today, is nearly twice the size of early bagels in the Big Apple. This change happened in the 1980s.

Today, bagels in the city also come in so many different varieties—including some that may even surprise you. You can find everything from French toast to rainbow bagels with cream cheese options that range from chocolate chip cookie dough to bacon cheddar and everything in between!

Wondering what sets New York bagels apart from other bagels? It's believed that New York City's water may have to do with why bagels in the Big Apple are so much better than everywhere else. It's believed the city's water has just the right ratio of magnesium to calcium, which makes its bagels softer and, ultimately, chewier.

Random Facts

1. The first roller coaster could be found on Coney Island. The ride was created by LaMarcus Adna Thompson in 1884. Passengers had to get off the roller coaster halfway through the ride so the car could be switched to another track.

2. Teddy bears got their start in New York City. The inspiration behind the idea of the teddy bear was President Theodore Roosevelt's refusal to shoot an injured black bear when he was hunting. Morris and Rose Michtom, who owned a candy store in Brooklyn, sewed a plush bear. They called it "Teddy's bear," after Teddy Roosevelt. The toy became such a hit that the store stopped selling candy in order to focus on teddy bears.

3. Cronuts were invented by a New York City pastry chef named Dominique Ansel. The croissant-donut hybrid first came out in May 2013 and still draws in huge crowds at the Dominque Ansel Bakery!

4. Children's museums started out in New York City! The Brooklyn Children's Museum, which opened in 1899, was the first museum in the United States that was designed for children. The Brooklyn Museum was also the first museum to offer "hands-on" exhibits.

5. Stephen Bruce, who co-founded the restaurant Serendipity 3, came up with the recipe for frozen hot chocolate. He kept his recipe a secret for 40 years before revealing it: crushed ice, 14 different types of cocoa (types unknown), and whipped cream topping.

6. The club sandwich got its start at the Saratoga Club-House in Saratoga Springs, New York.

7. The Mr. Potato Head toy was invented by George Lerner, a Brooklyn native. His invention first came about when he made plastic accessories to stick on real potatoes. Hasbro purchased the invention and released the all-plastic version of the toy in

1964. Mr. Potato Head was the first toy to ever be advertised on TV.

8. In 1898, Nikola Tesla invented the world's first remote control. Of course, the first remote didn't control a television, considering the TV wasn't invented until 1927. So, what did the first remote control operate? A boat! At the time, nobody believed the technology could even exist.

9. A chef named Charles Ranhofer at Delmonico's restaurant in Manhattan came up with the first Baked Alaska recipe in 1867. He created the cake to celebrate the United States purchasing Alaska from Russia, which is how it got its name.

10. The Reuben sandwich was created by Arnold Reuben, who was the owner of Reuben's Deli in 1914. As the story goes, an actress who was starring in one of Charlie Chaplin's films came into the deli feeling famished. She asked Arnold to make her a combination sandwich. He threw together the few ingredients which were left on the shelves of the deli, which resulted in corned beef, Swiss cheese, and sauerkraut on rye bread with Russian dressing.

11. Sweet'n Low was founded by an entrepreneur from New York City named Benjamin Eisenstadt. He and his chemist son figured out a way to create saccharin form. Prior to Sweet'n Low, saccharin could only be manufactured in pill or liquid form. Eisenstadt named the artificial sweetener after the poem "Sweet and Low" by Alfred Tennyson.

12. Kodak was invented by a New Yorker! In 1884, George Eastman invented the roll film. Four years later, he would go on to create a push button camera. His camera was so easy to use that its motto was, "You press the button, we do the rest."

13. Tuxedos got their start in upstate New York. There was a village called Tuxedo Park, which was an exclusive resort that was founded by a guy named Pierre Lorillard IV. Lorillard, who was a tobacco tycoon wore a tailless black jacket and black

tie to a ball at the Tuxedo Club in 1886. People started to wear the fashion, which Lorillard named after the resort. The origins of the word "tuxedo" may surprise you. It came from an Algonquian word that means "round foot" or easy to surrender. It was an insult that was originally aimed at the Wolf Tribe of New York.

14. Loafers have been a timeless and popular style of shoes. Loafers originated from Syracuse, New York. The design came from James Barrett's factory, which was well-known for its handmade products.

15. Jell-O originated from New York. Peter Cooper, who was well-known for developing the first steam-powered locomotive, developed powdered gelatin. Cooper's invention was patented in 1845. Pearle Bixby Wait from LeRoy, New York got a trademark for Jell-O in 1897. He and his wife added colors and fruit flavorings to the gelatin dessert.

16. New York is to thank for one of America's most popular antibiotics. Research that was performed at Bristol Laboratories in Syracuse helped with the development of the first synthetic form of penicillin. Though they were able to develop it in 1948, the first manufactured synthetic penicillin didn't come about until 1958. The drug was mass produced for the Armed Forces.

17. Eggs Benedict was invented in New York City. It's widely known as a hangover cure and for good reason! It was created by a hungover man who was staying at the Waldorf Astoria. The maître d was so impressed with the man's order that it was added to the hotel's menu, with a couple of changes: ham and an English muffin!

18. The fried Twinkie originated from Brooklyn! They were created by an England native named Christopher Sell. They came about because Sell tried deep-frying a lot of food items until he found something that tasted good. You can still find fried Twinkies at The Chip Chop Shop in Park Slope.

19. Scrabble was designed by an architect named Alfred Mosher Butts, who was a resident of Jackson Heights, Queens. Butts, who was a big fan of anagrams, designed the game in 1931. There's a street sign on Butt's corner in Queens, which honors the game's letter-scoring system.

20. The Tom Collins cocktail drink originated from New York City. It came about in 1874 when a guy played a prank on one of his friends at a bar in the city. He told him that a guy named Tom Collins had been in the bar talking about him. His friend went looking for the guy. The prank continued and many people started looking for the elusive "Tom Collins." The prank, which later came to be known as the Great Tom Collins Hoax of 1874, spread to Pennsylvania and St. Louis, Missouri. Newspapers printed alleged sightings of Tom. A bartender in New York City eventually created the cocktail, which is made of gin, lemon juice, sugar, and carbonated water. Whenever anyone would come into the bar looking for the famous Tom Collins, they would unknowingly be ordering the drink.

Test Yourself – Questions and Answers

1. Which food *did not* get its start in America in New York?

   a. Hot dogs
   b. Corn dogs
   c. Pizza

2. Who started Nathan's Famous hot dogs in Coney Island?

   a. Nathan Handwerker
   b. Nathan Famous
   c. Charles Feltman

3. Which popular camera brand was started in New York by an inventor named George Eastman?

   a. Sony
   b. Canon
   c. Kodak

4. Which popular cake recipe originated from the Astoria Waldorf?

   a. Red velvet cake
   b. German chocolate cake
   c. Pineapple upside down cake

5. Which popular junk food came from New York?

   a. Corn chips
   b. Popcorn
   c. Potato chips

Answers

1. b.

2. a.

3. c.

4. a.

5. c.

CHAPTER FIVE

NEW YORK'S UNSOLVED MYSTERIES, SUPERNATURAL, AND OTHER WEIRD FACTS

Have you ever wondered what unsolved mysteries have happened in New York? Do you know what creepy folklore haunts the Empire State? Some of these facts may shock you. Some of them will give you goosebumps. Some of them are just plain weird. Read on to find out more about some of the creepiest and most bizarre things that have happened in New York.

"Amityville Horror" Took Place on Long Island

You've probably seen the movie *The Amityville Horror* or its remake. The movies and the book of the same name are based on a real-life story that took place in a house located at 112 Ocean Avenue on Long Island.

Whether you've seen the film or not, chances are there are a lot of details about the story you've never heard about.

When people think of "Amityville Horror," they mainly think of the Lutzes' version of the tale: moving into a haunted house. But before George and Kathy Lutz (and her three children) moved into the Amityville Horror house, a dark tragedy took place there.

Ronald DeFeo Jr. shot his parents, two brothers, and two sisters in the house. He murdered his family members in their beds.

Just one month after Ronald DeFeo Jr. was convicted of the killings, the Lutz family moved in.

The DeFeo's furniture was still in the house when the Lutzes moved in. They paid an additional $400 for the furniture.

The Lutz family only lived in the house for 28 days. According to an interview given by George Lutz in 2005, the family didn't know they would never return to the house. The children were frightened one night, and the Lutzes called a priest who was aware of their situation. He suggested they go somewhere for the night, but they never returned.

A few weeks after the Lutzes left the house, paranormal investigators Ed and Lorraine Warren took a photograph in the house. The picture, which has since been nicknamed the "Demonic Boy Photograph," shows a child with glowing eyes—even though there were no kids in the house at the time of their investigation. Some believe John Matthew DeFeo's spirit is in the photo.

Although this might disappoint some people, there's a good possibility the Lutzes' experience in the Amityville Horror house may have been a hoax. William Weber, Ronald DeFeo Jr.'s lawyer, publicly stated that he and the Lutzes created the story together to "make a splash."

Even so, George and Kathy Lutz maintained that it was true until their deaths in 2006 and 2004, respectively. The children have also maintained the story over the years, though one of the sons claimed that George greatly exaggerated what went on inside the house.

If you want to get a peek at the house, know that the address has since changed at the request of the new owners. The house is now located at 108 Ocean Avenue.

Interestingly, there haven't been any reports of ghosts since the house has been under new ownership.

Nessie's Cousin May Live in Lake Champlain

It's believed that the long-lost cousin of Nessie, the Loch Ness Monster, can be found in New York's Lake Champlain. The monster, who has been nicknamed "Champ" or "Champy," has been sighted long before Nessie was ever spotted in Scotland.

The first sightings of the legendary Lake Champlain monster date back to when the Native American tribes in the area—the Iroquois and the Abenaki—spoke of seeing the creature. The Abenaki tribe called it "Tatoskok," which means "big serpent."

It has been said that the first European to report seeing Champ was Samuel de Champlain, who Lake Champlain was named after, in 1609. However, no evidence proves this to be true. It has been claimed that Samuel de Champlain described Champ as "a 20-foot serpent thick as a barrel, and a head like horse," but this quote has been found to be fake.

More than 300 sightings of Champ have been reported. To this day, people continue to report sightings.

One of the most famous sightings of the lake monster was by Sandra Massi in 1977. Massi photographed Champ, who bore a striking resemblance to Nessie in the photos.

The Fauna Communications Institute in collaboration with the *Discovery Channel* recorded noises coming from Lake Champlain resembling a beluga whale or dolphins. Beluga whales and dolphins do not live in Lake Champlain.

In 2005, a fisherman and his stepson captured video footage of Champ. Most people who have viewed the footage see the head and neck of a creature that resembles a Plesiosauria. Two former FBI forensic image analysts said the video was real and hadn't been manipulated.

The legend of Champ has drawn tourists to the Lake Champlain region. In fact, the "Champ Day" festival is celebrated in the region every July.

So, what exactly *is* Champ? Some experts believe Lake Champlain might have a breeding population of Tanystropheids, a reptile from the Middle Triassic period that resembles a long-neck dinosaur. Others believe he might be a member of the crocodile family, a Longnose Gar, a Lake Sturgeon, or even a large snapping turtle.

Whatever Champ is, it seems pretty convincing that *something* creepy is lurking in those waters.

A Neighborhood Called "The Hole" in Queens is a Body Dumping Ground

An area in the neighborhood of Ozone Park, Queens is known as "The Hole." The area spans 10 blocks between Queens and Brooklyn.

Few people actually want to live in The Hole. The land is so sunken in that it doesn't drain into the New York sewer system, making it prone to floods. The few people who live in the area keep boats in order to get from place to place during these floods.

However, the flooding isn't the only reason The Hole has hardly any residents. Ozone Park is home to John Gotti, head of the Gambino organized crime family. In 2004, one of Gotti's neighbors went missing after he accidentally hit John Gotti's son. This led to an FBI investigation, which uncovered a deep, dark secret.

The Hole was being used as a mobster burial ground. The two deceased mobsters were Philip "Philly Lucky" Giaccone and Dominick "Big Trin" Trinchera. They had been "dispatched" by John Gotti.

At the time, federal agents believed there were more bodies to be found in The Hole, but none were uncovered.

This wasn't the first time bodies had been discovered in The Hole, however. In 1981, children who were playing in The Hole found a body. That body was Mob-related, too. It had turned out to be Alphonse "Sonny Red" Indelicato, a member of the Bonanno organized crime family.

An Heiress Disappeared from Fifth Avenue and No One Ever Saw Her Again

On December 12th, 1910, a wealthy heiress and socialite named Dorothy Arnold left her family home in the Upper East Side and went out onto Fifth Avenue.

Dorothy, who was the daughter of a wealthy perfume importer, ran a few errands and bumped into her friend who she had a short conversation with outside a bookstore around 2 p.m. No one ever saw Dorothy again.

Her family realized she was missing a few hours later when she didn't come home for dinner. In hopes of avoiding publicity, they avoided contacting the police right away. They hired a private investigator before turning to the police after six weeks.

The police and her family tracked her last moves from the day she vanished. Marriage records were checked to see if Dorothy had eloped and fled, but there was nothing on file.

The case garnered a huge amount of publicity. Newspapers throughout the world reported on Dorothy Arnold's disappearance and followed up with leads and tips every day. Tips came in from all over the world, likely due to the family's offering of a reward of $1,000 (which is equal to about $26,000 today).

People claimed to spot Dorothy throughout both the United States and in other countries, including Italy and Chile.

According to *The Evening World*, a shop owner claimed Dorothy came into his shop in 1911 for men's clothing as a disguise. He also claimed she asked about steamer fare.

The same year, Dorothy's father received a postcard. The card read, "I am safe." While her father said it looked like her handwriting, he believed someone had copied her writing style.

One popular theory was that Dorothy had been pregnant and died during complications from an abortion. Police investigated an illegally-operated abortion clinic run out of a basement in Bellevue,

Pennsylvania, which had been known as "The House of Mystery" because women disappeared after going to the clinic. One of the doctors who worked at the clinic claimed Dorothy Arnold had died there due to abortion complications. The doctor said that her body had been burned in the furnace like all of the other women who had gone missing.

Dorothy's father believed his daughter had been kidnapped and murdered.

George Griscom Jr., a guy who Dorothy had been romantically involved with, believed she had committed suicide due to her failure as an aspiring writer. She had received a rejection for a story she'd hoped to have published days before her disappearance.

After Dorothy's disappearance, George Griscom Jr. was vacationing in Italy. In early 1911, Dorothy's mother and her brother John went to Italy where Griscom Jr. was staying to interrogate him about any information regarding her disappearance, but Griscom claimed to know nothing. Griscom then spent thousands of dollars on newspaper ads asking Dorothy to come home and claimed he wanted to marry her once she was found.

In 1916, a prisoner in Rhode Island claimed to bury a wealthy woman in a cellar at the same time of Dorothy's disappearance. The prisoner claimed he'd been hired by a man named "Little Louie," whose description matched that of George Griscom Jr. No evidence proved the prisoner's claims to be true, however.

To this day, the disappearance of Dorothy Arnold remains unsolved.

New York is Home to One of the Most Haunted Towns in the United States

Did you know one of the most haunted towns in America is located in New York? You've probably heard of the town before. It was made popular when Washington Irving wrote "The Legend of Sleepy Hollow."

Although Irving's tale was fictional, some of it is based on true legends about the town of Sleepy Hollow. One of the true parts of the tale? The legend of the infamous "Headless Horseman." During the American Revolutionary War, a German soldier was captured and beheaded. It's long been said that a headless apparition—AKA the Headless Horseman—has been spotted throughout the grounds of Patriot Park. Another place you might spot him? The Old Dutch Church and Burial Grounds.

The Sleepy Hollow Cemetery is believed to be one of the town's most haunted places. A number of famous people are buried in the cemetery, including: Washington Irving, Andrew Carnegie, Walter Chrysler, Elizabeth Arden, and William Rockefeller. People have claimed to see apparitions in the cemetery and hear unexplained whispering.

These are just a few of the most haunted spots in Sleepy Hollow!

A Human Was Once on Display at the Bronx Zoo

One of the most bizarre moments in New York history is when the Bronx Zoo featured a human exhibit called "The Missing Link" in 1906. The exhibit featured Ota Benga, a man from the African Congo.

Benga came from a tragic background. His wife and children had been killed when there was an attack on his village. He was captured by slave traders to a man named Samuel Phillips Verner, who planned for Benga to be exhibited in the United States.

William Hornaday, the director of the Bronx Zoo, hired Ota Benga to maintain the animal habitats at first. When he realized people were more intrigued by Benga than they were in the animals, Hornaday set up an exhibit with him.

Benga took a liking to an orangutan in the zoo's Monkey House exhibit. Hornaday told him to hang his hammock there. On the first day of the exhibit, zoo visitors found Benga in the Monkey House. A sign was added to the exhibit that read, "The African Pygmy,

'Ota Benga'." The sign included Benga's height, weight, and other details.

People became outraged over the exhibit. They were infuriated by the zoo having a human on display like he was an animal. The zoo allowed Benga to roam the grounds at first before eventually removing him from zoo grounds altogether.

Verner wasn't able to find future employment for Benga. Benga was introduced to human society and later shot himself in the heart when World War I prevented him from returning to the Congo.

The American Museum of Natural History's Missing Jewels

The American Museum of Natural History was robbed on the night of October 29th, 1964. Two guys from Miami Beach broke into the JP Morgan Hall of Gems and Minerals and stole 24 gems.

Three noteworthy gemstones were taken during the jewelry heist. They were the Star of India, the largest sapphire in the world; the Midnight Star, the blackest sapphire in existence, and the De Long Star Ruby, the world's most flawless ruby.

It's been estimated that the 24 stolen gems are worth the equivalent of $3 million today.

The robbery showed the museum's security system wasn't working properly. The burglar alarm had been dead for months. The gem room's halls' windows were also left open two inches for ventilation and there were no burglar alarms in place.

The thieves were arrested shortly after the heist.

The Star of India, the Midnight Star, and the De Long Star Ruby were all recovered and have been returned to the American Museum of Natural History, where they can still be found. Unfortunately, 14 of the 24 stolen jewels have yet to be found.

John Lennon's Ghost May Haunt an Apartment Building in New York City

John Lennon was shot dead outside his apartment building, the Dakota, in Central Park West. Years after his death, his widow Yoko Ono reported seeing his ghost sitting at the piano in the apartment they lived in together. Creepy, right? Well, it gets creepier.

John Lennon isn't the only ghost that's been known to haunt the Dakota. In fact, Lennon claimed to see an apparition himself, who he nicknamed the Crying Lady Ghost.

Other Dakota residents have reported sightings of a ghost of a girl who's estimated to be around seven years old. She smiles, laughs, and greets people when they encounter her in the hallways.

Edward Clark, the original owner of the Dakota, is said to have had a strong interest in the paranormal. He used to frequently hold séances to communicate with the dead.

There May Be Buried Treasure on Liberty Island

It has been said that Captain William Kidd buried his treasure on Liberty Island. Captain Kidd lived in New York City for four years in a house on Pearl Street, which would have allowed him to keep an eye on the island.

Captain Kidd was later hung in London in 1701 on one count of murder and five counts of piracy.

Although there may be buried treasure on Liberty Island, people have been looking for it for three centuries and turned up nothing.

There is a legend that says the treasure may be protected by ghosts, however. It has been said that a century after Captain Kidd's deaths, soldiers from Fort Wood tried to locate the treasure. They went to a psychic and followed her instructions on where to find it. When they dug in the area she'd led them to, their shovels hit a chest—and then a skull. An apparition rose from the ground with a cutlass in hand. The soldiers fled the area. When they returned, the chest was gone.

Captain Kidd was known for burying his treasures throughout the world. In 2015, an archeologist discovered buried treasure in Madagascar that is believed to have belonged to Kidd. Who knows? Maybe there *is* something on Liberty Island!

The Mystery of the Empire State Building Bermuda Triangle

You've probably heard of the Bermuda Triangle, an area in the Atlantic Ocean that is known to wreak havoc on a ship's navigation system and swallow ships. Well, the Big Apple once had a similar phenomenon a few years back.

In 2008, anytime people would drive within a five-block radius of the Empire State Building, their cars would suddenly die and not restart again. Every day, one tire and auto center in Hell's Kitchen would pick up the cars and move them a few blocks away. The cars would miraculously restart again.

It's believed that the radio signals for the broadcast beacon on the Empire State Building's tower were disabling the vehicles' alarm systems and preventing them from being able to restart. Seems like a pretty good theory, right?

Around 2013, the phenomenon suddenly stopped happening... but the broadcast beacon is still there. Strange, right? We think so, too.

The Legend of Cropsey: The Bogeyman Who Became Real

Beginning in the early 70s, there was an urban legend about "Cropsey," the bogeyman of Staten Island. Cropsey was said to be a homicidal madman.

Parents used to warn their children about Cropsey to convince them to be good. It helped them get their kids inside in time for curfew.

Even though Cropsey was an urban legend, girls in the area were going missing at the time.

There were several stories about Cropsey. In one of them, he was an escaped mental patient who was said to have a hook for a hand. He would drag children back to the abandoned ruins of Seaview Hospital, a former tuberculosis sanitarium.

Another one of the stories involved a camp located across from Willowbrook State School, a (now abandoned) mental institution on Staten Island. Cropsey was said to be a well-respected member of the community who went mad when his son allegedly died at the camp. To get his revenge, he would scour the woods for campers to kill. Camp counselors would use the story to get campers to behave.

This urban legend turned true in 1988 when Andre Rand, a former janitor at Willowbrook State School was found guilty of kidnapping four girls. The body of one of his alleged victims, Jennifer Schweiger, was found buried behind the former mental institution. The other three girls' bodies were never found. The jury could not reach a verdict on murder charges but was able to find him guilty of kidnapping. In 2005, he was tried again for the kidnapping of another girl who went missing in 1981. Rand was again found guilty.

Police believed Rand took part in Satanism and used the children for sacrifices. It was also believed that he may have passed the children around to his homeless and mentally disabled friends who lived in Willowbrook's underground tunnel system.

Andre Rand is currently serving 25 years to life in prison. In 2037, Rand is eligible for parole.

A documentary called *Cropsey* was released in 2009 and centers on both the urban legend and Andre Rand's conviction. Two movies— *The Burning* and *Madman*—were based on the urban legend of Cropsey.

A Woman Went Missing After Investigating the NYC Underground Vampire Community, Never to Be Seen Again

On July 16th, 1996, a freelance journalist named Susan Walsh disappeared from her apartment complex. She left her son with her ex-husband, who lived downstairs. Walsh was never seen again.

Early investigations centered on Walsh's ex-husband and the boyfriend she was living with. The page for July had been torn out of the calendar in her apartment, which had initially led investigators to believe that one of the men was behind her death. Although her ex-husband refused to let the police do forensic testing in their home, both he and her boyfriend were ruled out as suspects.

Another theory was that she was being stalked. Days before her disappearance, Walsh had been recorded in a group interview for a documentary her friend was working on, called *Stripped*. The documentary was about women working in the sex industry, and Walsh was a former exotic dancer. In the recording, she had mentioned having a "stalker."

Walsh didn't tell anyone who she thought the stalker was, but 10 years later, the *New York Post* published an article stating that Walsh's boyfriend at the time of her disappearance claimed another one of her ex-boyfriends had been stalking her.

Many believe Susan Walsh's investigative journalism may have had to do with her disappearance. Walsh had written an article for *The Village Voice* in which she claimed the Russian Mafia owned a strip club chain and were forcing young girls into the sex industry. Some believed the Russian Mafia was responsible for her disappearance.

But the most intriguing theory of all links her disappearance to the New York City underground vampire community. During the weeks leading up to her disappearance, Walsh had been working on an article about the vampire community in Manhattan. The article ultimately ended up being rejected.

Is it possible that Susan Walsh got too close to the vampire cult? Some have even wondered if she might have joined them, though her family claimed she would have never left her son or without letting anyone know where she was going.

An author and vampire expert named Katherine Ramsland went undercover in the underground vampire community to try to find out what may have happened to Walsh. She later wrote a book about it called *Piercing the Darkness: Undercover with Vampires in America Today*.

Ramsland claimed that the underground vampire community in Manhattan was ultimately harmless. They took part in consensual blood sharing, blood consumption, and other unique fetishes, but Ramsland doesn't believe the vampire community had anything to do with Walsh's disappearance.

Ramsland does note that the vampire community does gain benefits from the public viewing them as a threat. Several people from the vampire community had committed crimes. Could Susan Walsh have just met the wrong person from the cult at the wrong time?

Walsh's disappearance was featured on *Unsolved Mysteries*. Her disappearance remains an unsolved mystery to this day.

The Legend of the Hudson River Ghost Ship

Well, here's a different kind of urban legend for you. Forget about Bigfoot, vampires or UFOs. Ever hear of the Hudson River Ghost Ship? It's also been called the Hudson Valley Ghost Ship or the Brooklyn Ghost Ship. Whatever you want to call it, the legend is pretty creepy.

Ever since New York was known as New Amsterdam, there have been reports of a mysterious ghost ship floating down the Hudson River.

It has been said the ship appears without a flag and in the form of an apparition. Many believe the ship is the ghost of the Half Moon, Henry Hudson's ship which was destroyed in 1618. Others have theorized that the ship may be the ghost of an old prison ship. Whatever the case, sightings are reported to this day.

One man who reported seeing the Hudson River Ghost Ship says it's a wooden ship with three empty masts. The eeriest part about his description was that the ship was silent until it was about 50 feet away from him.

Over the years, the ship has come to be known as the "The Storm Ship." The ship is said to appear just prior to a storm sets in. Some sailors believe seeing the ship means bad weather is coming and take it as a sign to stay off the waters. Some even believe the ship appears before someone dies.

We're pretty sure that if we saw the ghost ship, we'd be nowhere near the water!

The Wall Street Bombing Mystery

Did you know there was a terror attack in New York City that happened long before the September 11th attacks? Coincidentally, this attack happened during the month of September, too.

On September 20th, 1920, a bomb exploded from a horse-drawn wagon in front of 23 Wall Street. The wagon had been loaded with 500 pounds of small iron weights and dynamites.

Thirty-eight people and one horse were killed from the attack, with hundreds more being injured from the shrapnel and glass that fell out of building windows.

No one took credit for the bombing. At the time, many people believed the communists were responsible for the attack, but no person or group ever claimed responsibilityfor the terrorist attack.

The city was anxious to reopen Wall Street the following day, which resulted in important evidence being destroyed. An investigation that lasted three years turned up nothing.

In 1944, the FBI said they believed Italian anarchists were responsible for the bombing, but even this theory has never really been proven.

We may never know who was responsible for the Wall Street bombing.

The Hotel Chelsea is Believed to be Haunted

The Hotel Chelsea in Manhattan is said to be one of the most haunted spots in New York City. The hotel, which has had a number of celebrity guests, tends to attract a lot of people who are on the hunt for ghosts.

The fact that the Chelsea might be haunted isn't all that surprising, considering it's dark and tragic past.

Sid Vicious from the Sex Pistols is believed to have stabbed his girlfriend, Nancy Spungen, at the Chelsea in 1978. He was arrested and set to stand trial for her murder, but he overdosed on heroin in 1979. People have reported seeing and hearing Sid Vicious and Nancy Spungen around the hotel floors.

Elevators are said to mysteriously stop at random floors. Legend has it that it's the ghost of Sid getting on the elevator because he's too lazy to take the stairs.

Famous poet Dylan Thomas also died at the Chelsea in 1953. His death was caused by pneumonia. Guests have reported seeing Thomas's face near Room 206, the room he died in.

Other people have reported hearing high-pitched screams and footsteps throughout the hotel. In 2009, three women captured skeletons in a photo in the closet, even though there wasn't actually a skeleton in the room. They claimed the lights in their room kept flickering on and off, the sink kept turning on and off, and there were strange bubbles that rose from the drain.

Don't believe it? The only way to find out is to spend a night at the hotel yourself!

Random Facts

1. There was one unsolved homicide in New York City on the day of the September 11th attacks. Henry Siwiak, a Polish immigrant, was shot in Brooklyn. He has been named "the last person killed in New York on 9/11," but his death wasn't relevant to the attacks. It's believed that the circumstances behind his murder may have been solved if so much police attention hadn't been diverted to the 9/11 attacks. It has been theorized that his killer might have believed he was responsible for the attacks since he was wearing camouflage at the time of his death and spoke poor English.

2. There was a riot in New York City in 1922 over straw hats. Yes, you read that right. People fought. Over straw hats. Why? Well, it was believed that straw hats were only appropriate summer attire. Wearing them in autumn was considered not only inappropriate, many considered it to be offensive. Similar riots broke out through all of the Northeast, but the original riot started in thee Big Apple. The riot, which lasted for three days, happened when straw hat hating men terrorized the streets of New York. They snatched and destroyed straw hats, and young men got into fights. Thankfully, no one died during the riot, but there were several injuries.

3. A common fear among New Yorkers is alligators in the sewage system. These fears aren't entirely baseless—there have been 12 sightings of alligators in New York City sewers over the years. People began to panic about coming face-to-face with an alligator in the Big Apple when the *New York Times* published an article titled "Alligator Found in Uptown Sewer" in 1935. It's believed the alligators found in the city were exotic pets that escaped down sewer grates and open manholes, but it's a widespread legend that people were flushing baby alligators down toilets.

4. There have been numerous reports of sightings of UFOs in New York over the years. In 2017 alone, there were 169 sightings across the entire state with 23% of those sightings hailing from the Big Apple. There were 39 sightings across New York City that year, according to the National UFO Reporting Center. Of those sightings, 10 were reported in Queens, nine were reported in Manhattan, three were reported in the Bronx, and two were reported on Staten Island. This is a switch from 2016 where the most UFO sightings were reported in Manhattan.

5. There's an urban legend known as Central Park's Skating Sisters. People have reported seeing apparitions at Wollman Rink in Central Park. It's believed they're the spirits of the Van der Voort sisters, Janet and Rosetta. Their overprotective father rarely allowed them to leave the family home without being accompanied, except for when they went ice skating. The sisters grew into lonely spinsters who died months apart in 1880. Since then, their ghosts have been spotted. The sisters are said to wear red and purple dresses with a bustle, and their feet don't touch the ground. It's also been said that they appear more when overprotective parents are around.

6. Richard Colvin Cox is the only cadet to have ever disappeared from the military academy in West Point, New York. He allegedly told his friends he was going to have dinner with a friend named George. Cox was never seen again. Police received an anonymous tip that a murderer named Robert Frisbee was linked to Cox's disappearance. Although Frisbee was in West Point at the time and matched George's description, no evidence linked him to Richard Colvin Cox.

7. A postal carrier named Joseph Brucato was caught hoarding 40,000 pieces of undelivered mail in the firetrap of his apartment. Brucato had been hoarding the mail for a decade. It included bills, birthday cards, junk mail, coupon booklets, and

anything else you can imagine. Brucato blamed his depression and alcoholism for his sticky fingers.

8. A widespread myth is that New York City is home to 8 million rats. If you suffer from a rat phobia, try not to worry *too* much when you're in the Big Apple. The Department of Health claims that there are really only 2 million rats in the city.

9. There have been numerous sightings of Big Foot and his tracks in Upstate New York. If he's out there, New Yorkers seem to be welcoming of him. There's a local ordinance to protect Sasquatch in Whitehall, New York, and two festivals in the area (The Sasquatch Calling Festival and the Chautauqua Lake Bigfoot Expo) celebrate the legendary creature.

10. Mountain lions no doubt exist in the wild, but it's been said that the cougar is extinct in the Northeastern region of the United States. People often report mountain lion sightings in Upstate New York. It's even been rumored that the Department of Environmental Conservation releases mountain lions into the wild to keep the deer population under control. The DEC denies these claims and says that any isolated sightings in New York have been mountain lions that were previously being held captive or one incident in which a cougar traveled 1,800 miles from South Dakota to New York state.

11. Arnold Rothstein was murdered in New York City in 1928. Rothstein was a kingpin of the Jewish mob who was well-known for gambling and racketeering. Rothstein was most famous for fixing the World Series in 1919. He allegedly paid the players of the Chicago White Sox to deliberately lose the World Series so that he would win $350,000. Rothstein was never charged with the crime, however. In 1928, Rothstein was shot in the stomach when he walked into a room at the Park Central Hotel for a poker game. Although Rothstein survived for a few days, he never told anyone who had shot him—though it was

suspected that he was assassinated by someone who he owed money, as he owed more than $500,000 in gambling debts.

12. An urban legend says there was once a time traveler in Times Square. In 1950, a man dressed in clothing from the Victorian era randomly appeared in the middle of the intersection. He is said to have appeared confused and disoriented. The man was hit and killed by a taxi. At the morgue, it was discovered that the man had letters and banknotes in his pocket with the year 1876 written on them. The paper didn't appear worn or aged.

13. In Rochester, New York, there's a legend about a lady in white. As the tale goes, the woman's teenage daughter went missing after a walk one day. The woman spent every day walking along the shores of Lake Ontario in search of her daughter before eventually jumping off the cliff and into the lake to commit suicide. Today, teenagers who go to the lake claim to see her ghost.

14. Today, violent crime rates are the lowest they've ever been in New York City. In 2017, there were only 290 homicides in the Big Apple. This is the lowest number since the 1940s. In the 1980s and early 1990s, violent crime rates spiked due to a crack epidemic in New York City.

15. The Landmark Theater in Syracuse, New York is believed to be haunted by the ghost of a woman who died when she fell off a balcony.

16. In 2003, people were frightened to learn a tiger was being kept in an apartment in Harlem. Antoine Yates got the tiger, which he called Ming, when it was just a cub. The cub eventually grew into a 500-pound tiger who ate buckets of chicken every day. Yates got Ming a companion: a 7-foot alligator named Al. Yates was caught with the tiger after it attacked a rescued house cat. The veterinary hospital let authorities know the cat's wounds were suspicious.

17. Yates wasn't the first to keep a wildcat in the city. Back in the 1950s, a gangster named Crazy Joe Gallo kept a lion in the

basement of a club owned by Mondo, a "midget mascot" for the Mafia. Joe Gallo used to try to intimidate people by taking the lion for walks through the neighborhood.

18. Three men pretended to be cops at a GameStop on Staten Island so they could skip the lines to get their copies of *Grand Theft Auto V*. They were later pulled over and charged with criminal impersonation.

19. A seventeen-year-old in Bushwick, Brooklyn was charged with terrorism after he posted an emoji of a police officer in between two emojis of guns on his Facebook wall. The NYPD claimed the "terroristic" emoji threats made them fear for their safety and public safety.

20. The Rolling Hills Asylum in East Bethany, New York is believed to be haunted. Patients who have died at the mental institution are believed to haunt the floors.

Test Yourself – Questions and Answers

1. Who is the first European who allegedly saw the Lake Champlain monster?

    a. Henry Hudson
    b. Samuel de Champlain
    c. Dylan Thomas

2. Captain William Kidd's buried treasure might be found where?

    a. "The Hole"
    b. Staten Island
    c. Liberty Island

3. There's been panic about which of the following animals being found in New York City's sewers?

    a. Alligators
    b. Snakes
    c. Tigers

4. Which famous person died at the Chelsea Hotel?

    a. Dylan Thomas
    b. Sid Vicious
    c. Arnold Rothstein

5. The legendary Staten Island bogeyman was named:

    a. "Little Louie"
    b. Cropsey
    c. Bogey

Answers

1. b.
2. c.
3. a.
4. a.
5. b.

CHAPTER SIX

NEW YORK SPORTS: BASEBALL, FOOTBALL, AND MORE!

You probably know New York is home to the most popular baseball team in the United States, but do you know the legend behind why their uniforms have pinstripes? Do you know which international sporting event has been held in New York twice? Do you know which athletes are from the Empire State? Here, you'll find the answers to all of these questions, along with other New York sports facts!

Mike Tyson's Career Started Out at a Juvenile Detention Center in New York

Mike Tyson, former heavyweight champion, is considered to be a legend. Did you know his career was started in New York?

Mike Tyson was born in Brownsville, Brooklyn in 1966. Tyson grew up in and around neighborhoods with crime rates. He often got into fights with kids who made fun of his lips and high-pitched voice. By the time he was 13, Tyson had been arrested nearly 40 times.

Tyson ended up in the Tyron School for Boys, a juvenile detention center in Johnstown, New York. It was there that Tyson began to box. His talent was discovered by a former boxer named Bobby Stewart.

Stewart took Tyson under his wing and trained him. Stewart later introduced Tyson to trainer and boxing manager Cus D'Amato. D'Amato ran a gym in the Catskills. When Mike Tyson's mom died when he was just 16 years old, D'Amato became his legal guardian.

Mike made his first boxing debut when he was 18 in Albany, New York. Tyson defeated his opponent, Hector Mercedes, in a knock-out during the first round. Tyson went onto win all but two of his first 28 fights before winning his first heavyweight championship in 1986.

After he was convicted of rape in 1992, people believed Tyson's career was over but it wasn't. In 1996, he went out to win the WBC and WBA titles.

In 2011, Mike Tyson was inducted into the Boxing Hall of Fame.

New York Has Hosted the Winter Olympics Twice

The Winter Olympics have been held in Lake Placid, New York twice.

The 3rd Winter Olympics were held in Lake Placid back in 1932. The games were opened by Franklin D. Roosevelt, who was the Governor of New York at the time.

Some of the highlights from the 1932 Winter Olympics include:

- Eddie Eagan became the first and only Olympian who won gold medals in both the winter and summer Olympics. At the 1920 Summer Olympics, he won a gold medal in boxing. In 1932, he won the gold in bobsleigh.

- Three-time winning Olympic champion Sonja Henie won her second gold medal in figure skating.

- The United States won a total of 12 Olympic medals, half of which were gold medals.

In 1980, the 13th Winter Olympics were also held in Lake Placid. Highlights from that year include:

- Artificial snow was used in the Olympics for the very first time.

- The USA's men's hockey team won the gold medal, defeating the Soviet team 4-3. The team wasn't projected to win. Their achievement became internationally known as the "Miracle on Ice."

- Eric Heiden won four gold medals and set one world record in speed skating. He became the first Olympics champion to win all five of the speed skating events and the first of three to ever win five gold medals at the same Games. To date, Heiden still holds the record of being the only Olympics champion to win five gold medals at a single Winter Games.

- The People's Republic of China entered the Olympics for the first time.

- The games were opened by United States Vice President Walter Mondale, marking the last time the Olympics were opened by an American Vice President.

And There's a Lake Placid Olympic Museum!

You can visit the Lake Placid Olympic Museum, which honors the 1932 and 1980 Winter Olympic Games.

A number of artifacts can be found at the museum. Some of these include Olympic torches, antique ice skates, bobsled equipment, Olympic uniforms, medals, official Olympics posters, and more. You'll also find artifacts relating to the champions of the Olympics games from 1932 and 1980.

The museum also commemorates Charles Jewtraw, an Olympics gold medalist from the Lake Placid region. Jewtraw was the first speed skater to win a gold medal at the 1st Winter Olympics in 1924.

You can also visit the Olympic Center, which has been named the Herb Brooks Arena. This is where the "Miracle on Ice" took place!

The New York Yankees Weren't Always Called the Yankees

It's hard to imagine the New York Yankees being called anything other than the Yankees today, but did you know the team was once named something else first?

In 1901, the New York Yankees were founded in Baltimore, Maryland. John McGraw owned the team, which was known as the Baltimore Orioles. The American League voted to move the team to New York.

When the Baltimore Orioles moved to New York in 1903, their name was changed to the New York Highlanders. Their first stadium was at Hilltop Park in Manhattan.

Even though they were called the Highlanders, a lot of sportswriters began to refer to them as the "Yanks" or "Yankees" because they were in the American League.

In 1913, the team was renamed the Yankees. At this time, they moved to the Polo Grounds stadium, which they shared with the New York Giants.

The New York Yankees' Pinstripe Uniforms May Have Been Designed for Babe Ruth

While this is technically an urban legend, it seems to be commonly accepted as the truth. It's been said that Babe Ruth, who is undeniably the most famous baseball player of all-time, is the reason the New York Yankees have their pinstripe uniforms.

Babe Ruth was a pretty large guy, at least as far as baseball players go. Rumor has it that the team chose to go with pinstripe uniforms to help make Babe Ruth look thinner than he really was.

Some argue that this can't be true. The team initially adopted their pinstripe uniforms in 1912, back when they were still called the Highlanders. Babe Ruth didn't join the team until years later. Could it all be a total coincidence? We're not really sure, but the theory seems to be commonly accepted by most Yankees fanatics.

The New York Yankees and the New York Giants Were the First Teams to Retire Players' Numbers

When a baseball number is retired in the MLB or the NFL, it's to ensure no future players will wear them. People will only ever associate the number with that particular player.

Lou Gehrig was the first player in MLB history to have his number, 4, retired by the New York Yankees.

Today, Lou Gehrig is best-known for his disease, <u>amyotrophic lateral sclerosis</u>. That disease is now named after him and referred to simply as "Lou Gehrig's Disease."

The disease is what forced the former New York Yankees player into voluntary retirement on July 4th, 1939. The disease had begun to affect his performance. Gehrig died just two years later at the young age of 37.

Gehrig played for the Yankees from 1923 to 1939. During that time, he set a couple of records. He had the highest number of grand slams, which was later broken by Alex Rodriguez. He also held the record for the most consecutive games played at 2,130. That record wouldn't be broken for another 56 years when it was surpassed by Carl Ripken, Jr.

The second player in MLB history whose number was retired was Babe Ruth.

The New York Giants were also the first football team in the history of the NFL to retire a player's number. In 1935, Ray Flaherty left the team to become the head coach for the Redskins. His jersey number was the No. 1.

Babe Ruth Was Sold to the New York Yankees to Finance a Broadway Production

Today, he may be recognized as the New York Yankees' greatest legend, but unlike Lou Gehrig, Babe Ruth's careers didn't start and end with the Yankees.

Before he became a Yankees player, Ruth played for the Boston Red Sox first. In 1919, the New York Yankees bought him for more than $125,000, which is estimated to be about $1.45 million today.

Harry Frazee, owner of the Red Sox at the time, was also a theatrical agent, producer, and director. Rumor has it that the money Frazee sold Ruth to the Yankees for went to support the Broadway musical *No, No, Nanette*.

Although Babe Ruth was hesitant about leaving the Sox, he agreed to an initial two-year contract at $10,000 a year.

A lot of Red Sox fans blamed Frazee for selling Babe Ruth to the Yankees. His decision has been called "The Curse of the Bambino." Fans blamed the move for the lack of championships the Boston Red Sox accrued from 1918. The dry spell finally ended in 2004 when the team finally won against the St. Louis Cardinals in the October Classic.

A New York Baseball Team Has Played Some of the Longest Games in MLB History

Did you know that a New York baseball team has played not just one but *three* of the longest games in Major League Baseball history? And—surprise—it's not the New York Yankees!

The longest game played by the New York Mets was against the Atlanta Braves. The game lasted a total of eight hours, fifteen minutes. This includes rain delays.

When the game finally ended at 3:55 a.m., the Mets won 16-13.

New York is Home to the Baseball Hall of Fame

The National Baseball Hall of Fame and Museum is located in Cooperstown, New York.

The Hall of Fame was founded by Stephen Carlton Clark in 1939. Clark, who owned a local hotel, had hoped to draw tourists to Coopersburg, which had taken an economic hit during the Great Depression. Today, the Hall of Fame is considered the most significant establishment for the study of baseball in the United States.

So, what exactly can you expect to see at the museum? The exhibits contain thousands of MLB-related artifacts. You'll see pictures, watch video footage, and listen to audio that will help you learn more about the game.

Some of the many exhibits you'll find at the Baseball Hall of Fame and Museum include: Babe Ruth: His Life and Legend, Diamond Dreams: Women in Baseball, Pride and Passion: The African American Baseball Experience, Baseball at the Movies, Taking the Field: The 19th Century, and Today's Game.

You'll also want to check out the Hall of Fame Plaque Gallery, which is home to the bronze plaques to more than 300 players who have been inducted into the Hall of Fame.

The Super Bowl Has Been Won by New York Teams a Total of Five Times

Did you know the Super Bowl has been won by New York NFL teams five times? The New York Giants have won the Super Bowl four times, while the New York Jets have won it once.

The Giants won the Super Bowl during the following years:

1. 1987: The Giants defeated the Broncos by 39-20.

2. 1991: The Giants won against the Buffalo Bills with a score of 20-19.

3. 2008: The Giants beat the New England Patriots, winning 17-14.

4. 2012: The Giants defeated the New England Patriots by 21-17.

The Giants are tied with the Packers for the team with the 3rd highest number of Super Bowl titles.

The Jets won the Super Bowl in 1968. They defeated the Baltimore Colts with a score of 16-7.

The New York Rangers Are One of the Oldest Hockey Teams in the NHL

Did you know the New York Rangers were one of the first National Hockey League teams to be formed? The team was formed in 1926. It was one of the "Original Six"—the first six teams that entered the NHL. The other teams from the Original Six include: the Chicago Blackhawks, the Boston Bruins, the Detroit Red Wings, the Montreal Canadiens, and the Toronto Maple Leafs.

The New York Rangers began breaking records their very first season in the NHL. Their first season, they finished with the highest record in the league. Rangers player Bill Cook was also the highest scorer that season.

In 1928, the Rangers won their first Stanley Cup. They were the first—and remain the only—team to win the Stanley Cup within two years of joining the league.

In the first six years, the Rangers went to the finals four times.

Both Hockey and Basketball Games Are Played at Madison Square Garden

Did you know that both hockey games *and* basketball games are played at Madison Square Garden?

The MSG arena is home to both the NBA's New York Knicks and the NHL's New York Rangers. In fact, games from both teams have been played in the arena on the very same day. Wondering how that can even be possible?

During hockey season, the ice can be found underneath the stage that's used for the basketball court. It's kept frozen with insulated material.

While the New York Knicks play their home games at Madison Square Garden, they haven't always had the greatest luck there. Their second worst loss in team history happened at MSG when they lost by a 50 points loss to the Dallas Mavericks.

The New York Rangers' retired numbers can be found hanging from the rafters of the MSG arena. One of those numbers belonged to the most well-known Rangers player, Wayne Gretzky.

Nina Kuscsik is a Brooklyn Native

Nina Kuscsik, a native of Brooklyn, is famous for setting several historical records for female long-distance runners.

In 1970, she became the first female to run the New York City marathon. Kuscsik won the races two years in a row in 1972 and 1973. In 1972, she was also the first woman to win the Boston Marathon.

At the time, the prizes for winning the marathon for women were wreaths and a bowl of stew. Today, female marathon champions are now able to earn six-figure rewards—a feat that Kuscsik is often credited for.

Twelve-Time Olympic Medallist Ryan Lochte is From New York

Twelve-time Olympic medalist Ryan Lochte is a household name. He ranks second in men's swimming, just behind Michael Phelps. Did you know he's a New York native?

Ryan Lochte was born in Rochester, New York. He grew up in Bristol, New York and attended Bloomfield Central Schools until his family moved to Florida when Ryan was 12 years old.

Lochte first began to learn to swim when he was living in New York. His father was a swim instructor and often kicked Ryan out of his swim classes for misbehaving. It wasn't until junior high school that Ryan really got serious about learning to swim. He began to train harder after he lost at the Junior Olympics.

Ryan Lochte went on to six gold, three silver, and three bronze Olympic medals. Lochte holds the world record for short course 400-meter individual medley and both the long and short course 200-meter individual medley.

In 2016, Lochte sparked a lot of controversies when he lied about being robbed in Rio de Janeiro, Brazil during the Summer Olympics. Later accounts of the incident were different from the first version, which made people question the validity of the story. Lochte was put on probation from swimming for 10 months.

Baseball Might Become the State's Official Sport, But Not Every New Yorker Would Agree with That Decision

There have been talks about making baseball New York's official state sport. In a lot of ways, the decision makes sense.

New York is home to the Yankees, the most popular (and arguably the most successful) team in the MLB. Many of the greatest MLB players of all-time played for the Yankees, such as: Babe Ruth, Lou Gehrig, Joe DiMaggio, Yogi Berra, Derek Jeter, Mariano Rivera, and Alex Rodriguez—just to name a few of the *many*.

New York City is also one of only four metropolitan cities that's home to more than one baseball team.

There are also two minor league baseball teams in New York City.

The Baseball Hall of Fame is also located in New York and for good reason. New York City is rich with both baseball history and notorious legends.

But despite all that, football is the most followed sport in New York City! Many have argued that football should be the official state sport... if one is ever chosen at all.

Random Facts

1. NBA legend Michael Jordan was born in Brooklyn, New York, but his family moved to Wilmington when he was a toddler. Jordan later went on to defeat the New York Knicks when he played for the Chicago Bulls.

2. A number of records were set by the New York Yankees. The Yankees have won the most consecutive World Series titles — and they've done it more than once. They won between the years of 1996 and 2000 and then again between 1927 and 1932 and 1937 and 1941. Mariano Rivera has pitched the most World Series games. The only MLB players to ever hit three home runs in a World Series were Babe Ruth and Reggie Jackson. Derek Jeter is the only MLB player to be named both the All-Star MVP and the World Series MVP in the same year (2000). Orlando Hernandez has the highest strikeout rate of any MLB player who has pitched in the World Series. Yogi Berra held the record for playing more World Series games than any other Yankees player.

3. Although the New York Giants are considered a New York football team, they're based out of New Jersey. Their home stadium is MetLife Stadium in East Rutherford, New Jersey. When the team was founded in 1925, however, they played at Polo Grounds in Manhattan and later spent two decades playing at Yankees stadium. Currently, the only NFL team that actually plays in the Empire State are the Buffalo Bills.

4. The Buffalo Bills are the only New York NFL team who hasn't won a Super Bowl championship. They also are the only team in the NFL who has lost four Super Bowl games in a row in the years of 1990, 1991, 1992, and 1993. Their losses became a joke and the team lost a lot of fans due to their consecutive losses. At one point, it was even said that "bills" stood for "Boy, I love losing Super (Bowls)."

5. In 1927, the New York Yankees had a lineup known as "Murderers Row." It included: Babe Ruth, Lou Gehrig, Bob Meusel, Earle Combs, Mark Koenig, and Tony Lazzeri. These first six batters were carefully chosen to intimidate the opposing pitcher. Between the years of 1923 and 1962, they won 20 World Series titles with their all-star lineup.

6. The New York Yankees have the highest number of World Series titles of any team in the MLB. As of 2009, they've won a total of 27 World Series titles. The team with the second highest number of World Series titles is the St. Louis Cardinals, who only have 11 titles.

7. Nancy Lieberman was born in Brooklyn and was raised in Far Rockaway, New York. She has been considered one of the best women's basketball players of all-time. Lieberman was nicknamed "Lady Magic," which was a nod at "Magic" Johnson. Lieberman has been inducted into both the Basketball Hall of Fame and the Women's Basketball Hall of Fame.

8. The New York Jets were originally called the Titans of New York when they were established back in 1959. Like the Giants and Yankees, they first began playing at Polo Ground in Manhattan. When the team went under new ownership in 1963, they were renamed the Jets and were moved to Shea Stadium.

9. The New York Giants were the first football team in the NFL to retire a player's number.

10. As of 2012, the New York Giants had never lost an NFC Championship Game.

11. The New York Mets' full legal team name is the New York Metropolitan Baseball Club, Inc. At one point, owner Joan Whitney Payson considered naming the team the Bees, the Continentals, the Avengers, the Meadowlarks, or the Islanders.

12. The New York Giants' full legal team name is "The New York Giants Football Team." The word "Football" was added to

the name in 1937 because they wanted to differentiate themselves from the former New York Giants baseball team, who later moved to San Francisco.

13. Former New York Yankees manager Joe Torre was born in Brooklyn, New York. Under his management, the Yankees won four World Series titles. Prior to managing the Yankees, Torre played for the Milwaukee/Atlanta Braves, St. Louis Cardinals, and New York Mets. Torre holds the world record of scoring 2,000 hits as a baseball player and 2,000 wins as a baseball manager. As of 2018, Joe Torre was the chief baseball officer for the MLB.

14. The New York Knicks' legal franchise name is the New York Knickerbockers. Ned Irish, the owner of the team, wanted the name to be distinctive of New York. "Knickerbocker" originated from Washington Irving's pen name Diedrich Knickerbocker, under which he wrote a satirical history book called *A History of New-York from the Beginning of the World to the End of the Dutch Dynasty*. The name "Knickerbocker" had been used to describe Dutch settlers in New Amsterdam and later all New Yorkers. Irish had his staff members vote on the name of his basketball team and the New York Knickerbockers got the highest number of votes.

15. The Mets have a number of regional landmarks in its logo, such as Woolworth Building, the Empire State Building, and the United Nations Building. The bridge in the logo is meant to represent all five boroughs.

16. Country musician Garth Brooks tried out for the New York Mets in 2000. After a sad 0-17 at bat, the Mets opted not to add them to their rotation. At the time, it was believed to be a big publicity stunt. However, Brooks later went on to try out for the Kansas City Royals in 2004. It was there that he got his only hit. We think he should probably stick to country music.

17. The New York Mets are the first MLB team to trade a player back to his original team. Harry Chiti was originally traded

from the Cleveland Indians to the New York Mets with the agreement that the Mets would trade a player back to the Indians later on. When the time came, they gave Chiti back to Cleveland.

18. Vince Lombardi, the head coach of the Green Bay Packers in the 1960s, was born in Brooklyn.

19. The Knicks made a trade for Brooklyn native Carmelo Anthony. In the beginning, people didn't think the trade was worth it. Since then, Anthony has proven to be one of the Knicks' best players and made it to the Hall of Fame.

20. In 2000, Woody Johnson paid $635 million for the New York Jets. Johnson outbid Charles Dolan, whose company Cablevision owns Madison Square Garden, the New York Rangers, and the New York Knicks.

Test Yourself – Questions and Answers

1. The Winter Olympics have been hosted twice in which of the following New York towns?

    a. Lake Champlain
    b. Lake Placid
    c. Rochester

2. According to urban legend, why do the New York Yankees uniforms have pinstripes?

    a. Because it was Babe Ruth's favorite pattern
    b. Babe Ruth thought pinstripes would bring good luck to the team
    c. Pinstripes would slim Babe Ruth's larger figure

3. Which famous sports legend was *not* born in New York?

    a. Babe Ruth
    b. Michael Jordan
    c. Mike Tyson

4. Which Hall of Fame can be found in Cooperstown, New York?

    a. The Basketball Hall of Fame
    b. The Baseball Hall of Fame
    c. The Football Hall of Fame

5. Which country musician tried out for the New York Mets?

    a. Blake Shelton
    b. Keith Urban
    c. Garth Brooks

Answers

1. b.
2. c.
3. a.
4. b.
5. c.

DON'T FORGET YOUR
FREE BOOKS

OTHER BOOKS IN THIS SERIES

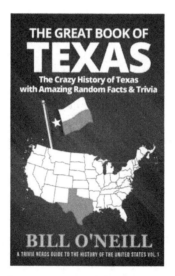

Are you looking to learn more about Texas? Sure, you've heard about the Alamo and JFK's assassination in history class, but there's so much about the Lone Star State that even natives don't know about. In this trivia book, you'll journey through Texas's history, pop culture, sports, folklore, and so much more!

In The Great Book of Texas, some of the things you will learn include:

Which Texas hero isn't even from Texas?

Why is Texas called the Lone Star State?

Which hotel in Austin is one of the most haunted hotels in the United States?

Where was Bonnie and Clyde's hideout located?

Which Tejano musician is buried in Corpus Christi?

What unsolved mysteries happened in the state?

Which Texas-born celebrity was voted "Most Handsome" in high school?

Which popular TV show star just opened a brewery in Austin?

You'll find out the answers to these questions and many other facts. Some of them will be fun, some of them will creepy, and some of them will be sad, but all of them will be fascinating! This book is jampacked with everything you could have ever wondered about Texas.

Whether you consider yourself a Texas pro or you know absolutely nothing about the state, you'll learn something new as you discover more about the state's past, present, and future. Find out about things that weren't mentioned in your history book. In fact, you might even be able to impress your history teacher with your newfound knowledge once you've finished reading! So, what are you waiting for? Dive in now to learn all there is to know about the Lone Star State!

MORE BOOKS BY BILL O'NEILL

I hope you enjoyed this book and learned something new. Please feel free to check out some of my previous books on Amazon.

Made in the USA
Coppell, TX
21 November 2019